MW01493706

MIND OVER GRIND

HOW TO *BREAK FREE* WHEN WORK HIJACKS YOUR LIFE

GUY WINCH, PhD

SIMON & SCHUSTER

New York   Amsterdam/Antwerp   London
Toronto   Sydney/Melbourne   New Delhi

Simon & Schuster
1230 Avenue of the Americas
New York, NY 10020

First Simon & Schuster hardcover edition February 2026

SIMON & SCHUSTER and colophon are registered trademarks of Simon & Schuster, LLC

Simon & Schuster strongly believes in freedom of expression and stands against censorship in all its forms. For more information, visit BooksBelong.com.

For information about special discounts for bulk purchases, please contact Simon & Schuster Special Sales at 1-866-506-1949 or business@simonandschuster.com.

The Simon & Schuster Speakers Bureau can bring authors to your live event. For more information or to book an event, contact the Simon & Schuster Speakers Bureau at 1-866-248-3049 or visit our website at www.simonspeakers.com.

Interior design by Wendy Blum

Manufactured in the United States of America

10 9 8 7 6 5 4 3 2 1

Library of Congress Control Number: 2025945006

ISBN 978-1-6680-6933-2
ISBN 978-1-6680-6935-6 (ebook)

 Let's stay in touch! Scan here to get book recommendations, exclusive offers, and more delivered to your inbox.

For Efi,
who taught me many of the
lessons in this book

CONTENTS

CONTENTS

MIND
OVER
GRIND

INTRODUCTION

Sunday Evening

Work—The Gift That Keeps on Taking

I DECIDED TO BECOME a psychologist when I was 14 years old. The choice was heavily influenced by comic books and included more than a whiff of escapist fantasy: I'd go to graduate school and open a private practice in a faraway land, the birthplace of many a superhero—New York City. To teenage me, psychology seemed like a true superpower. I would scale people's defenses with leaps of compassion, overpower their problems with insight, and shield them with empathy.

Sixteen years later, I graduated with a doctorate in clinical psychology from New York University and opened a private practice in Manhattan. On the first anniversary of my practice, I left my office and walked to my new apartment. I had recently moved to a safer neighborhood, and for the first time since arriving in New York City, I didn't have to check for muggers when taking out my keys. I was living the life I had fantasized about all those years ago. Tired from a grueling week and eager to unwind, I got into the elevator with a neighbor who was an emergency room physician. The elevator rose, shuddered, and stalled between floors, at which point my neighbor—the man who dealt with emergencies for a living—began poking at all the buttons and banging on the door while exclaiming, "This is my nightmare! This is my nightmare!"

Trapped in a small space with my frantic neighbor and realizing we would now have to stop at every floor, I looked at him and said with annoyance, "And *this* is *my* nightmare." My neighbor glared at me, humiliation leaking into the panic on his face, and resumed banging on the door. I felt my cheeks flush. Where was my compassion? The man was clearly in distress. I could have easily calmed him down. Instead, I had mocked his vulnerability and made him feel even worse. Why had I acted so unkindly?

When I got home, I closed my eyes and tried to identify what I was feeling beneath the swirl of emotions the incident had triggered. One feeling stood out immediately—exhaustion, a fatigue so deep no amount of sleep could touch it. I felt detached, jaded, like someone who had been practicing psychology for decades and was tired of it.

Those were symptoms of burnout. But how could I be burnt out? Burnout was cumulative, a result of months and years of chronic stress and pressure. I had only been in practice for a year. I quickly realized that it wasn't the one year of private practice that was the problem; it was the six years of overwork that preceded it.

I had come to the United States with big hopes and dreams but with literally no money. I was fortunate to receive a full scholarship from New York University, but as generous as that was, it wasn't enough to make ends meet in New York City. In addition to being a full-time graduate student, I had to take three part-time jobs. But it wasn't just the overwork that had caused my burnout; it was the stress that came with chronic financial insecurity, like worrying about not being able to pay rent or afford food. I lived in a tiny room, I walked everywhere because I couldn't afford the subway, I regularly skipped meals when I ran out of money, and I worked 10 to 12 hours a day, seven days a week, with only two or three days off every year.

That explained why my first six years in the United States had led to burnout.

It did not explain why I had continued overworking in the seventh year once I was a licensed psychologist and no longer needed to push myself to such extremes.

I had fallen into the trap that so often ensnares those who spend years in survival mode for financial or safety reasons. All your energy and mental resources are focused on basic needs like food and rent. You are in constant problem-solving mode, figuring out how to manage with inadequate resources, what you can skip, what you can do without. In survival mode, self-reflection, emotional processing, and long-term planning take a back seat. Asking yourself how you feel is pointless if there's nothing you can do about it anyway.

I had my own private practice, a green card, and financial stability, yet I was still driving myself to exhaustion like my survival depended on it. I recalled an exchange with a colleague a few months earlier and winced at the memory. She was telling me about her new job in the psychiatric outpatient department of a local hospital and asked me if I ever got the Sunday Blues—the anxious dread many people feel on Sunday evenings of starting the workweek. I told her I never did.

"What's your secret?" she asked.

"I work seven days a week," I answered, with misplaced pride. "You can't dread the start of one workweek if the previous one never ends." She raised a concerned eyebrow. I ignored it. Much like red flags, eyebrows are too often dismissed when our friends raise them.

The irony of a mental health professional being so blind to their own emotional well-being wasn't lost on me. But it wasn't just my emotional health that was languishing. My practice had become my exclusive focus; I thought about my clients all the time, even when I was home. I had no time nor energy to socialize, date, or to pursue any hobbies or passions. I was sleeping poorly, eating unhealthy foods, barely exercising, and ignoring the friends and colleagues who reached out to me.

Somehow, work had hijacked my entire life, and I hadn't even realized it. Chances are work has hijacked yours too, in ways that you too might not have realized.

Over the past couple of decades, there has been an explosion of scientific research into how the workplace impacts our emotional health and our relationships, both at work and outside of it. The findings paint an alarming picture of how deeply work has penetrated into our lives and minds and the damage it is doing, often without us being aware of it.

This Is Your Life on Work

The number of people experiencing *intense work stress* in today's workplace has been at the highest levels recorded for the past five years. In a 2024 American Psychological Association poll, 43% of workers reported high stress, and 67% reported symptoms of burnout. No surprise then that thriving at work was also at an all-time low. Intense stress and burnout are serious conditions that pose equally serious threats to your physical health and emotional well-being, including increased risk of cardiovascular and gastrointestinal disease, diabetes, respiratory infections, anxiety, depression, alcohol and substance abuse, suicide, and general mortality.

Activities that pose such severe risks to health and well-being typically come with a warning label. Work does not.

Our health and well-being aren't the only things that work has hijacked; the current workplace also compromises our ability to do our jobs well. Studies found that excessive work demands cause us to make significantly more mistakes, to be less efficient and productive, and to unwittingly self-sabotage in ways that increase our stress and exhaustion and add to the strain we already feel.

Work also hijacks our emotional intelligence. Intense pressures on the job impair our ability to recognize our feelings and needs and to accurately read those of our colleagues. As a result, we're less likely to manage our emotions effectively or to manage our relationships at work as well as we could. In part, that's why disconnection and loneliness at work are so prevalent, why we're more likely to experience more conflict with our coworkers than we are to encounter cooperation and understanding, and why so many of us are having meltdowns. It is also why we sometimes feel like we love our profession but hate our job.

Work has even hijacked our moral code. Studies of unethical behavior have identified a common psychological process that occurs in high-stress workplaces that leads people who would rarely act unethically in their personal lives to behave in ways that become more unethical over time. In many cases, this process happens without the person realizing how extreme their conduct has become. In some companies and organizations, certain kinds of immoral, unethical, and even illegal behaviors are the norm. In one survey, *38%* of workers said they would act unethically if asked to do so by a manager.

Our work also impacts our personal time and family lives in far more ways than we realize. We dramatically underestimate the extent to which we bring home stresses and tensions from our jobs and how this work invasion causes conflict within our most cherished relationships.

You might have noticed that difficult days at work are often followed by arguments and conflict at home, but you probably haven't realized how work impacts your unconscious feelings toward your loved ones. That's why you might love your partner but feel emotionally distant from them at times and why family members' efforts to engage you can feel irritating and inconsiderate. This transfer of stress and tension from work to home can be unrelenting; studies found that when *you* are overly stressed from work, *your partner* can develop symptoms of burnout.

Work even hijacks our thoughts. A consistent finding is that the more stressful and distressing your day is, the harder it will be for you to stop thinking about work in the evening, no matter how desperate you are to switch off. You're trying to enjoy alone time or time with friends and family, but your mind keeps bombarding you with replays of worries, hurts, and irritations from your workday. No matter how many times you drag your focus back to the present, you end up stewing about work again a few minutes later.

Even if we can switch off at night or on the weekend, we are still not free of work's negative influence. Another body of research discovered that work impacts how we spend our leisure time—and not in a good way. The more intense the workday, the more exhausted we are when we get home, the more likely we will be to spend the evening relaxing, binging shows, and doomscrolling. That might seem like a fine way to recover from an intense day at work, but studies have confirmed that we then are likely to wake up the next morning lacking vitality and still feeling worn out.

Work has hijacked other aspects of our self-care as well. For example, most cancers are treatable when caught early, and half of the adults who had cancer in the United States are diagnosed as a result of their annual checkup. Yet, in a recent survey, 23% of adults said they skipped their annual medical checkups because they conflicted with work hours. Other studies found that high work stress makes us more likely to eat unhealthy foods and to skip exercising, and less likely to stay on top of basic tasks such as cleaning, bill-paying, grocery shopping, and household repairs. These drops in self-care often accumulate so significantly they can meet the definition of self-neglect such that we would qualify for a home aide were the condition not entirely self-imposed. Today's workplace is so unhealthy that it's causing functional people to stop functioning outside of work almost entirely.

In today's workplace, work stress operates like a pinball machine. It shoots out and hits one domain of our lives after another, exacerbating stress in each domain it touches, dinging from work to our personal lives and back again. These vicious cycles keep stress in play far longer and it is this overexposure that is causing the rise in burnout. Some workplaces are much worse than others, but these ravages impact all workers, not just those who are stuck in toxic cultures or saddled with abusive managers. In fact, being excited, driven, and passionate about your work can set you up for the same problems, no matter your profession, industry, geography, or culture. So can being self-employed, as I found out in my early career. That's what makes the current workplace so problematic—it is an equal opportunity abuser. Some workers are harmed significantly, some only moderately, but it damages all workers to some degree.

The Price We Pay to Work

Today's workplace is brutal for many and a grind for the rest. Soaring rates of stress and burnout have consequences that extend far beyond the workplace to society at large. In a 2024 survey, 77% of workers reported that work stress was affecting their physical health. Another found that 120,000 deaths per year—twice as many as the number of US soldiers who died in the Vietnam War—and up to 8% of annual health care costs in the United States could be attributed to the pressure employees face.

The need for change is as obvious as the solution. If employers invested in the emotional health of their employees, both employers and employees would benefit: performance, productivity, engagement, creativity, loyalty, and team functioning would go up, while mistakes, sick days, absenteeism, and turnover would go down. Many employers are aware of these findings, yet beyond lip service and token responses (e.g., mental health employee resource pages), few authentic efforts are being made to reduce stress in the workforce, and those that are being made have done nothing to arrest the downward trend in employee mental health.

One of the more blatant sources of stress and emotional harm in the workplace is hostility and aggression. Incidents of bullying, harassment, bias, and incivility are at epidemic levels too. The Workplace Bullying Institute noted that in 2017, 19% of employees reported having experienced bullying in the workplace. By 2024 that number was up to 32%. Add in the 14% of workers who reported witnessing bullying, and you have almost half the workforce experiencing a hostile work environment by that standard alone. Studies found that experiencing toxic behaviors in the workplace makes you eight times more likely to develop symptoms of burnout.

The workplace is hierarchical; change can only be driven from the top. In workplaces that maintain a culture that is intolerant of aggression at every level of the organization and emphasize a strong core value of respect, aggressions and even microaggressions are quite rare. These workplaces can still be highly stressful, but they demonstrate that with the right leadership and culture, it is possible to dramatically reduce hostility and aggression. Yet, most companies are too busy driving quarterly earnings to care about their employees' welfare, and burnout is the inevitable result.

Change is not likely anytime soon, and we need to be able to survive until it arrives. We might not be able to compel many companies to prioritize people over profits or to lead with compassion, but we aren't powerless. There's one aspect of our work experience that we control—ourselves. Work might be a battlefield, but we are not without weapons. How we manage our own emotions and psychological functioning can make a huge difference. For example, one thing that happens to us psychologically when stress exceeds a certain intensity is that we go from managing it productively to managing it so unproductively that we actually make things even more stressful for ourselves.

Here's why that happens.

How Stress Makes Us Mismanage Stress

Stress is defined as our brain and body's responses to challenges and pressures of all kinds. The relationship between stress and performance is best represented by a bell curve in which stress is on the vertical axis and performance is on the horizontal. When stress is too low (the far-left side of the curve), our performance tends to be poorer because the lack of pressure can make us complacent and unmotivated. As stress increases, our functioning improves because the rise in pressure forces us to pay more attention and use more of our abilities. The top part of the curve, where stress is moderate, is our Goldilocks Zone of optimal functioning—where the stress is "just right," and we do our best work. Past that Goldilocks Zone, the stress begins to exceed our capacity to manage it effectively, and our performance declines.

This explanation of how stress impacts performance has been around for decades, but we now have a better understanding of what actually goes wrong past the tipping point at the top of the curve—how we end up undermining ourselves and making the stress worse. Intense stress can make work feel like a modern-day battlefield, but it is not one our brains have evolved to negotiate well because this battle—our job—never ends. Our efforts to psychologically adapt to this constant struggle often cause more harm than good.

Here is what goes wrong.

When the demands and pressures of our job become intense, we naturally seek to conserve our mental energy so that we can meet those demands. We do this by going into autopilot mode—we put our head down and go from task to task and from meeting to meeting without pausing to reflect on how we're doing or why we're doing things the way we are. Meanwhile, our brain will deploy automatic and unconscious mental processes to manage our decisions and coping mechanisms behind the scenes so that we don't have to consciously mull over every action and step.

The problem is that our unconscious mind lacks the sophistication and executive functions that our conscious mind can draw upon, such as long-term planning, prioritizing, or anticipating consequences. These strategies and approaches our unconscious mind uses when we're on autopilot might benefit us in the moment, but they compound our stress in the long run, making the grind much worse. That additional stress will then make us even more likely to default to automatic coping, manage the pressures counterproductively, and increase our stress even more.

These *vicious stress cycles* are self-reinforcing and difficult to break. This is one of the reasons burnout symptoms are at an all-time high and why so many of our efforts to improve our work-life balance fail to alleviate our exhaustion. The impact of such relentless stress cannot be mitigated by a few hours of healthy activities; we have to find ways to reduce these vicious stress cycles.

These mental processes are largely unconscious. There is no push notification to alert us when our stress management is about to flip from productive to counterproductive. Trying to be in conscious control all the time isn't the answer either. It's impractical—attempting to be thoughtful and intentional all day would exhaust our attentional capacities by 10 AM. It's also unnecessary—our automatic processes do a good enough job of running things behind the scenes most of the time. The trick, as you will see in later chapters, is to know *when* to disengage your autopilot and *what to do* once you have.

To summarize: (1) **The stresses of the current workplace are damaging our productivity and well-being:** The more demanding our jobs are, the more likely it becomes that our functioning at work will be impaired and our emotional health and relationships outside of work will suffer. (2) **We are making things worse for ourselves:** The more mental strain we experience during our workday, the more likely we will be to default to unconscious self-sabotaging strategies that increase our stress even further. (3) **We don't realize that we**

are sabotaging ourselves: Much of this self-undermining happens outside our awareness because work pressures are likely to make us default to our psychological autopilot to get through the day. **(4) Loving our job doesn't protect us:** Being engaged and excited about our work puts us at just as much risk because labors of love are still labors.

Okay, enough bad news, let's talk solutions.

To break free from the various ways work has hijacked your life, you will need to: (1) reduce your overall work stress, (2) know when to disengage your autopilot so you can prevent unconscious self-sabotage and assert deliberate control, (3) minimize the impact of work stress and strain by learning how to recover from them more effectively, and (4) nurture key aspects of your life and relationships that work has diminished.

This book will offer you an array of science-based tools and techniques to regain control, reduce your stress and risk of burnout, enhance your productivity and satisfaction at work, gain a healthier work-life balance, boost your emotional and physical health, and repair the damage that work pressures have inflicted on your relationships. These tools and techniques have benefited hundreds of my clients as well as the leaders and managers of companies and governmental agencies where I've given workshops.

Along the way, I will also explain some of our basic psychological operations—how our stress response works, what our coping mechanisms do and how to use them effectively, how to regulate and manage our emotions, how blind spots cause us to repeat our mistakes, how to reconnect to meaningful aspects of our identity that have fallen by the wayside, how to get the most out of our emotional intelligence, how to set boundaries with work, how to recalibrate our moral compass, why avoidance supersizes anxiety, how to know when overworking is becoming dangerous, and more.

Lastly, if you're questioning whether you are in the right job or career, as I did when I got burnt out many years ago, this book will help you decide if you should stay in your job or make a change.

Here is what you will *not* learn in this book.

You will not learn how to fight the system: not how to take on your uncaring employer, nor how to push back against overworking, nor how to complain about bias or harassment, nor how to confront abusive bosses, nor how to get help from human resources for any of the above. As much as I would love to offer advice in these areas, I cannot. It would be too dangerous. In many companies, doing any of those things could easily put your career and job in jeopardy. I have seen too many people speak up and find themselves in the next round of cuts, too many managers retaliating against those who went up against them, too many human resource departments forced to defend the company at the expense of the employee, and too many employers who yelled at, humiliated, and belittled employees who dared question them about anything. The fact that almost half of workers are hesitant to speak up about the unhealthy nature of their workplace is yet another sign of how unhealthy the workplace is.

In short, this book will not help you change your workplace; it will help you survive the workplace you're in. The book follows five of my psychotherapy clients over the course of a few months to a few years in their jobs, detailing the struggles they had at work and the fallout that impacted their personal lives and relationships during that time.* As a group, these five people and I (I share my own struggles with work too) represent many of the challenges workers face today. Alongside them, you will learn tools, strategies, and solutions for dealing with those challenges, the science that undergirds them, and how to personalize them to your specific situation.

The book is organized by the days of the week to symbolize the accumulation of stress over time and the progressively harsher situations so many of us encounter in today's workplace. You might have noticed that we started this introduction with Sunday evening, not Monday morning. Monday is when the workweek begins in actuality (for those who work a traditional workweek), but for many, it begins psychologically the night before, when anticipatory dread creates an *introduction* to the workweek in the form of the Sunday Blues. Let's begin by discussing how to make Sunday evenings less dread-full.

---

* To protect the privacy of my clients, I've changed names and certain identifying information. To avoid identifying details, one character is a blend of two people whose stories and experiences were remarkably similar.

Banishing the Sunday Blues

When I got burnt out early in my career, I realized that I had to stop working seven days a week and take Sundays off to rest and relax. The goal I set for myself was to get so blissed out that I might even experience a touch of the Sunday Blues. Success felt more like a wallop than a touch. The nosedive in my mood and the heaviness that gripped my chest as the weekend wound to a close was just as unpleasant as advertised.

Here's why the Sunday Blues happen: your brain's default response to threats is to sound the alarm so that you can prepare for what lies ahead. Since work is fundamentally stressful and challenging, your brain considers it a threat and dutifully floods you with dread on Sunday evening to warn you that *the workweek is coming!* By sounding the alarm, your brain is helping you prepare for the emotional and psychological dangers that lie ahead.

To reduce your Sunday dread, you need to make the "threat" seem less immediate and therefore less urgent. The best way to do so is to layer another activity between the end of the weekend and the start of the workweek— preferably a pleasant, enjoyable, meaningful, or connective one. Layering in an activity that you can look forward to on Monday mornings will push work further back in the queue and make it seem less urgent because there's a whole other agenda item to focus on beforehand.

For this strategy to be effective, you will need to make a big deal about the activity and message to your brain that you are looking forward to doing it. The more of an "event" you make of it, the greater the buffer your brain will perceive between Sunday and the start of the workweek and the less dread you should experience as a result. If your job is ridiculously oppressive, this technique might not be sufficient to banish the Blues entirely; these things are hard to predict, but it is worth trying nonetheless.

You could schedule breakfast with a friend (self-message: *I'm excited to see Jimmy for pancakes tomorrow*), get in a workout before heading to your job (*I love starting the day doing something healthy for myself*), or spend an hour on a project at home (*I really enjoy working on my Halloween costume*). Using this brain hack has helped dozens of my clients minimize the Sunday Blues. Yes, it might mean going to bed earlier or getting less sleep, but the sleep you will get is likely to be more restorative because you'll be less stressed-out.

Lastly, when possible, try to avoid making the first task when you get to work on Monday mornings a stressful or difficult one. If that's not in your control, try to find an aspect of that first task that's interesting, satisfying, or entertaining, and focus on that when you think about work. For example, if you have a long, tense staff meeting first thing every Monday, you could wear the new outfit you bought over the weekend and look forward to feeling good in it, or get excited about hearing how your colleague's surprise birthday party for her husband went, or get curious about whether two of your colleagues resolved the tension between them after the argument they had on Friday or whether their sniping will continue.

Creating a buffer between the end of the weekend and the start of your workday on Monday should reward you with a more pleasant Sunday evening and a more restorative Sunday night's sleep.

Are you ready for Monday?

CHAPTER ONE

Monday Morning

Back to the Grind—How Good Stress Goes Bad

"MONDAYS ARE A KILLER," Tony exclaimed at the start of our video session. His deep frown lines and heavy brow made him look troubled and angry, belying his sweet and upbeat disposition. His six-foot-four frame and three hundred pounds of muscle didn't correct the impression. Neither did his neck-cracking habit. "I need a good workout this evening," Tony said while twisting his jaw to one side. He was a successful stock trader—a notoriously stressful job, especially when markets were volatile, which, at the time, they were.

I nodded in agreement. Mondays are indeed the most stressful day of the week because we jump from the calm of the weekend into the hustle of work. They are also the day in which incidents of incivility and rudeness in the workplace are highest, fostering a vicious cycle: stress fosters bad moods and irritability, which make people more prone to rudeness and incivility, which amps up our stress and worsens our moods. Tony wasn't being literal when he said Mondays were a killer, but he wasn't far off the mark. More strokes happen on Mondays than on any other workday, particularly for men, while for both genders, a third of all cerebral hemorrhages take place on Mondays. Even deaths by suicide are higher on Mondays than on any other day of the week.

Tony's preferred mode of stress management was weight lifting. Lots of it. Pumping iron obviously worked for him because he rarely looked tense, even now, during trading hours. "It isn't the trading that's stressful; it's the people," he told me when we started working together. Tony was the top trader in his office, and that put a target on his back. "Competition energizes me when it's about the trades," he explained, "but I have zero patience for office politics and playground squabbles. I don't play those games." Unfortunately, the number two guy in the office did. Tony called him Scar, like the character in *The Lion King* who killed his own brother to take the throne. Unable to outperform Tony in trades, Scar focused on sabotaging Tony's relationships by making him look bad to his coworkers.

When Jason, a new trader, joined the team the previous year and immediately struggled, Scar took him under his wing to "mentor" him. At first, Tony was supportive of the move as Jason was overwhelmed and out of his depth, and Tony felt bad for him. But Scar's motives became clear when they resumed in-person meetings after the pandemic shutdowns. The first time Tony gently disagreed with Jason, Scar rushed to the new trader's defense and accused Tony of "throwing his weight around." From then on, whenever Tony offered Jason feedback, regardless of how respectfully and constructively he did so, Scar would look at Jason with feigned concern and tell Tony to back off. Jason, relieved to have someone to blame for his poor performance, leaned into the victimhood as if he were actually aggrieved.

After a couple of rounds of this, Tony got fed up with Scar's theatrics and went to their boss for advice. The boss dismissed Tony's concerns as "childish infighting between colleagues." What made these incidents with Jason truly distressing for Tony was that he was both very empathetic and highly guilt-prone. A difficult childhood with a mother who blamed Tony for her every emotion left him with an incorrectly calibrated guilt response and a predisposition to experience other people's feelings as being more urgent than his own.

Guilt-prone people are often disadvantaged in the workplace because they tend to feel guilty at any sign of distress in other people, even if they did little or nothing to cause it. They might apologize unnecessarily, which can diminish their credibility and authority, or have trouble saying no to additional tasks or responsibilities when they're already overwhelmed. The fear of causing discomfort or distress to others can make them avoid confrontation when they have been wronged, and they're vulnerable to emotional manipulation when negotiating. Developing strategies to manage guilty feelings, set boundaries with those who seek to take advantage of them, and increase their assertiveness can help mitigate these disadvantages.

But Tony did none of those things. His lifelong strategy for dealing with his crippling guilt was to avoid inadvertently upsetting people by treating *everyone* with respect and consideration. For Tony, kindness wasn't just a tactic; it was a value he held dearly. He was far prouder of his reputation as being "one of the good guys" than he was for being the top trader. His strategy helped minimize guilt-inducing occurrences, but as avoidance does, it also prevented him from developing more adaptive approaches to managing guilt overall.

Tony recognized that Jason was being manipulated by Scar and that the new hire played along because it served his own purposes. But Jason's pained expression whenever Tony said anything to him in meetings, and Scar's fake concern for the "stricken" junior colleague, made Tony feel guilty nonetheless. For guilt-prone people, knowing that you're being manipulated into feeling guilt does not diminish the guilt you feel.

Tony was in the middle of telling me about Scar's latest trouble-making efforts when he glanced sideways and stopped midsentence. It was still trading hours, and he had warned me he might have to step away for a few seconds to make a trade. He apologized for the interruption, clicked off his video and microphone, and reappeared thirty seconds later, smiling apologetically. "Sorry," he said. "I might have to do one more trade in a moment, but that should be it." Sure enough, a few minutes later, Tony's eyes flickered to the side again. "Sorry," he repeated, "last one." He muted the video again but must have missed the microphone icon because I heard him stand, take three quick steps, and bellow at the top of his lungs, "Sell twenty million!! Sell twenty million!! Now!! Now!!!"

I was so startled, I came this close to joining the Monday casualty list. A moment later the video went on, and Tony was back on the couch, perfectly calm. "Sorry, but we should be in the clear now." He looked at me. "Is everything alright?"

My heart was still racing. "Your mic didn't mute," I explained. "Is that normal, to scream like that when you're making a trade?"

"Oh, my gosh, I'm so sorry!" Tony exclaimed, looking stricken himself. "Are you okay?"

"I'm fine," I reassured him with a smile.

"Sorry. I raise my voice when the trades are urgent," Tony explained. "The people executing the trades are in a noisy and chaotic room, so it's the only way to get their attention. We all do it. And don't worry, I check in with them to make sure they're not offended. I'm the only trader who does," he said with a smile. "They think it's 'cute.' They rib me about it all the time."

Tony's ability to appear so calm after having screamed his head off seconds earlier was remarkable. In fact, it was practically gazelle-like. Gazelles, like many wild animals, have a highly calibrated stress response. They will go back to feeding within seconds of narrowly escaping a chasing lion. One moment they are about to be eaten alive, the next they're munching on shoots and shrubs like it was antelope-night at the salad bar. Short bursts of stress like those or like the ones Tony experiences while making a trade are not necessarily harmful, and they can even be beneficial. What gives stress its bad reputation is the damage it causes when it goes from being acute and short-lived to being ongoing and chronic.

Short bursts of stress can be good for you because they can make your *stress response* more efficient. Your stress response includes the physiological and psychological activation that occurs when you encounter a challenge or threat and your ability to return to calm once that threat has passed. Tony's stress response was highly efficient, as evidenced by his rapid return to calm after making a high-stakes trade. Acute stress is beneficial because it can prepare you to meet challenges by sharpening your focus and reaction time and by enhancing your immune system functioning (which gets activated as a response to a threat). Certain types of stress can even trigger the release of oxytocin—the bonding or cuddle hormone, which is why so many lifelong friends and romantic partners can trace their origins to meeting in a waiting room for a job interview or orientation week when starting college.

Like Tony's workouts, stress can help us build muscles—mental and emotional ones—in the form of resilience. But just as muscles need time to recover from intense activation, our body needs downtime to recover from stress. When we experience stress too frequently or for prolonged periods, the wear and tear can cause damage significant enough to be life-changing and even life-ending. Unfortunately, in today's workplace, chronic stress is practically the norm. The culprits are legion: toxic cultures, after-hours emails, unreasonable deadlines or sales targets, overlapping role responsibilities, critical bosses, startup-funding shortfalls, anticipated mergers, reorganizations, and an endless array of other circumstances can induce weeks and months of relentless stress. To understand why chronic stress can be so destructive, let's take a slow-motion look at what happened in Tony's body when he made that second trade during our session.

When he glanced over and saw his stock hit its target price, his adrenal glands unleashed a surge of adrenaline and cortisol (the stress hormone), and his sympathetic nervous system flew into action, activating his fight-or-flight (or freeze) response. As he leapt up from the couch, Tony's breath quickened, and his pupils dilated so he could see better (super useful when running away from a lion; less so when making a trade). His heart rate and blood pressure increased as he strode to the phone, and his blood vessels constricted, directing oxygenated blood away from less urgent tasks like digestion and toward his muscles so he could fight or flee (or shout) more effectively. As he made the call, stress hormones elevated his blood sugar to give him immediate energy and to prepare his immune cells to fight foreign invaders and heal after injury.

When Tony ended the call, his brain, registering that the "emergency" was over, activated his parasympathetic nervous system (PNS) to counteract the activation his sympathetic nervous system (SNS) had initiated. Think of the *SNS* as setting up and hosting the party—moving the furniture, putting out extra food, and cranking up the music to get everyone dancing—and the *PNS* as shutting off the music, sending the guests home, putting everything back in its place, and doing cleanup. Your SNS might be a more exciting environment, but without your PNS, the party would keep going indefinitely, and your place (your body) would get trashed.

Now imagine what would happen to your body if the work stress you experienced went on for months, and your physiological arousal systems did not get to rest or reset. Having your blood pressure and heart rate elevated for sustained periods could lead to hypertension, heart disease, stroke, and other cardiovascular problems. Repeated disruptions to your digestive system could cause heartburn, ulcers, or irritable bowel syndrome. The cortisol that directed your body to store energy for the "emergency" would also make you crave carbs and other energy-dense foods—useful for fighting on the battlefield, but when your battles take place in a meeting room, those extra calories are likely to end up as deep belly fat. Constant tension would lead to headaches and muscle pain, as well as sleep problems, which in turn could impair your concentration, focus, and other aspects of your cognitive functioning.

And then there's the psychological harm stress can do. Being on continual alert from "threats" like looming deadlines, micromanaging bosses, or scheming coworkers could foster dread, negative thoughts, and pessimistic perceptions and lead to anxiety and depression. Over time, your immune system would weaken, and you could suffer from decreased fertility. If you menstruate, your cycles could get disrupted. Chronic stress has even been associated with short-ened telomeres—the DNA sequences at the end of our chromosomes that protect them from fraying—causing premature cell death and shortened life expectancy.

Plus, each of these symptoms could have ripple effects. They can weaken the immune system, making you vulnerable to disease. Muscle pain can dis-rupt mobility and lead to atrophy and weight gain. They can lead to anxiety and depression, which in turn can lead to alcohol consumption or drug use. Stress-related exhaustion can impair your coping mechanisms, expose you to even greater stress, and lead to burnout. Fortunately, the stress highway has exit ramps courtesy of your parasympathetic nervous system—provided you are able to activate it, which is difficult to do when stress is chronic.

Tony's stress response was extremely impressive, but it was also context-specific. His ability to manage the stress of making multimillion-dollar trades was excellent. His ability to manage interpersonal conflict of any kind was weak. In his case, his discrepancy in stress tolerance was substantial, but those kinds of gaps are by no means unusual.

Your Stress Tolerance Is Adaptable

Every profession has its own unique brand of stress that seems untenable to outsiders but is manageable to those in the field. I recently passed by a street fair in Europe where I saw a "human statue" of Atlas—painted gold from head to toe, wearing a loincloth, and carrying the world on his back—stand still while surrounded by a large flock of pigeons that were being fed by eager children. Every few minutes, some kid would stomp toward the flock and cause the pigeons to take flight and swarm over poor Atlas. Remarkably, he never broke his pose. Standing completely still in very little clothing while overfed birds circled directly overhead seemed incredibly stressful to me, but when I asked him if it bothered him, Atlas shrugged.

What allowed the street performer to take the occasional pigeon dropping in stride was that our ability to deal with stress is quite elastic. Imagine your stress tolerance as a balloon. When the intensity and duration of the stress to which you are exposed falls within your psychological comfort zone (the confines of the balloon), you can manage it effectively. When the stress goes beyond your comfort zone, one of two things can happen. If the stress increases gradually, the balloon will expand to accommodate it. But if the stress increases sharply or goes on for too long, the balloon will inflate beyond its limits and "pop." Your coping mechanisms will falter, you'll feel overwhelmed and anxious, and your ability to think clearly and perform your normal tasks will be compromised.

In other words, much like tolerance for any other kind of psychological pressure, such as risk, conflict, boredom, or anxiety, your stress tolerance increases with exposure. This is why your first few days or weeks in any new job are likely to feel overwhelming—you haven't yet adapted to the various challenges and uncertainties of the new role. But after a while, those same stressors feel more manageable because repeatedly dealing with them has expanded your balloon—your comfort zone and tolerance. Most of us can think back to situations in life that initially seemed incredibly stressful yet ended up stretching us without breaking us.

We can often stretch our range quite significantly, but our adaptability has limits. We each have what I call *psychological design limitations*—the point beyond which our capacities get maxed out in a given situation—at which we can no longer expand our stress tolerance.

I used to be terrified of public speaking, and for good reason—I used to stutter. In high school, I dreaded being called on in class, and I avoided speaking as much as I could when socializing in groups. As I got older, it became more stammer than stutter, but the stutter came back with a vengeance in stressful situations. At age twenty-nine, when I had to present my doctoral thesis before a committee (a highly stressful event known as "defending your dissertation"— the word *defending* being apt), I stammered so badly at first that I could barely complete a sentence. The idea of speaking onstage in front of thousands of people, something I do regularly today, would have seemed nightmarish to me at the time. What got me there was a series of unrelated experiences over many years that gradually inflated my stress-tolerance-for-public-speaking balloon.

My tolerance for screaming, however, remains low, so when, toward the end of our session, I saw Tony glance sideways again, I quickly hovered the mouse over the volume setting, just in case a trade was about to happen. Tony tensed, but he didn't stand up. His eyes darted back and forth as he reread the message. Clearly exasperated, he said, "Scar called a meeting to discuss tensions within the team. He knows our boss doesn't want to be involved, so it makes him look like a leader even though he's the one who's created the problems in the first place. Well, they can have it without me—I'm not playing his games."

"Is anyone else not going?"

Tony looked over at a different screen and shook his head. "Everyone is going." Tony groaned, "I guess I have to go, but it's ridiculous. I didn't do anything wrong, and people know it. Scar can have his team discussion, but he's not going to convince anyone."

"Tony, I don't think Scar is planning to have a simple discussion. He called the meeting, so he'll run it. He'll try to make Jason seem like a helpless victim."

"And me the big bully."

"While your colleagues watch and judge from the sidelines," I added.

Tony moaned, "I hate confrontation. I can't deal with a meeting like that."

"The most important thing is to stay calm and not lose your cool. You're tall and jacked. If you get too tense and frustrated, you'll seem intimidating, and that will feed into the bully narrative." As a therapist, I don't comment on people's appearance unless it is relevant to the situation. Tony was so muscular that I had seen other clients do a double take when they saw him in the waiting room. It was a factor he needed to consider.

"I hate this," Tony muttered. "For real, I can't handle it."

I suggested that we role-play various directions the meeting could take, figure out best tactics, and come up with ways for Tony to counterattack Scar while staying calm and grounded. Still, I worried that regardless of how the meeting went, tensions in the team would only increase as a result. Given the bogus nature of Jason's grievances, they were unlikely to be resolved, and the public airing of "accusations" against Tony would embroil the entire team and create exactly the kind of interpersonal tensions to which he was most vulnerable. That alone could damage his ability to do his job well, which was exactly the result Scar was after.

Stress Impairs Your Mental Functioning

Our mental bandwidth is limited in that we have a finite reservoir of cognitive and emotional resources from which to draw. High stress can take up big chunks of our bandwidth because our coping mechanisms have to work hard behind the scenes to keep our emotions from overwhelming us and impairing our execution of the task at hand. Our brain typically manages those processes automatically, outside our conscious awareness, although we can also take over and deploy our coping mechanisms consciously and deliberately should we choose to do so.* Our unconscious mind might be able to perform several mental operations at once but our conscious mind cannot, because it's restrained by the limits of our attention.

To illustrate how these limitations operate, let's peek in on what was going on in Tony's brain later that night. He was in the kitchen, chopping salad for dinner and helping his oldest with her spelling homework while his wife bathed

---

* I will be using the terms *unconscious, unconscious mind, automatic processes,* and *out of our awareness* interchangeably even though they have slightly different meanings. None of these terms should imply that our unconscious mind is self-aware or able to think in such ways—it is not.

their youngest. Tony might have believed he was multitasking in that moment, but he was not. In fact, we can only pay true attention to one task at a time.

Wait, you say, but I fold laundry like a champ while talking on the phone to my sister, isn't that multitasking?

No. What you (and Tony) are actually doing is task switching—rapidly shifting attention back and forth between two tasks (phone and laundry or salad and homework). Tony had task switched between those same two tasks the evening before without a problem. But now, his brain had to work harder behind the scenes to manage his stress and worry about the upcoming meeting. That took away from the bandwidth he had available for other mental operations, which is why it took his daughter saying, "No, Daddy," for him to realize he had asked her to spell "Dijon" instead of "dog."

Realizing that he was preoccupied brought the events of the day back into Tony's conscious awareness, at which point he stopped spelling and chopping entirely. He imagined Scar berating him in the meeting and his colleagues looking at him with disappointment. It took a second nudge from his daughter for him to refocus on spelling and chopping.

Thinking about stressful events will always compromise your mental bandwidth because of the effort required to manage the emotions stress evokes (e.g., fear, anxiety, worry, anger, helplessness). *Intense stress always taxes your mental operations.* The greater the stress you experience, the more compromised your executive functions will be.

The other consequence of experiencing high stress and pressure in your work is that, as we saw in the Introduction, there comes a point at which our stress management flips from productive to counterproductive. Let's break down why and how that happens.

Your Brain Isn't Always on Your Side

Tony was supposed to spend the rest of the evening preparing for the meeting the next evening. But when he opened his laptop and saw his schedule for the next day, he realized that preparing for the meeting would take time away from his real work, the work he actually got paid to do, the work for which he needed to be focused and sharp. He felt a surge of resentment. That was what Scar wanted, to rattle him and keep him busy with office politics so that his trades would suffer. Tony refused to let Scar get the upper hand. He decided to go to bed early so that he got a good night's sleep. He could go over his notes from our session in the office tomorrow.

But once Tony got to work, he got caught up in trading and doing his regular tasks, and before he knew it, it was time for the meeting. He thus got to the conference room far less prepared and far more nervous than he might have been had he taken the time to prepare.

When we face stressful, anxiety-provoking, or otherwise unpleasant tasks in the workplace, the temptation to procrastinate or downright avoid them can be strong. Many of us yield to those temptations because, like Tony, we're skilled at justifying avoidance and delay, even when doing so is against our best interests. And by "we," I mean our unconscious mind. To understand why this behavior is so common, let's look at what was happening psychologically for Tony when those decisions were made.

Tony dreaded the meeting because it involved his kryptonite—interpersonal conflict. The prospect of having to sit through Scar accusing him of repeatedly bullying Jason (when Tony had simply offered advice and guidance) while his colleagues looked on made Tony extremely stressed and anxious. As we know, one of the ways our brains deal with such pressures is to default to unconscious coping mechanisms in order to preserve our limited conscious bandwidth for more important tasks like getting our work done. As previously mentioned, our unconscious mind lacks self-awareness and favors coping strategies that offer quick, simple, and immediate emotional relief. Since the task before him was stressful, Tony's unconscious mind "helped" him avoid those unpleasant emotions by allowing him to procrastinate until the next day, and then it "helped" him do so again throughout the day at the office.

Procrastination is not about avoiding obnoxious tasks; it is about avoiding the unsettling emotions those tasks evoke, and it usually happens with our unconscious at the helm. True, we sometimes procrastinate after what might seem like thoughtful deliberation, but that "thoughtfulness" rarely entails serious consideration of the consequences of our avoidance. Every time Tony had an opportunity to prepare for the meeting, his stress spiked, and his unconscious mind swooped in to offer relief by getting him to do something else instead. He justified the avoidance by reframing efforts to prepare for the meeting as *doing what Scar wanted* or *taking his focus away from his work*. The consequences of being unprepared for the meeting could easily impede Tony's ability to focus on his work far more than would taking an hour to go over his notes—he knew that. But our unconscious mind excels at using our intelligence "against us" by manufacturing compelling excuses and justifications to get us to do the not-so-wise thing.

The human brain might be the most brilliant machine in the universe, but it requires adult supervision. There are moments in which we need to disengage the autopilot and make ourselves do the hard thing—supervise our own behavior—and the urge to procrastinate is one of those moments.

The real problem with procrastination is not the single delay but the accumulation of stress it creates. Putting off a stressful task during an already pressured workday might seem reasonable in the moment. But that task will then hover in the back of our mind throughout the day, the pressure to complete it mounting every hour. Delaying an unpleasant task only magnifies the stress that task causes—allowing it to occupy mental bandwidth for far longer than it would have had we tackled it right away. This unnecessary stress and occupation of mental bandwidth often extend beyond the workday because the tasks we tend to procrastinate on at work are likely to preoccupy us in the evening when we're trying to unwind and to jolt us awake with worry at 3 AM.

Procrastination is an example of how work stresses and pressures make us undermine ourselves by defaulting to unconscious mechanisms that compound our stress in the long run. As such, one of the most basic things we can do to reduce stress is to minimize procrastination and avoidance.

Harness the Power of Nuisance

As we'll see in the next chapter, what determines how stressful and disruptive a situation will be is how we frame that situation to ourselves. If we framed obnoxious tasks in less threatening ways, the automatic urge to avoid them would be weaker and easier to overcome.

Tony couldn't just tell himself that Scar's meeting wouldn't be stressful; his unconscious mind would reject that assumption because it wouldn't register as believable. To get around this limitation, we need to frame stressful tasks in ways that preserve their unpleasant quality yet make us more motivated to tackle them—by thinking of them as *nuisances*. Nuisances are defined as *minor* irritations, like flies, pebbles in our shoes, or itchy underwear tags. We usually don't procrastinate when faced with a nuisance; we tackle it immediately. When you face an obnoxious task, train yourself to flag it as one of the unpleasant ones and say to yourself: *What a nuisance. Let's get it out of the way.*

Seeing ourselves in dual roles is useful for minimizing procrastination too. Specifically, having compassion for your future self—the Friday-You that gets stuck doing everything Monday-You avoided. Studies found that we tend to think of our future selves as strangers, which is why we do things that are harmful to that future version of us (e.g., smoking) and fail to do things that would be helpful to us in the future (e.g., saving money). In one study, participants were told that to get credit for the experiment, they would either have to drink a disgusting brew that day or later on in the school year and to commit to how much of the stuff they would drink. Students who were told they would drink the brew that day chose two tablespoons, but students committing their future selves chose half a cup—a similar amount to which they were willing to commit a stranger to drink. Creating a relationship with future versions of themselves helped subjects be kinder to their present self by avoiding procrastination. I was excited to read those studies because I have been doing exactly that for years, and it has helped me reduce procrastination significantly.

How I do so might sound silly, mostly because it is, but it is also remarkably effective.

When I catch myself about to postpone an unpleasant task, I say to myself, *That's going to make next week more difficult for Next-Week-Guy, don't saddle him with that*, or *Tomorrow-Guy will be very grateful if you did this for him now.* I also make sure to thank Yesterday-Guy or Last-Week-Guy when the next day or week arrives, and the task I would have dreaded doing is already done. The goal is to create more of a relationship with your future self.

Tony had no relationship with his future self, and he didn't frame the upcoming meeting as a mere nuisance. He did the opposite—he defined it as fundamentally tense and unpleasant because it involved interpersonal conflict. That not only encouraged procrastination, it set him up to experience the meeting as much more stressful than he would have otherwise and to perform more poorly in it as a result.

How we frame work stresses and pressures has a dramatic effect on our perceptions of those pressures and, consequently, on our performance. Over time, those kinds of inflated tensions and strains can impact our entire careers.

CHAPTER TWO

Monday Afternoon

Challenge or Threat—The Only Thing to Stress About Is Stress Itself

TONY ARRIVED FOR OUR next session soon after the team meeting with Scar. He exhaled long and hard, clearly relieved that the meeting was over. He told me he hadn't prepared as much as he could have because he got caught up with work but had made sure to get into the right frame of mind before going in.

"I took a deep breath and told myself, *You got this*, a couple of times," he reported. "Scar started the meeting and immediately gave Jason the floor. I thought Scar would use the opportunity to grandstand, so I was thrown off by that. Jason accused me of bullying and intimidating him since he joined the team. He looked so nervous and uncomfortable that I was afraid to interrupt him because that would just make his point. He had transcripts of all our meetings and went incident by incident, reading quotes of things I'd said to him. He made them all sound threatening, though I never said them that way. Like if I said, *If I were you, I'd spend more time going over research reports*, he made the *If I were you* sound menacing, like a threat, and he added sinister finger-pointing that never happened."

"How did you respond?"

"It was obvious that even though he was looking at me, he was speaking to the team. They were the ones he was trying to convince, not me. I didn't want to play games, so when it was my turn to respond, I just addressed them directly. I told them I was sure they remembered that while the words were accurate, my tone was kind, and I did not point or make threatening gestures. That definitely made some heads nod. But before I could go on, Scar interrupted me, outraged. He said, *Jason bravely shared his feelings with you, and your response is to deny his emotional experience? You think he made up that he felt belittled by you? You did it to him just now. You didn't even look at him; you focused on everyone but him, like he didn't matter. How else is he supposed to feel?*"

Tony said, "For a second, I wondered if Scar was right. Jason certainly looked insulted; had I hurt his feelings? But then I remembered that Jason had pulled the same look every time Scar had accused me on his behalf, so it was just BS. I was about to respond when Scar gave me the hand to shush me and said, *If you insist on treating Jason that disrespectfully, there's no point in having this meeting.* Then he stood up. Jason quickly stood up too. Everyone else exchanged looks. When Scar saw that no one else was standing, he softened his tone and said, *Look, we're all tired, and clearly this isn't going to get resolved tonight. Let's go home.* People started to get up. I realized I couldn't let Scar have the last word, so I pointed at him and said, *You're the bully, not me!*"

Tony shook his head, "Huge mistake. Scar stared at my finger and said, *Are you going to claim that you didn't point now either?* He rolled his eyes at me and left. It was totally humiliating. Everyone avoided looking at me and just filed out. I blew it. I screwed up big-time."

I couldn't argue; the meeting definitely did damage. But it was hard to fault Tony. He was way out of his comfort zone, and Scar, a skilled manipulator and tactician, had orchestrated the meeting to perfection. Having Jason deliver the accusations neutralized Tony's ability to interrupt, as he would have looked like a bully had he done so. Using quotes from meeting transcripts reinforced the impression that Tony's issue with Jason was long-standing, and pushing Tony to lose his cool made him appear far from the kind and supportive coworker he actually was and more like the bully Scar claimed him to be. I was also pretty certain that had Tony responded to Jason directly (instead of looking at the team), Scar would have made a bigger deal of Tony denying Jason's "emotional experience" and broken up the meeting for that. Scar had set up the meeting such that Tony could not win no matter what he did.

When I explained that to Tony, he understood he'd been set up to fail, but he was still angry with himself for what happened at the end. "I went in knowing that the one thing I could not do was lose my cool, and I did." Tony was right; that was the one directive he had been determined to follow. The factors that made him fail to execute the most important aspect of the meeting were the same ones that cause all of us to manage stress effectively in some critical moments and fail miserably in others.

The Thin Line Between a Challenge and a Threat

Our ability to manage high-stress situations at work depends to a large degree on one specific factor—how we perceive the situation and frame it in our conscious and unconscious minds. The specifics of the situation matter of course, but what matters more is your mindset. Differences in mindset yield dramatically different outcomes in pressured situations. Specifically—whether you perceive the situation to be a challenge you feel equipped to meet (*challenge state*) or a threat that could potentially sink you (*threat state*).

Hundreds of studies have demonstrated that your brain and body respond very differently in each of those mental states. Challenge states are associated with adaptive mindsets, positive emotions, improved performance, a more efficient cardiovascular response, better-balanced hormonal responses, and more involvement of the prefrontal cortex (responsible for cognitive functions such as impulse control and focus). Threat states, on the other hand, are associated with errors, second-guessing, poorer performance, and more leakage of fear, self-consciousness, and other distracting emotions.

It's remarkable that such huge differences are determined based solely on how we perceive and frame the stressful situation, but it highlights how much our experience of stress is determined by our mindset and mental state. Whether you enter a challenge or threat state isn't determined by an objective assessment of your skill sets in a given (stressful) situation, but by your conscious and unconscious feelings, motivations, and beliefs about whether you'll be able to handle that situation well. You can try to manage your *conscious* feelings and beliefs about the situation to increase your likelihood of entering a challenge state (by telling yourself "You got this!" like Tony did), but your *unconscious* perceptions and beliefs could still sabotage you and flip you from challenge into threat.

The challenge-versus-threat theory identifies three factors that determine your mindset: (1) whether you believe you have sufficient resources to succeed (e.g., skill sets, training, support), (2) whether you feel a sense of control in the situation, and (3) whether your primary motivation is to attain a positive outcome (e.g., nail the presentation and impress the boss) or to avoid a negative one (e.g., don't get nervous and embarrass yourself). Feeling in control and equipped to meet the challenge and being motivated by achievement are associated with a challenge state and enhanced performance. Having an inadequate sense of control, questioning your ability, and seeking to avoid a negative outcome are associated with a threat mindset and poorer performance.

Let's revisit what happened to Tony in the team meeting through the lens of these three factors.

Feeling set up to succeed: Tony was supposed to go over the potential scenarios we didn't cover in our session by himself, including one in which Jason confronted him directly. But because the task was so uncomfortable for him, his unconscious mind "helped" him avoid it by getting him to procrastinate. As a result, he was not as prepared or as confident as he could have been.

When you face a stressful situation at work (e.g., high-stakes presentations, meetings, and negotiations; conflicts between or within teams or difficult bosses, vendors, or coworkers) preparing well is critical because it helps you both practically and psychologically (confidence). Inadequate preparation can make you question whether you have sufficient practice, skills, and resources to succeed and thereby predispose you toward a threat state.

Having a sense of control: Completing his preparation would also have allowed Tony to feel more in control because he would have felt better equipped to anticipate what might happen and how best to respond to each scenario. It would also have saved him from being put off guard at the outset, and it would have increased his chances of maintaining his emotional equilibrium when Scar unexpectedly declared the meeting over.

Today's workplace isn't known for giving employees control over their jobs. However, what matters isn't whether you *are* in control but whether you *feel* in control, and the latter is far more attainable than the former. To gain a sense of control in a stressful situation, you need to identify the factors you can determine and focus on them. Job interviews are stressful and unpredictable, but there is much you can still control: your appearance (by what you wear), manner (by inhabiting the role for which you're interviewing), professionalism (by getting there on time, preparing answers for questions they're likely to ask you, and preparing questions for them that show you did your homework). Focusing on the elements you can influence will make you and your unconscious mind feel more in control and therefore more likely to enter a challenge state.

When Scar brought the meeting to an abrupt halt, Tony lost whatever sense of control he had left. That drastically shifted his motivation from succeeding to not failing.

Being motivated to succeed: When you're motivated to succeed, and you envision the goalpost, you are more likely to charge toward it. For example, if your goal is to wow your boss with your presentation (and you feel prepared and in control), you're likely to stay focused and go through your deck like a champ. But if midway, your boss starts shifting in her seat and looking out the window, you might worry that she's getting bored and go into damage control. You then might start rushing through your deck, skipping slides, and going off script—none of which are likely to impress her.

That's what happened to Tony. When Scar ended the meeting, Tony became focused on avoiding a negative outcome, which led him to improvise and accuse Scar of being a bully without explaining himself, giving examples, or laying out his case the way we had practiced in our session.

Like most people, Tony didn't have a full understanding of the challenge-versus-threat theory. But there is one occupation in which high-stakes, stressful situations happen so regularly, everyone knows it extremely well—professional athletes. Athletes in all sports learn the psychology behind challenge and threat mindsets and train accordingly. In some sports, like tennis, you can literally see when players struggle to maintain their composure and confidence when they fall behind so they can stay in a challenge mindset. In fact, what separates the greats from the rest is their ability to manage intense pressure without their mindset shifting into a threat state.

Much as athletes do, we too can manage our mindset when we face highly stressful situations at work by putting in the effort to help us feel prepared and in control and by defining attainable successful outcomes. We also need to work on maintaining our mindset when things go poorly, as they invariably do at times, so that one bad stumble at work does not set us up to make another. That's the problem Tony faced after the team meeting left him feeling stressed and anxious about the fallout.

"I don't know how I'm going to face those people tomorrow," he said. "The entire office will be talking about what happened. There'll be awkward stares and whispers and gossip. I can't deal with that, I really can't." Tony was doing something many of us do when a situation fills us with dread—he was making it worse.

When you're anxious and stressed about a situation at work, it's important to remind yourself that your conscious thoughts and verbalizations (e.g., "I can't deal with that") convey messages to your unconscious mind that could put you in a threat mindset. You therefore need to monitor your internal dialogue, and what you say aloud, so that you don't allow your worries to set you up for failure. That might sound like an impossible task to many. But it isn't *whether* you acknowledge your distress but *how* you do so that matters. Your unconscious mind is always listening. But you can use that to your advantage.

How to Avoid Psyching Yourself Out

When you face a stressful or intimidating situation, telling yourself you won't be able to handle it will *psych you out* and sabotage your chances of performing at your best. Such thoughts and declarations will amplify your stress and dread, freak out your unconscious mind, and put you into a performance-inhibiting threat state. No professional soccer player would tell herself she couldn't handle the stress of a big game because doing so would be as damaging as taking a hammer to her kneecap.

Tony understood this when I explained it to him, or rather his conscious mind did. But our unconscious doesn't respond to reason and logic. If you tell someone who has a fear of flying that traveling by plane is orders of magnitude safer than traveling by car (which is true), their conscious mind might believe it, but their unconscious will still flood them with anxiety when they get on the plane.

When you catch yourself saying or thinking any version of *I won't be able to handle it*, stop and correct yourself using the brain-hacking technique I gave Tony—*The Mind Whisperer Exercise*. It works this way: since the stress you feel is being generated by your unconscious warning you of looming danger, you have to convince it to stop sounding the alarm. Another principle of how our automatic processes operate is *believability*—your unconscious will reject statements that fall outside the range of what it considers to be reasonable. Since it already knows you're stressed, it won't accept that there's no danger or that the danger is minor. But it will accept that you'll be able to handle whatever danger there is.

Instead of telling yourself, *I won't be able to handle the stressful thing*, say, *That thing is going to be stressful, but I'll handle it*. By reassuring your unconscious that you're already on alert (*That thing is going to be stressful . . .*), it won't need to work so hard to warn you of the looming danger. And by saying . . . *but I'll handle it*, you're communicating that you *will* be able to handle *it*—which refers to both the thing itself and to the stress, which downgrades the level of threat the danger presents.

Much like with all psychological messaging, whether to ourselves or to others, consistency is critical. The more consistent you are, the greater the likelihood of your message being received. Since your unconscious is always listening, try to correct every expression of *I won't be able to handle that* to *That will be stressful, but I can handle it*.

Once you prevent yourself from amplifying your stress inadvertently, you'll need to reduce the stress you already feel by regaining a sense of control and beefing up your resources (the other two elements that determine challenge or threat mindsets). As mentioned, we don't have to have full control to feel in control—a little goes a long way. Small and seemingly minor demonstrations of impact, agency, and proactivity can be enough to give you a sense of control in the situation and to convince your unconscious of the same.

How small? A short list could do it—the names of people who could advise or support you, the resources you could gather to gain insight or advice (e.g., articles, books, podcasts), the personal strengths you could bring to bear in the situation, and even a prepared script, including responses to possible attacks, so you don't have to come up with them on the spot. Tony would feel less stressed on the day after the meeting if he thought through strategies he could use in advance.

"The first few hours will probably be the most uncomfortable," I acknowledged. "You'll worry about what people heard and what they think, and you might even feel nervous and self-conscious. How will you manage those feelings?"

"Poorly."

"I meant, what's your plan for handling them?"

"Get there early, hide in my office, sneak out as soon as I can?"

I shook my head. "That would be a mistake."

Tony's predicament—having to face the judgments and whispers of his coworkers—was a common one. When you fail to land the big account, are passed up for the promotion everyone believed you had in the bag, get berated by your manager in a big meeting, screw up a critical presentation, or get into a screaming match with your colleague in the hallway, everyone is likely to know about it. Facing people afterward can feel intimidating and embarrassing, and the impulse to hide might be strong.

Resist it. Hiding will only make things worse. Those who aren't among your friends or supporters will interpret your avoidance as an admission of incompetence, inadequacy, ineptitude, a bad temper, or, in Tony's case, guilt. Meanwhile, the people who are on your side will take your cue and think you want them to give you space, so they'll be less likely to offer you support, and you might interpret their absence to mean that they too are judging you.

The best you can do in such difficult situations is to take what little control you can. Set the tone for how you want to be treated by acting in ways that invite the kind of responses you want. If you want support from those you trust, seek them out. If you want things to go back to normal, behave as if things *are* normal. You'll probably have to fake it at first, at least slightly. A casual *Oh well, you can't win 'em all* vibe is best—as if you have shrugged off the incident and have moved on. Doing so will send others a clear signal to move on as well.

I suggested to Tony that he think of a few people who would be in his corner and approach them no differently than he always had. Hopefully they would take his lead and give him a sense of normalcy. The best thing to do when you're about to face a dread-inducing situation at work is to have a relaxing evening and get a good night's sleep beforehand.

However, doing so will likely be a challenge.

The stresses and pressures of our job don't magically disappear at the end of our workday; we bring them home with us whether we intend to or not. Our work can hijack our most private spaces—including our very thoughts.

CHAPTER THREE

Monday Evening

The Blitz—How to Stop the Nightly Intrusion of Work Thoughts

ONE INTERESTING THING ABOUT work stress is that we don't experience most of it *at* work. We are usually too busy during the workday and focused on getting tasks done to pause and reflect on what we're going through. We are much more likely to mull over distressing events *after* the workday ends— during our commute home, while having dinner with family or friends, when watching a show, or when we're trying to fall asleep later that night.

This mulling happens because we all have a fundamental psychological need to make sense of our experiences, especially challenging ones. The more distressing or upsetting your workday is, the more compelled you will be to brood and ruminate about it after hours. You will replay situations in your mind, dwell on how frustrating, unfair, or aggravating something was, stew on how he said that insulting thing or how she gave you that look. And the more you ruminate, the less present you will be in whatever you are doing.

Ruminating about work in the evenings was a huge problem for Sally, a single mother in her thirties who I had started seeing in therapy when one of my sliding-scale slots opened up. As many therapists do, I reserve some appointments for people who cannot afford my regular fee. Doing so gives back to the community, it keeps my practice varied, and it grounds me professionally and personally.

Sally opened her first session by getting right to the point. "When I was in college, I saw a documentary about London during World War II. Did you know the people there got bombed every night?" I nodded. I was born in London and heard about the Blitz from my grandparents when I was growing up. "That's what it feels like in my head," Sally continued, "like I'm being bombarded by thoughts about work every night." Her face softened. "I'm away from my daughter all day. When I get home after work, I have such limited time to play with her before I have to get her ready for bed. But instead of enjoying it, all I can think about is how much work I still have to do. I try to catch myself when I zone out and refocus on my daughter and our time together, but it doesn't work. Two minutes later, I'm composing an email in my head or obsessing about my co-lead on the nightmare project I have going on at my job." Sally sat up straight. "That's why I made the appointment. I want to be more present with my daughter. Help me make the blitz stop."

Sally had started a new job just a few months earlier, a highly demanding one that was rendered even more challenging by the arrangement she had negotiated with her employer. Sally could leave the office every day at 4:30 PM so she could get home and have time with her daughter, provided she got her work done—which she was highly motivated to do given the job offered a game-changing performance bonus. Securing the bonus was critical for her because it could free her from a trap too many single working mothers faced.

"I've been ready to move up in title and pay for the past two years," Sally explained, "but I've been stuck on the *childcare cliff.* Until this role came along, every job offer I got included an increase in pay that was just enough for me to lose childcare subsidies but not enough to cover private childcare. So, I couldn't take any of them."

Many hardworking single parents (and plenty of dual-income families) fall into this problematic salary range and can't move forward in their careers because of it. Sally also had to overcome the *mommy penalty.* Women make 83 cents on the dollar compared to men, but each child under five years old reduces the mother's earnings by 15 percent. Sally's new job would leap her over the childcare cliff *if* she secured the bonus. To do so, she would need to deliver every project she was assigned on schedule. If she were late on even a single one, she would get nothing. It was a real gamble because the salary alone wasn't enough to cover her expenses. She would have to go into credit card debt to pay for her nanny.

"I'm taking a big risk," Sally admitted, "but the bonus would cover twice the amount of the debt so I could pay it all back and get a bigger apartment." Her eyes lit up at the prospect. "I could finally have a bedroom of my own."

The company's human resources representative, who himself had two children, went as far as to caution Sally that her predecessor typically worked till 9 PM every night but was never able to secure the bonus in his three years in the role. The odds were clearly not in her favor.

But Sally didn't need any favors. Her father had been in the military and died when she was thirteen years old. Her mother, a personal trainer, was diagnosed with breast cancer only months later and died shortly after Sally graduated from high school. Her time with them was far too short, but the foundation of independence and self-discipline they had given her helped her get through the pain, grief, and loss and set her on a journey of self-improvement and personal growth.

Sally would need all the skills and resilience she had gained because the demands of her new job were intense. So too was the nightly assault of ruminations that disrupted her quality time with her daughter. But that wasn't the only damage her ruminating was doing to her health and well-being.

The Difference Between Healthy and Unhealthy Thinking

Ruminating is a form of self-reflection, which is why people are surprised when I characterize it as unhealthy or maladaptive. After all, isn't therapy based on self-reflection? It is, but there are several ways to self-reflect, and not all of them are useful. The purpose of *healthy* self-reflection is to process challenging events in order to gain understanding, insight, acceptance, or perspective, or to find solutions, or figure out a plan of action. That kind of thinking eases distress and, by doing so, helps you let go of the troubling incident. But ruminating—brooding about the events while swirling in the unpleasant emotions they trigger—offers no insights or solutions. It just amplifies your angst.

The word *rumination* comes from how cows digest food. For those unfamiliar with the joys of cow digestion: they chew and swallow, then they regurgitate the food back up and chew it again. So yes, it's slightly disgusting, but it works for cows because, by chewing over their food, they extract more nutrition from it. However, when we ruminate, little "nutrition" is extracted because we don't gain insight or action plans; we just rotate through distressing thoughts.

You've probably spent an entire evening replaying an argument you had with someone at work earlier that day—wishing you had said this instead of that, coming up with mic-drop moments you'll never use because the argument already happened. Telling the offending person off in your head might give you a tang of sweet satisfaction, but it will soon be drowned out by the bitter aftertaste of the anger, resentment, and aggravation you stirred up by ruminating. And those flavors will linger long after the satisfaction has faded.*

Ruminating always leaves you with viscerally unpleasant feelings because recalling *emotional* wounds has a side effect that recalling *physical* wounds does not—it reactivates the pain the wound caused. If you tell the tale of how you broke your leg while trying to catch a Frisbee last summer, your leg will not hurt as a result. But telling the story of how a colleague took credit for your idea will make you feel upset and frustrated all over again, even if it happened twenty years ago. Every time you ruminate about upsetting events, you reactivate the same feelings you had when the incident occurred. Or in the case of ruminating about a future worry, you activate anxiety and the feelings you would have if the worrisome event came to pass.

While rumination intensifies visceral feelings of stress and angst, healthy

---

* Ruminating about happy events is, unfortunately, far less common. When we do dwell on positive emotions, we do so briefly, and they rarely pop into our minds intrusively (except when we are romantically infatuated). Therefore, when I discuss rumination, I'll be referring to how we reflect on upsetting and distressing moments, not pleasant ones.

forms of self-reflection such as problem-solving ease them. That's how you know you're ruminating—you feel it in your body in the same heavy ways you typically experience stress or the other unpleasant feelings you're reactivating. Sally experienced stress as tightness in her chest. I'm a member of the stomach-knotting club. Tony felt stress as tightness in his neck and tension in his muscles. Others might experience heart palpitations or gastrointestinal distress.

Ruminating is extremely common; we all do it far more than we realize, not just in our heads but with our nearest and dearest. Think back to your last highly frustrating or stressful situation at work. How many colleagues, friends, or family members knew about it? I've asked people I work with to keep track of the number of hours they ruminate about work during a stressful period, and the average is over 10 hours a week. Sally ruminated for almost 14—an average of two hours a day (including weekends). Keep a record during your stressful periods at work, and you'll probably be surprised by how much time you're wasting on a harmful activity that offers little value.

The reason after-work ruminations are so common is that our unconscious mind holds a specific belief about our job that we don't necessarily share—that our work is the most important thing in our lives. Remember, your unconscious mind thinks in literal and simplistic terms. Not only do you spend more of your waking hours working than you do with your family or friends, your work is what enables you to address most of your needs.

The psychologist Abraham Maslow proposed that we are compelled to satisfy lower-level needs before focusing on higher-level ones. He envisioned a pyramid in which the basic needs at the bottom, like food, water, shelter, and clothing, had to be met before we could consider any others. Those basic needs are paid for by our jobs. Once those needs are covered, we move up to the next tier on the pyramid—safety and security, which are also heavily influenced by our job and socioeconomic status. Further up the pyramid is family and connection. For many, our job and our "work tribe" is how we fulfill vital aspects of our need to belong, where friendships are created and romantic relationships can ignite. Higher up on the pyramid are needs for self-esteem, self-efficacy, respect, recognition, and accomplishment—in which our work is often central. Work also comprises a significant aspect of our identity and how we address needs at the top of the pyramid, such as creativity, self-determination, and self-actualization.

In short, work is foundational to virtually every aspect of our lives. That's why our unconscious mind considers it our top priority and why it operates to ensure that work remains our top priority, often in direct opposition to our actual needs and wants—like when we're trying to switch off or have quality time with loved ones.

How Ruminating Impacts Your Well-Being

Ruminating doesn't just reactivate distressing emotions. It also triggers our stress response, and not in a healthy gazelle kind of way but in an unhealthy there-goes-the-evening kind of way. Ruminating about our boss telling us off in a meeting will put our body in fight-or-flight mode because our unconscious responds to all threats similarly, whether the danger is from our enemy throwing spears or our boss throwing shade.

Ruminating triggers the release of cortisol into our bloodstream after it had already been doing laps there all day. As a result, our body won't get a chance to come down from the stress of the day, and our internal systems won't get a much-needed respite. Breaks from stress and high activation are critical for short- and long-term health and well-being. So much so, that ruminating about work after work hours is associated with significantly higher risks of cardiovascular disease, higher levels of HDL cholesterol, and higher blood pressure. Other studies have found that ruminating about work causes sleep disturbances—trouble falling asleep or waking up repeatedly during the night—and mood disturbances (from activating intensely unpleasant feelings). It's associated with eating unhealthier foods (we use food and substances for comfort and mood management), and it even impairs our cognitive and executive functions—the very skills we need to do our jobs well. In one study, people who ruminated intensely about work while at home were five times more likely to report lapses of attention the next day, and twice as likely to have trouble completing projects.

Consider that in addition to all that damage, every hour you ruminate after hours is tantamount to unpaid overtime because you're mentally back at work, even if you're not accomplishing anything. Wait, I take that back—you are "accomplishing" things—you're damaging your emotional and physical health, compromising your productivity, ruining your leisure and family time, and impairing your quality of life.

If you're thinking, *Fine, I will definitely stop ruminating*—not so fast. It isn't that simple. Ruminations are very difficult to control because they're intrusive thoughts, not deliberate ones. They're also extremely compelling. It always feels like we're doing something important when we're ruminating, like we're figuring something out even though we're not.

Another complicating factor is that the more stress and pressure we experience during the workday, the stronger the urge to ruminate will be. And as Sally found out, some forms of work stresses are far more likely to trigger intrusive ruminations than others.

Horrible Coworkers

"My first week in the office, I was a frantic mess," Sally acknowledged. "My boss expected me to hit the ground running, but the workload was crazy and I started falling behind. I had to do something, so I turned to my best friend for support."

"What's your friend's name?"

"Spreadsheet."

For a moment, I fully entertained the notion that some parent actually named their kid "Spreadsheet," but then Sally pointed to her phone, and there was a spreadsheet on the screen.

"Now, every minute of my day is planned," she explained. "I'm up at five, light therapy lamp for ten minutes—outdoor sunlight is better, but I can't leave my daughter. I do a four-minute Tabata training—twenty seconds of burpees, ten seconds of rest, eight times, then a cold shower to sharpen my stress response. I get dressed, do ten minutes of mindfulness meditation, brief the nanny while doing my makeup, bike to the office, start at seven, lunch at my desk, home by five. Dinner with my angel—I'm doing intermittent fasting, so I eat with her. Then we play until bathtime, I bathe her, read her a story, and put her down by eight. I do another hour or two of work, pull out the sofa bed, do a guided meditation, and go to sleep."

"You can fall asleep after going sixteen hours without a break?" I asked.

"Not at first. But I upped my sleep hygiene and put in blackout shades. I refine my systems continually, both at home and at work. From what I can tell, the dude before me wasn't maxing efficiency, which is probably why he never got his bonus. I started listening to productivity and optimization podcasts on my bike ride to and from work to get ideas, though some episodes are super long, so I put them on one-point-five speed."

I smiled. "To match your natural setting."

Sally laughed. "You get me. Anyway, my team is on board with the new systems, so that part is under control." She pointed to her temple. "But this part isn't. I need to manage my thoughts better so I can enjoy the time with my daughter. She's sharp. She can tell I'm checked out. If she's not getting enough out of our time together, I might as well go back to my old job."

"Sally, I worry that what you're doing isn't sustainable, even if you do get a handle on your thoughts. What about your personal needs? When do you get to have a life?"

"Next year. If I get the bonus, I can pull back and still have childcare covered. If I free up five hours a week, I could even date."

Sally's plan seemed like a recipe for burnout, but she was adamant about sticking to it. She checked her watch, saw that thirty minutes had already elapsed, and said, "Look, I know what I'm doing sounds iffy. But it's my only shot at a better life, and it's only for one year. Can you help me control my thoughts or not?"

"Yes. But with tons of reservations."

"Cool. I'll add them to my spreadsheet." I must have looked dismayed because she said, "That was a joke. Mostly." She took out a notebook and pen. "Okay. Fix me."

Earlier in my career, I might have refused Sally's request. Agreeing to help her mitigate the damage of overworking without first examining her history and the possible unconscious motivations that were leading her to neglect her emotional health would have seemed irresponsible. But my beliefs about my role as a therapist have evolved over the years. Granted, some of my former teachers might say *devolved*. In graduate school, I was taught that regardless of what a person's "presenting problem" was, I should make my own independent assessment of what the person needed and guide their therapy accordingly. That never sat well with me. Therapy is expensive and time-consuming, and we therapists are, after all, service providers. Today, if a client wants to work on a specific issue and not others, I consider that their prerogative. If I think their proposed focus and direction are too narrow or not beneficial, I tell them so. But unless someone is asking for something ineffective, harmful, or outside my areas of expertise, I give them what they want. In Sally's case with a caveat.

"I can't fix you, but I can help you fix yourself," I said to her. "However, once you get a handle on your ruminating, I insist we discuss how you can get breaks from the stress now, this year. Going from morning till night isn't sustainable. Burnt-Out Mommy will be even less present with your daughter than Ruminating Mommy is."

Sally agreed. I asked her what she was ruminating about most. "The hell project I mentioned earlier," she responded. What made the project hellish for Sally was the leader of the team she had to collaborate with. Her rather salty description of him included a string of F-bombs capped with a wish for him to engage in a physiologically implausible feat of self-gratification.

Interpersonal conflict has been found to be an especially potent driver of rumination. Other issues that my clients have spent hours chewing over include looming layoffs; experiencing bias due to factors such as gender, race, culture, age, disability, sexual preference, religion, or appearance; being micro-managed; lacking control or agency; and incidents that result in embarrassment, humil-iation, or feelings of helplessness. Sally and her team were responsible for the content and design of a new interface, but they couldn't complete their work until her co-lead's team did the tech build, and her hellish colleague was in no hurry to do so.

"We have a hard deadline and a strict timeline of deliverables," Sally explained. "Eric, that's my co-lead, sends me a link three days behind schedule and asks me to sign off on their work. I click it, and it's a total joke. The images are the wrong size, the text isn't laid out correctly, and there's zero functionality. We had a meeting, and he accused me of looking for problems and being unreasonable. He was so arrogant and smug that even his team looked uncomfortable."

"That bad?"

Sally held up her phone and showed me her co-lead's LinkedIn picture. I had to stifle a snort-laugh. The image practically screamed entitlement and conceit. Given his choice of headshot, he also suffered from a severe lack of self-awareness. "I see your point."

"Thank you. So, a week later, Eric sends me the sign-off again. Some things were fixed, others not. Now we're a full week behind. I asked my boss for advice, but she was useless. All she said was that she was confident I'll figure it out. It's incredibly frustrating."

Studies have found that unfinished tasks, especially time-sensitive ones, can get ensnared in our brains like kitten claws in a tea doily and foster such intense ruminating that it impairs our sleep. Unfortunately for Sally, one thing that can make unfinished tasks register as even more stressful is when our bosses have high expectations of our ability to complete them.

Workplace incivility does the same thing. When someone is condescending, rude, disrespectful, derogatory, or makes us feel excluded or rejected, we can stew on it for hours, and Sally's co-lead served her a steady diet of such insults. "I went over to Eric's office to deal with him one-on-one, and he gaslit me—told me it's practically ready—and accused me of being uptight and difficult. I insisted he give me a firm delivery date. He pretended to get a call and shooed me out of his office like I was an intern. We have to have a functioning version in one week. I Slacked him this morning. Guess who's on vacation for the next five days?"

My stomach was in knots just from listening to Sally's predicament. No wonder she was ruminating so intensely. "Okay, let's get to the fixing," I said to Sally. She sat up, ready to take notes.

How to Banish Ruminations

What makes ruminations so compelling and difficult to dismiss is that they're not centered around the incident or person but around the *intense emotions* that person or incident provoked. The more intense those feelings are, the more your thoughts will swirl around them like they are an emotional black hole. You could even find yourself *rumination-surfing*—going from one incident that evoked those specific feelings to another for hours on end.

Sally's ruminating often focused on lies and betrayal. "I'm bathing my daughter and find myself replaying how aggravating it was to have my co-lead lie to my face about the completion dates. That reminded me of my previous job where my boss promised to promote me for two years in a row but never did, and then denied he ever promised me anything. The next thing I know, I'm thinking about how my old boyfriend swore up and down that he wanted kids and then broke up with me the day I told him I was pregnant."

Hearing how Sally had been mistreated by bosses and boyfriends made me want to explore those issues further, but I respected our agreement and focused the rest of the session on the three steps of rumination banishment: (1) Attack the ruminations' source of power by weakening the emotions fueling them—lowering their emotional intensity will make it easier to resist the urge to indulge them. (2) Convert ruminative thoughts into healthy and productive ones or, if that's not possible, disengage from them using a brain hack. (3) Develop a strong intolerance for ruminative thoughts.

1. The Science of Emotional Management

In my talks, I often ask the audience to think about a distressing event and how they managed the intense emotions it caused. People often yell out, "Tequila!" or "Sex!" or "Sobbing!" which often do go in that sequence—but I rarely get actual strategies. The term psychologists use to describe the automatic and deliberate strategies we use to moderate the intensity and duration of our feelings is *emotional regulation.**

Much of the emotional regulation we do occurs automatically and unconsciously, like how we intuitively dial down expressions of anger at work. Snapping at our bosses when they say something disrespectful might be justified, but it would not serve us well. Our unconscious knows that, so it automatically keeps a lid on our emotional reactions and prevents us from responding as we might in a different context.

We can also regulate our emotions consciously and deliberately. Tony did that when he first learned about the meeting Scar called. To calm the stress and anxiety he felt about having to defend himself in front of the whole team, he referred to the meeting as "ridiculous." By minimizing its legitimacy, he diminished the threat and, consequently, the stress it triggered.

Our automatic (unconscious) and intentional (conscious) emotional regulation strategies keep the intensity of our feelings within manageable levels so that they don't overwhelm us. However, our capacity for emotional management has limits. When the intensity of our emotions exceeds our ability to contain them, they spill over, and we become overwhelmed and flooded by them—a psychological state known as *dysregulation.*

Dysregulation is a temporary loss of the ability to control your emotions. You might burst into tears, shut down entirely, experience panic, become highly agitated, act impulsively, have difficulty thinking clearly, or become irrational. Even small provocations can trigger outsized reactions. "Losing it" in such ways isn't just distressing, it's often embarrassing and even harmful because we say and do things when we are dysregulated that we wouldn't otherwise. Some people get dysregulated more easily than others, but we all have our breaking point.

Most jobs expect us to adhere to unspoken codes of conduct (e.g., behave professionally, be respectful to higher-ups, avoid outbursts, welcome customers with a smile). Doing so requires a constant deployment of emotional regulation techniques and strategies. For example, you might seek *emotional support* after

---

* The terms *emotions* and *feelings* refer to slightly different things in psychological theory and research, but I will be using them interchangeably.

the meeting with your boss or use *distraction* when you don't want to dwell on a frustrating interaction (e.g., by swiping, scrolling, or gaming). Like Tony did, you might use *avoidance* to steer clear of a stressful meeting and then come to *acceptance* when you realize that avoidance isn't an option.

The most common emotional regulation strategy is *suppression*—pushing down your emotions to hide your true feelings and to adhere to display rules (the unspoken and spoken expectations that dictate which emotions should be expressed or suppressed at work, such as being expected to smile graciously when your colleague gets promoted instead of you and not show how devastated you are). Suppression is effective but strenuous because you're not just pushing down the original feeling, you're acting as if you have an entirely different one, and you have to keep up the "act" for as long as the original emotion lingers.

Sales, nursing, teaching, politics, litigation, airline service, customer service, therapy, and other professions can require using suppression continually. Over time, using suppression in the workplace has been found to have a significantly negative impact on emotional health, at least in the United States and other countries in which individual well-being is prioritized. Interestingly, a recent large multinational study found that suppression had the opposite impact in countries in which social harmony and collective well-being were prioritized. For example, in China, suppression can feel dutiful because your efforts are contributing to the greater good (maintaining harmony), while in the United States, you are likely to experience those efforts as being imposed on you and therefore oppressive.

First Weaken the Emotion, Then Attack the Rumination

The most effective and efficient strategy to reduce the intensity of your emotions is *reframing* (also known as *cognitive reappraisal*). The goal of reframing is to weaken the emotion at the source by changing how you feel about the situation itself instead of just covering the emotion by suppressing it. You can do so by using one of three approaches: (1) *shift your perspective*, (2) *find silver linings*, or (3) *identify opportunities*. As I advised Sally, when battling work ruminations, you should use all three for maximum effect.

"Shifting your perspective will enable you to see the distressing situation from a new vantage point from which things seem less emotionally charged," I explained. "For example, you can shift your perspective in time by imagining that you're looking back at the present from five years in the future. Does the situation seem as important? Will you even remember it? Would it pass the *memoir test?*"

"What's the memoir test?" Sally asked.

"If you wrote a memoir about your life, would the incident be worthy of inclusion? Most of the things we ruminate about are not. In which case, you can reframe the situation as merely a difficult moment in what will hopefully be a long and successful career. This type of framing minimizes the importance of the event, which should help remove its emotional sting."

Sally looked up from her note-taking and said, "More examples, please."

"You could also shift perspective by broadening your lens. For example, you could remind yourself that there are more important things going on in your life, like a friend who lost her job or your daughter's health, so that the issue seems relatively less significant and less emotionally evocative. Or you can adopt a different point of view. For example, looking at things through the lens of departmental politics could show you where you fit into the larger chess game being played, which could help you take things less personally. Or using empathy to gain a better understanding of the offending person and possibly even have compassion for them, which can soothe anger, resentment, and frustration."

Sally was not a fan of the empathy approach, "I have zero compassion for that incompetent pile of—"

"Apparently not," I interrupted. "But what about his team? You said they looked uncomfortable in the meeting. Is it possible they're caught in the middle here? If they are, they might be willing to do the fixes you need, especially now that he's away."

Sally's eyes opened wide. "I can email him the new punch list and copy them. His out-of-office reply will bounce it back, but they'll get it. I can mention the original target date to imply that he was cool with them doing the fixes. Yeah, that might work. Okay, go on."

"The second approach to reframing is to find silver linings. Identifying the good in the bad will reduce the intensity of the distressing emotions, and it might even add some pleasant ones to the mix."

There is almost always *some* good that can come from challenging situations. For Tony, going to the office after the embarrassing team meeting will be stressful and upsetting, but it will also reveal who he may be able to trust and who might be in Scar's camp—valuable information for the reputation restoration efforts he needs to make.

One silver lining inherent in any hardship is that getting through it can help you build emotional resilience. Hardship doesn't automatically boost resilience, though. To make it count, we need to assess and acknowledge the various external resources (e.g., seeking advice or getting social support) and internal ones (e.g., practicing acceptance or prioritizing self-care) that helped make the hardship more manageable or tolerable. Knowing the elements that got us through one crisis gives us confidence that we can get through another.

Most bad situations also present opportunities—the third approach to reframing—but it feels annoying to look for them, so we often neglect to do so. For example, most people get irritated when their manager saddles them with extra tasks, but such situations can provide opportunities to acquire new skills or put you in touch with higher-ups and offer you a chance to impress them. Getting a disappointing performance review will sting, but it will pinpoint where you need to make efforts to improve, and doing so will give you an opportunity to demonstrate that you take feedback well and are capable of growth.

Sally came up with, "My team is definitely more bonded because of what happened. And if I can create a backchannel with the tech team, I could also use it going forward and work around Eric." Her eyes lit up. "If I make single moms look good, maybe my company would hire more of them and pay them better."

Reframing helps reduce the intensity and frequency of our ruminations enough to engage in step two—converting unhealthy forms of self-reflection into productive ones.

2. How to Convert Ruminations into Healthy Thoughts

The same studies that documented the many harms ruminating inflicts found that reflecting about the same kinds of events using problem-solving and solution-oriented thinking did not amplify stress, it eased it. To illustrate how to convert one form of thinking into another, let's use Sally's most frequent ruminative thought as an example: *I've got so much work to do.*

Ruminating about excessive workloads is as common as it is useless because we don't tend to do it when we are at work and getting things done; we do it outside of work and in ways that disrupt our efforts to de-stress. Remember that your unconscious doesn't care that you are troubled about a laborious expense report. It will interpret your distress as a sign of *looming danger*, not *looming paperwork*, and it will put your entire system into fight-or-flight.

"Fine," Sally said when I explained that to her. "But I do have a ton of work. How do I convert that stress into a healthy thought?"

"By framing it as a question to be answered or solved," I responded. "*I have so much work to do* is a scheduling question. What you're really asking is, *Where can I find room in my schedule for the specific task that's troubling me?* or *What could I move to make room for it?* Or even, *When can I go over my schedule to reassure myself that I have time to work on it?* Remember, the goal here is not necessarily to solve the problem but to convince your unconscious that you're on top of it so it stops activating your stress response."

Given her affinity for calendars and spreadsheets, going over her schedule was easy advice for Sally to adopt. Fortunately, our unconscious takes calendars as seriously as Sally does. In one experiment, worried participants were instructed to postpone their worrying to a later date and only think about the problem then. Scheduling their worry allowed many of them to let go of the issue in the moment. However, for that to work, you have to be sincere in your intention to address the worry later—your unconscious can tell if you are not.

Sally also needed to convert ruminations about her co-lead. To change interpersonal tensions and conflicts into problems that can be solved, consider whether the person would be open to a conversation. If so, what's a realistic outcome that would be worth pursuing, and what approach would be most effective to achieve it? If a conversation isn't possible or productive, figure out how to minimize interaction with that person or how to identify their triggers so you can avoid activating them.

"I'll give this all a try," Sally said, "but to be honest, when I'm with my daughter, I'm not always going to have the time to think through how to shift perspective or how to convert to problem-solving. Doing that would make me just as checked out as ruminating."

"Good point," I acknowledged. "There's a brain hack you can use to stop ruminating in those situations, at least temporarily—distraction. The urge to ruminate is like a craving; it comes in waves. Studies have shown that a two- or three-minute distraction is enough to allow the urge to pass. But—the distraction has to take up enough mental bandwidth to deprive the rumination of 'oxygen' until your brain resets, which means it has to require focus and concentration. Scrolling, viewing, or casual reading won't cut it because those activities are passive; they don't take up enough bandwidth. What does are puzzles, memory tasks, or other brain teasers like counting back from 100 by 7's (100, 93, 86 . . .), recalling the items in your fridge, or one you can do with your daughter—recalling the order of books on her shelf."

Battling ruminations is a form of cognitive retraining—you are literally teaching your brain to think differently. That takes time and effort and, most importantly, consistency. But you can accelerate the process.

3. Don't Tolerate Intrusive Thoughts

Ruminations are intruders that steal your time and attention, take you away from the things that matter, and impair your well-being—there is ample reason to push them away. "You have to develop an absolute intolerance for ruminating," I explained to Sally. "See them as intrusive hijackers of your thoughts and have real disdain for them, note the 'ick' the thought caused in your stomach and expel it from your mind."

"It's the 'ick' in the tech department I'd rather expel," Sally replied. "But fine, how do I develop this intolerance?"

"There are two steps." The first is to catch yourself ruminating and label the thought as "rumination." Training yourself to label ruminative thoughts as the uninvited intruders they are is highly doable with practice.

The second step is to foster disgust, disdain, and annoyance toward such intrusions. Indulging ruminations is like picking a scab off an emotional wound—use that imagery. Imagine your finger picking at crusty skin until pus oozes out. If that is too unpleasant for you, envision the ruminative thought as a skunk that snuck into your house. Would you allow it to join you on the couch? Every time you indulge a ruminative thought, visualize the skunk next to you and kick it out. With consistency and repetition, you can train yourself to catch such thoughts and expel them quickly. I did it myself years ago. That doesn't mean I no longer get bombarded with ruminations during stressful periods at work—I do. But I catch them quickly and use reframing, converting, and/or distracting so they get only a few seconds of stage time. You can and should do the same with anxious thoughts (many ruminative thoughts are anxiety-driven anyway), especially if the thought is catastrophic. For example, when you catch yourself thinking, *If I ask my boss for a vacation, they'll fire me, and I'll never find another job again*, label the thought as "anxiety" and envision it intruding into your space as you would a ruminative thought.

Sally tackled her ruminations with her typical gusto and did a great job scaling them back. But that wasn't her only triumph; she also got her co-lead's team to complete their part of the project while he was on vacation. When her co-lead returned and realized that Sally had worked with his team behind his back, he was furious, but there was nothing he could do to stop the product from launching on time.

Taking back control of your thoughts in the evening will help you feel more rested the next day. That turns out to be critical because starting the day tired and stressed will limit your mental bandwidth and make you more likely to default to automatic coping mechanisms instead of more deliberate ones. And given the stresses of the current workplace, your unconscious coping mechanisms are likely to do more harm than good.

CHAPTER FOUR

Tuesday Morning

Self-Sabotage—How to Avoid Using Harmful Coping Mechanisms

TUESDAYS CAN FEEL LIKE the longest day of the week—the previous weekend seems like a distant memory, and the upcoming weekend is almost a full workweek away. No wonder then that an analysis of social media posts indicated that Tuesdays were the day positive emotions at work were at their lowest. A low mood can make the ongoing stress and pressure of your job feel even more suffocating and require your coping mechanisms to work even harder to manage those stresses.

Coping mechanisms are mental devices that help us manage, reduce, or tolerate stressors from without and difficult emotions from within. Similarly to emotional regulation, our coping mechanisms can be deployed automatically and outside our awareness (unconsciously), as well as intentionally and deliberately (consciously). Our coping mechanisms are also subject to bandwidth limitations, which means that the more bandwidth we need to devote to managing stress and strain at work, the less we'll have to manage our coping mechanisms intentionally, and the more likely we'll be to default to automatic coping processes that can harm us in the long run.

Priya, a twenty-five-year-old personal assistant, had an impressive history of undermining her own best interests at work. Priya's boss, a film producer, traveled frequently, and his plans often changed with little notice. Consequently, she had to constantly scramble to rebook travel itineraries, studio visits, hotel reservations, and car services. She spent entire evenings packing, unpacking, and repacking suitcases, ordering groceries for her boss's return, throwing them out when he was delayed, and then reordering them all over again, all while falling behind on her other duties.

"My boss yells at me, like, all the time," Priya explained to her parents, who had brought her to family therapy. "He sees how mad stressed I get, but he doesn't care. He kept piling on more and more responsibilities." She turned to me, "I couldn't deal anymore, so I quit and gave him two weeks' notice. My parents reacted like it was the *end of the world*, so here we are."

"Honey!" Priya's mother exclaimed. "We're not here because you quit *one* job."

"How many jobs did you quit?" I asked Priya.

"Eleven," she responded.

"In six years," her father added. "A family friend told her he could easily get her a job as a senior PA because she had enough experience; she just didn't have it in one place. He told her, *Just stay in a single job for two years and you could move up.* She knows that, but she quits after just a few months anyway."

"You don't understand how totally stressful being a PA is or how difficult the bosses are," Priya responded defiantly. "They want me to be their secretary, their housekeeper, personal shopper, hospital pickup. You know what the nurses said when they saw me at the colonoscopy clinic last month? *Hello again.* That's how often I've been there. My mental health matters. I won't stay in a job if it's making me miserable."

"Your mental health matters to us too," her mother said. "That's why we're here. But honey, it isn't just the jobs. You dropped out of college after one year. You stop coming to family therapy after a few sessions every time we see someone. You quit *everything*."

"I left college because I wasn't going to classes and I didn't want to waste hundreds of thousands of your hard-earned dollars. Sorry if that disappointed you."

"She's always had a thing with money," her father said. "She'd rather sleep on strangers' couches than let us help with her rent."

"It's called couch surfing, and I only do it when I'm in between jobs."

"You're always in between jobs!" her mother exclaimed.

I let the bickering go on a little longer. When working with couples or families, it's important to see how they communicate around conflict because that was usually where the therapeutic work is needed. But one thing was already clear to me. Priya was unaware of how profoundly her automatic coping mechanisms were sabotaging her.

We Are Still Babies at Heart

The best way to gain an appreciation for what your coping mechanisms do is to consider what life was like without them when you were a baby. Newborns have no coping mechanisms with which to buffer distress of any kind, which is why everything makes them cry. Crying is our default and natural response to hunger, fear, fatigue, discomfort, or pain, and it alerts others that we need help. We start life by outsourcing our coping strategies to our caregivers, but we begin to learn how to self-soothe rather quickly, usually within our first year. Our coping mechanisms then continue to develop throughout our infancy, childhood, and early adulthood (and in some ways, throughout our entire lives).

Our coping mechanisms serve the same function airbags do in cars—when they sense an imminent "collision," they deploy instantly to cushion us from harm. The threats that trigger our coping mechanisms can come from outside us (e.g., our boss being on the warpath) or inside (e.g., anxiety, stress, or other strong emotions and sensations). Our coping mechanisms don't always deploy at full strength though; fatigue, hunger, pain, or general overuse can render them less effective. That's why being exhausted, hungry, or in pain makes us moody, emotional, volatile, and prone to tears—more like our child-self—because our coping mechanisms aren't working at their full capacity.

Want to feel young again? Forget Botox and fillers; exhaust your coping mechanisms. You're welcome.

There is a critical difference between the coping mechanisms available to our conscious mind and those deployed by automatic processes. When we're in conscious control of our coping mechanisms, we favor strategies that are *problem-focused*—aimed at addressing the source of stress directly. For example, Sally coped with the threat of missing her deadline and losing her bonus by tackling the source of stress directly (manipulating her co-lead's team into working with her directly while he was on vacation). On the other hand, our automatic coping mechanisms use strategies that are *emotion-focused*. Rather than eliminating or managing threats at the source, they focus on reducing our emotional distress by offering solutions that provide immediate relief, like distraction. Today, our go-to source of distraction is our phone. We surf social media, text a friend, or game in order to get a break from the stress of the moment.

The problem with outsourcing our coping mechanisms to a device that's always within reach is that we overuse it and become too reliant on distraction as a coping mechanism. Doing so prevents us from sharpening our problem-focused coping skills, and it shrinks our stress-tolerance balloon because we're not learning to handle stress but to avoid it. As a result, we're likely to experience the same pressures as more intense than we would have had we learned how to cope with them better.

That is exactly what happened to Priya.

When the pressures of her jobs mounted, she didn't discuss her workload with her bosses or find ways to manage the demands of her jobs more directly. Rather, she allowed the stress to mount until her coping mechanisms could no longer cushion it effectively, at which point her unconscious swooped in to grant her immediate emotional relief—by quitting. She then had to move out of her apartment and start looking for a new job while sleeping on friends' couches, all of which added far more stress to her life. Failing to get the two years of experience she needed to advance in her career also kept her on the bottom rung of her employment ladder.

Priya didn't deny that she had a pattern of quitting (after eleven times, she couldn't), but she justified her actions the same way many of us do when we're confronted with evidence of self-sabotage—we blame external factors (e.g., our bosses being difficult, the client being unreasonable). Our unconscious mind will urge us to act unwisely at times, but that doesn't absolve us of responsibility for those actions (or inactions). We might not have realized that automatic processes were making decisions for us, but we knew *what* we were doing, even if not *why* we were doing it.

Priya needed to see how she contributed to her predicament without her feeling blamed. That would be difficult for me to help her do with her parents there, but if I asked to speak with Priya privately, she would think I believed that she was the problem. Given her history of quitting therapy, I didn't want to risk that. So, I tried to get her to do something we could all benefit from doing whether we are in therapy or not—get curious about her patterns.

"Eleven jobs in six years," I said to Priya. "What do you think keeps going wrong?"

"Nothing goes wrong," Priya insisted. "It's like dating. You go out with someone, get to know them, realize it's not a good match, and break up with them." She turned to her parents. "You wouldn't want me to stay in a bad relationship, would you? Same thing with bad bosses."

Her mother turned to me with a *See what we're dealing with?* look.

"Priya, do you know why your parents are worried about you?"

"They're anxious, co-dependent empty-nesters?"

"Maybe, I don't know them well enough to say. What I do know is that it's not because you quit every job you start."

"Yes, it is," Priya's mother insisted.

Priya shot me a *See what I'm dealing with?* look.

"No," I said to Priya's mother. "What's triggering your worry is not the pattern of Priya breaking up with her bosses but that Priya doesn't seem worried about the pattern," I looked at Priya, "or at least curious as to why you keep repeating it. I agree with you; work *is* like dating, at least in some ways. One of them is that job interviews have a dual purpose. The employer needs to assess your fit for them, and you need to assess whether they are a good fit for you. It's possible you're focusing too much attention on getting the job and not enough on whether the job and the boss are a good match for you."

I paused for Priya to object. She didn't, so I added, "I can see other patterns as well, but that discussion would probably be more productive without your parents in the room." I turned to Priya's parents. "You see that Priya quit eleven jobs in six years, and that worries you. But what you don't see is that she did something else eleven times—she found new ones. That isn't easy to do. She had to contact agencies, submit résumés and cover letters, go to interviews, get herself in the right mindset to impress. Then she had to learn the ropes, adjust to the new boss's quirks, demands, and expectations. That takes serious motivation, dedication, and self-discipline. Those things should modify how worried you are, no?"

Priya looked at her parents, as if waiting for them to object. They did not.

"If Priya agreed to come for a few sessions by herself, would you agree to back off and not ask her about jobs during the time she and I worked together?" They nodded.

"Your decision, Priya. Are you okay with you and I meeting without them?"

"Would you do that, honey?" Priya's mother said, hopefully.

I jumped in before Priya could respond. "This is why Priya isn't worried," I said to her parents. "You're *so* worried, your feelings about this are *so* big, there's no room for hers. Unless you give her the space to have her own thoughts and feelings about her career, nothing will change." I said to Priya, "You know your parents; how difficult will it be for them to not bring up work or discuss their worries with you?"

"Like, impossible."

I smiled at her parents. "Are you willing to take on Mission: Impossible?" Her parents nodded reluctantly. "Great," I responded. "Priya and I will take it from here."

If I could help Priya recognize when she was becoming overly pressured at work, she might be able to start using problem-focused coping strategies to reduce those stresses so that her unconscious mind didn't swoop in to save her by pushing the eject button.

But first, I needed her to recognize the various ways she was undermining herself. It wasn't just the impulsive quitting that was problematic; Priya was doing something that made the normal pressures her job entailed far worse than they would have been otherwise—defining her entire job as stressful. It's a mistake many of us make and one that can do surprising damage.

Your Job Is Less Stressful Than You Think

After the terrorist attacks of September 11, 2001, I dedicated one of the low-fee ther-apy slots in my practice to firefighters. I have since worked with many. You might think that running into burning buildings is the epitome of stress, but none of the firefighters I worked with defined their job as extremely stressful. As one ten-year veteran explained, "You spend most of your time in the firehouse, not putting out fires." To be clear, there were moments and events that were extremely stressful—life-threatening situations always are. But those incidents were relatively rare.

What other aspects of their job caused them stress? The answers ranged from "When people aren't getting along, and there's tension in the firehouse" to "When it's my turn to cook because I always get complaints" to "Those shirtless firefighter calendars—not an expectation most of us can live up to."

Framing our entire job as stressful adds an unnecessary prism of distress to every task we do because our unconscious will respond by raising the associ-ated threat level accordingly. Doing so will also predispose us toward a threat mindset, which can significantly impair our performance and productivity. But perhaps the biggest problem with characterizing our entire job as stressful is that it simply isn't true.

When I asked Priya what percentage of her typical workweek involved highly stressful tasks, she said 90%.

What percentage of your workweek is highly stressful? Please note your response before you continue reading.

Few jobs are stressful 90% of the time, even if it sometimes feels that way. For example, a meeting that devolves into a shouting match can make your whole day feel tense even though the meeting itself only lasted an hour and the rest of the day was far less stressful. To help Priya get a clearer sense of which aspects of her job were stressful and which were not, I gave her an exercise I call *Locating Your Job's Stress Mines*. You will need to write down your answers.

1. Start by listing all the roles you inhabit (Priya wrote: personal assistant, office assistant, gofer, travel agent, concierge, secretary, and housekeeper).

2. Under each role, write the specific tasks that role requires (e.g., Priya's role as housekeeper included cleaning the office, serving beverages, hanging up coats, dropping off and picking up dry-cleaning, ordering food and groceries, accepting deliveries, etc. For her role as travel agent, she included making flight and hotel reservations, coordinating airport pickups, making restaurant reservations, arranging transportation, and canceling and rescheduling all the above). Include electronic communications such as emails, texting, and business messaging apps; the various meetings you attend (each type gets its own row); any managerial duties (e.g., supervision, feedback, development, pep talks); and the various entities you deal with (e.g., team members, vendors, clients, customers).

3. Next, estimate how many minutes or hours per week each task requires. If a task only happens monthly or quarterly, prorate the time accordingly (Priya spent roughly one and a half hours per week in face-to-face or phone communication with her boss. Her most time-consuming role was being a travel agent, on which she spent almost six hours a week).

4. Go through your list of tasks and indicate how stressful each task is on a scale of 1 to 10. (Priya spent 10 hours a week on housekeeping duties that she didn't love but were not stressful to complete. Her most stressful duty was the one and a half hours she spent in direct communication with her boss.)

5. For items that you rated as eight or above, detail what makes the task stressful (Priya hated meetings with her boss because he frequently criticized, lectured, and raised his voice). You might fear public speaking and therefore hate having to talk in staff meetings. Or you might dread dealing with a particularly unpleasant customer.

6. On the bottom row, total how many tasks per week are highly stressful and how many hours you spend doing them. Then calculate what percentage of your working hours that constitutes. To get the percentage, take the number

of stressful hours you work per week, divide it by your total work hours per week, and multiply by 100.

Priya's highly stressful tasks totaled 4 hours out of a 50-hour workweek. She had estimated her highly stressful tasks as comprising 90% of her work hours when they constituted less than 10% of them. How did your totals compare with your initial estimate?

Deactivating Your Stress Mines

The Stress Mines exercise gives you a more realistic assessment of how many highly stressful tasks your job truly involves. However, its real value is that once you know where your stress mines are, you can modify the language you use to describe your job. Instead of the stress-inducing thought, *My job is super stressful*, you can say, *I only have one stressful thing today—meeting with my boss at three*. By doing so, your coping mechanisms will only be on high alert for specific moments instead of for the entire week.

Most importantly, by being forewarned about when you will need to deploy your coping mechanisms (e.g., in preparation for the meeting with your boss), you are more likely to do so in a considered and intentional way. When I have meetings that I expect to be stressful, I take a few slow deep breaths (to calm myself), and then I brace myself as if I am going into battle. If a situation looks like it will be especially distressing, I set up a call with a friend or loved one ahead of time so that I can vent and get emotional support afterward. Doing such things will help you minimize the self-sabotage and avoidance your automatic coping processes would have opted for after needlessly being on high alert all day (e.g., distracting yourself with Reels as the meeting approached and then losing track of time and getting to the meeting late).

It's impossible to avoid all the pain points that come with our job, but we can achieve a meaningful reduction by approaching our stress mines with our shields raised. Mentally bracing ourselves—adjusting our mindset to one that anticipates tension or pressure before an unpleasant task—will help us get to the task with our coping mechanisms at full capacity, which will reduce the distress that mine causes.

Another way to reduce stress is to examine the tasks you ranked as moderately stressful and explore whether they can be delegated or minimized. Remember, stress is subjective; you might hate expense reports, but if the colleague joining you on the sales trip does not, they might agree to do yours if you took care of booking the hotels. Delegating is most useful when the task is one you do regularly because those are the ones that have the best return on investment (delegating always involves effort to explain and train the other person).

Once Priya learned how to deactivate her stress mines *in theory*, she needed to find a new job in which she could apply the skill in practice. She also knew that it would take time to find the right job and didn't feel comfortable "wasting" her parents' money on therapy until she did, so she decided to take a break from our sessions. She promised to reach out once she found a new job, and she assured me she wasn't quitting therapy, merely pausing it. Since she had clearly thought through her decision, I was less worried about it being motivated by unconscious avoidance, and I believed she would return.

Priya's coping mechanisms resulted in dramatic exits, but our unconscious impulses can also impact us in more mundane ways, leading to small errors that can have an outsized impact because we are likely to repeat them many times. But there are tools we can use to catch and correct these minor slips before they become major crises.

CHAPTER FIVE

Tuesday Afternoon

Familiar Patterns—How Stress Makes Us Repeat Our Mistakes

PRIYA CAME BACK TO therapy, but only once she was five months into a new job. The reason she delayed was that she was also four months into a new relationship. "Doing therapy when I was mad happy felt weird," she explained. Her new position was with a media company run by five partners who were supported by two personal assistants: Jan, a senior assistant who had been there for 10 years, and Kev, who had been the junior assistant until he got promoted when Priya joined.

"I'm responsible for *Dayles, Sosh, Scheds*, and *Tins*," Priya explained. "That's daily office needs, social media, weekly schedules, and travel itineraries. Basically, the stuff Jan and Kev hate doing—the *bores* and *chores*. Jan travels with the partners, and Kev joins them for conferences and whatever. But I never get to go to anything. I was cool with it at first because the job was chill, but a month ago, the vibe totally changed. Now the partners are all over me every time I get to work a few minutes late. Like, last week, I was almost at the office with the coffee orders when I realized I forgot the cinnamon sprinkle for the half-caf, triple-shot, extra-hot latte with steamed milk, so I had to go back. Cinnamon Sprinkle—I call the partners by their coffee order—made such a stink about me being late I cried in the bathroom for, like, an hour."

Using nicknames in the workplace is quite common, especially when doing so as a memory aid. "Sounds rough," I acknowledged. "But given that, congrats on not quitting."

Priya winced. "Uh-oh," I said.

"No, no, I didn't quit," she quickly clarified, "I *quiet* quit. I had to do something. The bosses are super tense and uptight. Like, they're just waiting for me to mess up again. I'm getting home late every night, and I'm not even learning anything. So, I decided to prioritize my work-life balance. If they need something done as soon as possible, I do it as soon as *reasonable*. If they email me after hours, I get back the next morning. So far, there's been zero pushback."

"How long have you been quiet quitting?"

"Two days."

"Ah. The jury's still out on the pushback, then. But look, you came face-to-face with the urge to quit, and you didn't. That's excellent. Now let's discuss quiet quitting."

Priya, like many quiet quitters, thought she was taking control by disengaging from her job, but she was not. Her decision was a classic less-pain-now-more-pain-later emotional-focused coping mechanism—the type favored by our unconscious mind. Disengaging from your job might relieve you of stress in the short term, but it doesn't actually solve anything. It won't help you develop professionally or advance your career, and it could easily get you fired the next time layoffs come around.

Quiet quitting is, in essence, a relationship-management technique: *If you, employer, make so few efforts to care about my needs, I won't work as hard to take care of yours.* The problem is that the "relationship" remains problematic and unsatisfying—nothing changes. If you used the bandwidth you gained by quiet quitting to look for a better opportunity, the strategy would make more sense. But Priya still needed eighteen more months in her role to be eligible for senior personal assistant positions, so leaving wasn't an option for her.

"We had worked on you addressing dissatisfactions with your manager rather than allowing stress to accumulate," I said. "Have you tried talking to . . . Cinnamon Sprinkle?"

"He's too busy. They all are. Scheds are totally blocked."

"Then what are you doing to manage the stress?" I inquired.

"I send my boyfriend exploding-head emojis, and he texts me hearts and flexed biceps so I stay strong."

Priya's boyfriend sounded supportive, which was good to hear. It was also the first time I heard her express frustration that she wasn't higher up on her professional ladder, which was encouraging as well. On the not-good-news front, her bosses were already "all over her" for being repeatedly late. This was the first I was hearing about Priya having a time-management problem, and it worried me. Given how stressful her situation was, her time management was likely to decline, not improve.

Intense job strain sets us up to make more mistakes because of our bandwidth limitations. The more pressured our job is, the more mental bandwidth we have to devote to managing those stresses, and the fewer attentional resources we'll have to devote to our tasks. We'll be more prone to making mistakes as a result. The errors we make might be small, but they could have outsized consequences. Having a number off in a spreadsheet or a financial model, forgetting a key clause in a contract, or being late to a critical meeting can lead to professional disaster.

Interestingly, when we're stressed and fatigued, we don't actually make dozens of different mistakes. We make a few *types* of mistakes, and then we repeat them in various situations. That's because we each have our personal blind spots—the factors and considerations that we typically miss, minimize, or misjudge—that cause us to stumble again and again.

What's curious about our blind spots is that they persist at all, given how often they trip us up. Time-management issues are a great example. While some people with poor time management don't get stressed by being late, Priya, like many, did. The rushing, panic, and embarrassment she endured when she was running behind felt very unpleasant, yet she kept making the same mistakes. As Jan, the senior personal assistant on Priya's team, said to her in a moment of frustration, "You take the same route to work every day; how have you not calculated when you should leave to get here on time?" In fact, Priya had done those calculations more than once.

To understand the kinds of psychological mechanisms that maintain our repetitive fails, let's break down why Priya was so often late to work.

How Mistakes Resist Change

A 2025 report found that 75% of college students struggle with poor time management and procrastination (such high rates are not unusual for college students). They then bring their bad habits into the workplace. Our fondness for procrastination tends to decline with age, but it does so rather slowly. In the meantime, being even seven minutes late for work or for meetings, missing deadlines, or falling behind on team projects can add a lot of unnecessary stress. It can also negatively impact our relationships at work, as well as our overall career, as it can make us seem irresponsible, disengaged, and unprofessional to others.

It also has ripple effects. A series of studies found that meetings that started late averaged more criticisms, interruptions, and other unpleasant manifestations of irritability than meetings that started on time. In other words, people who are late increase the stress to which they're exposed not just via the tension they experience while trying to get places but also due to the negative vibe they encounter when they arrive.

Priya had calculated how long it would take her to get to the office—most people with time-management issues usually do—but her math was off. She had a blind spot that plagued many with similar issues: *Overlooking the Small Stuff.*

Priya accounted for the big variables, but the minor details didn't show up on her radar. For example, she factored in how long she might wait for a train, how long the subway ride was, and how long it would take her to walk to the subway and from the subway to her office. But she neglected to account for the time it took to get from the subway station entrance to the platform and from the platform to the exit, or for having to wait in line to enter the highly trafficked elevators in her office. It was a similar story with her deliverables. She spent two weeks working on a report for an important meeting and finished it "just in time," only to be late for the meeting because she hadn't accounted for the time it took her to print out and collate a dozen copies.

To overcome your blind spots, you first need to disengage your autopilot—otherwise your unconscious mind will keep using the same flawed strategies—and then develop more effective strategies (e.g., considering the minor details). What makes this challenging, besides the fact that changing ingrained mental habits always requires effort, is that (1) when you are stressed and depleted, your unconscious mind will try to convince you that nothing bad will happen if you give yourself a break and do things the old way, and (2) the justifications for doing so are likely to register much more prominently than any objections.

Some of the following justifications and objections (in parentheses) might sound familiar: *I can squeeze in this quick thing without losing track of time* (you cannot), *No one will mind if I'm a few minutes late* (people usually do), *I finished what I was doing, so I'm ready to leave* (no, you're ready to start gathering your things to be ready to leave), *I've done the math* (you skipped the small details), *It will only take two minutes* (it will take ten), and *I have plenty of time* (things always take longer than you think they will).

Stress doesn't just increase our error-proneness in these ways; it also affects how we respond to those errors after we make them. The approaches we take to managing our mistakes in the workplace have been studied extensively in recent years. What matters is not whether we make mistakes at work but how we deal with them once they've occurred. Known as *error management*, there are two main approaches for dealing with mistakes. *Positive error management* involves owning our mistakes, finding the positives in them, and trying to learn from them. *Negative error management* involves trying to cover up our mistakes, avoid them, and therefore, not learn from them. How we manage our mistakes is also influenced by their consequences. There is evidence that when the consequences are significant (say, because our boss is already "all over us" and waiting for us to mess up again), adopting a negative error management strategy can increase stress and mental strain and predispose us to making even more mistakes going forward.

The reason more of us don't practice positive error management is that it's unpleasant. Delving into what went wrong and examining the often-distressing consequences of our mistakes is uncomfortable in and of itself, but we make it even more so by adding an unnecessary soundtrack of harsh self-criticism (e.g., *I'm such an idiot; I hate myself*). As natural as it is to self-flagellate after a failure, doing so is always unwise. Our self-worth and confidence are already bruised; the last thing we should do is damage them further. Making an emotionally challenging process even more unpleasant with negative self-talk will sap our motivation to learn from the mistake and set us up for entering a "threat mindset" going forward.

Parents might want to consider that negative self-talk has the same impact as yelling at a child in anger when they do something wrong—it will make the child focus on feeling bad or on fearing your anger and direct their attention away from their mistake and what they could learn from it. Taking a moment to regulate your emotions so that you can have a calm discussion with them about what they could do better next time is best for the child. The same is true for the adult *you* when you make a mistake; skip the angry self-talk and focus on how you can do better next time.

The trick to analyzing our errors is to approach them as if you were a *failure detective*—an objective third party who's there to identify the evidence and spot the patterns with no judgments. Concluding that you should double-check the spelling when ordering *Employee of the Month* plaques is useful. Calling yourself an idiot because the ones that arrived say *Employee of the Mouth* is not. Confronting our mistakes takes fortitude, so instead of criticizing yourself for your failures, congratulate yourself for having the emotional strength to examine them and learn from them.

I worked with Priya to help her recognize her blind spot and the justifications that kept her tripping on the same banana peel. But changing habits takes time, and I worried that given how tense things were in her office and given how little margin for error she had for additional failures, she might have to take drastic action.

"Priya, do you know how punctual people always get to places on time?" She shook her head. "They don't," I said. "They're always early. That way, on the rare occasion that something goes wrong, they can still be on time."

She recoiled at the implication. "You want me to get to work early? Spend even more hours in that office? I can barely stand being there as it is."

"I know. But a chunk of that is because you get stressed-out when you're late, and another chunk is because the partners are breathing down your neck. Getting to work early for a couple of weeks could eliminate the time pressure, and it might make Cinnamon Spice back off and give you a break."

"Cinnamon *Sprinkle*," Priya corrected me. "And it's not just him, Oat Milk and Hold the Foam are on my case too. But fine," Priya sighed, "I'll try."

Time management was not the only repetitive failure Priya had, but since they all required a similar three-step process, I wanted to make sure she knew how to handle that one before I brought up the others.

How to Overcome Repetitive Errors

Two main causes of repetitive errors are our blind spots and the unconscious justifications we generate for sticking with the same problematic strategies. To counteract those vulnerabilities, we need to (1) identify our repetitive errors and the blind spots that enable them, (2) introduce speed bumps to stop us from using the same ingrained, error-prone strategies, and (3) reassert conscious control so we can introduce new practices.

Let's review how Priya implemented this approach for time management and then apply these steps to other common workplace blind spots.

Poor Time Management: Most people with poor time management know they have a problem. The panic, flop sweat, and armpit drying in the restroom are hard to miss. We've also discussed their blind spot—overlooking the small stuff—and we've enumerated the justifications that keep them from asserting conscious control (e.g., *I won't lose track of time*).

That leaves the speed bumps.

Speed bumps are useful for preventing accidents, but they are inherently annoying because they force you to slow down when you're in a hurry to get somewhere. The mental speed bump I suggested to Priya was a checklist. Checklists are highly effective as mental speed bumps because they force us to be mindful and deliberate, which prevents us from defaulting to automatic processes and having another "accident." And they can be annoying for those same reasons—checking a list every time we take the same action can feel irritating and forced. But we only have to do that until we've acquired the new habit.

Priya created two checklists: one for the small stuff she needed to consider when calculating travel times (e.g., the time it took to gather her keys, coat, and bag or to traverse the long hallways from the elevator to her desk). The other was for the minor details associated with completing projects on time: formatting, printing, typo hunting, cross-checking, waiting for approvals, etc.

The general template for avoiding time-management errors is to use travel checklists to make commuting calculations more accurate and to practice working backward from a project's due date to plot out when each element needs to be completed. Like most of the exercises in this book, you should personalize the suggestions and tweak as you go. Take out irrelevant factors and add any vulnerabilities that come up in your failure-detective error analysis.

The next type of mistake Priya repeated was far more common and consequential.

Ignoring Critical Accumulations of Stress: Failing to recognize that she was reaching a breaking point had led Priya to quit her job eleven times. I struggle with the same blind spot. It was only after I became burnt out early in my career that I realized how out of touch I was with my own stress levels. Too many of today's workers discover they'd been ignoring critical accumulations of stress the way I had—by getting burnt out.

What makes this blind spot so common is that it is a literal one—we have no mechanism by which to directly observe how high our stress levels are at any given time—we lack an actual stress gauge. Yes, we can tell that we're stressed, or even that we are very stressed, but we cannot tell when we cross over into the danger zone for burnout or how deep we might already be within it. Even if our physical, mental, and emotional exhaustion indicate that we might be nearing the cliff, we're unlikely to know how close to the edge we are until we go over it.

To be clear, the fault for stress and burnout peaking in the workplace is due to the proliferation of emotionally unhealthy cultures. But given how ineffective so many companies have been at reducing employee stress, it's up to us to monitor our emotional health so that we do not sustain serious damage.

To prevent such outcomes, you will first need to catch the justifications your unconscious mind uses to keep you grinding away. Sally, the optimizing single mother, justified her mounting stress by telling herself versions of: *The stress is just temporary* (stress for months on end is considered chronic, not temporary), *I don't have a choice* (you can choose to not get burnt out), and *I can take it* (so far, but you won't see the cliff until you go over it). Other common justifications include: *Everyone is doing it* (people's circumstances and tolerances are different), *If I don't push myself, I'll lose my competitive edge* (chronic stress will dull your edge even more), and *That's what the job requires* (that doesn't mean you should ignore what you require).

To overcome this repetitive error, you do not need speed bumps to alert you that you are stressed; both Priya and Sally were well aware of that, and you probably are too. What they weren't aware of was the severity—how deep in the red zone they were. An effective speed bump would be one that alerted you that your stress levels were approaching a danger zone, or already inside one, so that you could avoid grinding your way to burnout.

How to Measure Your Stress

Studies of work stress typically use lengthy questionnaires and complex diary studies to assess the stress levels of the participants. However, some studies use a much simpler tool—a stress thermometer. That name makes the tool sound fancier than it is—basically, a simple line (horizontal or vertical) with numbers from 1 to 10 where 1 = no stress and 10 = extreme stress. Several times a day, mark the point on the line that best represents your current state: when you first get to work, after a stressful event (use the high-scoring items from the "stress mines" exercise in the previous chapter), and toward the end of the workday. It's best to note your scores daily for at least two weeks. Put reminders on your phone for the three daily measurement times or you might get caught up in the workday and forget to do the ratings. Or you can use one of the many available apps for tracking your mood and stress.

One potential issue with the stress thermometer is scale or proportion. When work stress goes on for extended periods, as it often does, it can be difficult to determine whether the stress you feel at a given moment is a 5 or a 7. Therefore, you'll need to set a baseline that reminds you of how it feels to have no stress and compare your current state to that. To set your baseline, find a video of you that was taken when you were relaxed, happy, and as stress-free as you get. Watch it, and try to recall how you felt in that moment. That is how a 1 on the stress thermometer feels for you. Use that comparison to rate how stressed you feel at the time of measurement.

Some of the studies that use these kinds of self-reported stress ratings have suggested specific cutoffs for stress "danger zones." I will share them here, but note that using them in this context has not been validated scientifically. With that in mind, average daily/weekly stress ratings of 5 and above could indicate that you might be generally stressed, and ratings above 8, if ongoing, might endanger your emotional health such that the urgency for you to reduce your stress is more immediate.

This book offers many tools and techniques for stress reduction. When your stress levels reach or exceed the danger cutoffs, you should use as many of them as you can to reduce stress, and you should keep measuring your stress levels until they're no longer in the danger zone.

The other approach to reducing stress is to counterbalance it by improving how you feel about your job and your experience at work. Priya's managers didn't have time to meet, so she believed there was nothing she could do to better her situation. But that was due to another blind spot that afflicts many workers, including other quiet quitters.

Professional Development Helplessness: Priya was frustrated by her managers' disinterest in developing her professionally. Managerial apathy has a big impact on how we perceive our work experience. Spending our entire day toiling away for people who seem indifferent to our needs adds a layer of stress to everything we do. On the other hand, workers who feel like they are learning and gaining valuable skills experience more job satisfaction and less stress as a result. The blind spot Priya shared with quiet quitters and others was believing that she needed her managers or company to drive her professional development. She did not. You probably don't either.

The justifications that blind us to the possibilities for professional development are: *My manager isn't interested* (they might not have the inclination or bandwidth, but that doesn't mean they'd be opposed to you pursuing these things independently), *My company doesn't offer resources for learning* (your colleagues might be all the resources you need), or *My current responsibilities aren't teaching me anything* (you can take on ones that do).

The speed bumps you introduce need to counter the feelings of helplessness that keep you stuck. I've worked with people across many industries who had similar frustrations about their jobs and managers. Almost all of them were able to further their professional development by using a method I call *role curation* (known in the research as *job crafting*). Role curation involves identifying opportunities to acquire new skills, strengthen existing ones, or take on more meaningful tasks in your current job.

To become a senior personal assistant, Priya needed two years in a single role, as well as proficiency with scheduling and project management software and, ideally, experience supervising a junior assistant. When I asked her how she might address the latter two needs in her current role, her first reaction was that she could not. I asked her to give it more thought.

"Maybe I can ask my bosses' permission to hire an unpaid summer intern?"

"That's a great idea," I responded. "How can you make it as frictionless for them as possible, so that it's easier for them to say yes?"

"I could tell them that I would recruit, train, and supervise her myself, so it wouldn't cost them any time or money. I could also look into upgrading our travel and scheduling software; the system we have sucks and everyone hates it. If I found a relatively cheap one and explained how much time it would free up for all three assistants, they might go for it."

Role curation is a straightforward process. We identify the skills and experience we need in order to advance in our career and then seek opportunities to gain them. We can volunteer to take on tasks that give us relevant experience, offer to assist a coworker with a skill set we need if they coach us on the basics, ask to switch responsibilities with coworkers who are using tools we would like to become more proficient at, or, like Priya did, convince higher-ups that we can serve their needs better if we updated existing systems or procedures or instituted new ones.

Any success we have essentially turns our current frustrating job into free schooling that prepares us to climb to the next rung on our professional ladder. Role curation can also help mitigate the resentment and frustration that comes with having apathetic or overwhelmed managers and an uncaring work culture because it will help us regain feelings of control, improve our mood and outlook, increase our job satisfaction, and decrease stress.

Tony the trader didn't need further professional development because he was already at the top of his ladder. However, his ability to stay there was in peril due to a blind spot that seriously limits the career aspirations of many people.

Ignoring Office Politics: Tony, like many workers, believed that what should matter is one's performance, not the "playground squabbles" that went on behind the scenes. Indeed, Tony continued to minimize the threat Scar posed even after his nemesis embarrassed him in front of the entire team. "The one good thing that came out of that meeting," Tony told me in our session that night, "is that now that things are out in the open, I'll watch every word I say to Jason from here on and prove to people that I'm not a bully. Scar won't be able to blame me for Jason's bad performance, and things will go back to normal."

I seriously doubted that. Tony was kind and good-hearted, and those character traits often came with a dollop of naivete and gullibility. Scar manufactured the problem with Jason and then inflamed the tensions between him and Tony over many weeks. Scar then orchestrated the team meeting, made Tony look bad in it, and staged a dramatic walkout. His goal was clearly to rattle Tony, and he was succeeding. If anything, Scar would feel emboldened to take things to the next level. But Tony was so desperate for the tensions to end that he couldn't see this possibility.

That's what makes this blind spot so dangerous—it can prevent you from recognizing serious threats from coworkers or managers. Ignoring the political landscape around you, including other people's agendas, puts you at a huge disadvantage. Interpersonal dynamics and behind the scenes machinations often impact careers more than actual performance does, whether they should or not. That is in part why so many incompetent workers get promoted and so many talented ones languish. The justifications Tony used to stay on the sidelines of these workplace Hunger Games were beliefs such as: *Good work always gets rewarded* (it does not), *My boss knows I deserve the promotion* (he might, but your colleague is lobbying harder than you are, and the squeaky wheel usually gets the grease), *I don't want to get my hands dirty* (you can engage ethically), and *I don't want to be in a confrontation* (if someone is undermining you, you're already in a confrontation).

To catch these justifications and take potential threats more seriously, you need speed bumps that will help you spot any underhanded maneuvering, lobbying, coalition-building, or reputation-harming moves your colleagues might be cooking up. The best way to do that is to have clear allies and sensitize yourself to the agendas of those who might pose a risk to you so you are more likely to catch the schemes they hatch. Having allies involves deepening your existing connections with colleagues (e.g., check in, have lunch, show interest) and actively cultivating new connections.

By sensitizing yourself to the agendas of your rivals, you'll become more alert to signs of trouble. To accomplish that, you need to list the people who might be inclined to undermine you and do a *perspective-taking exercise*. Start with the key players and those with whom you are in contact most frequently.

One at a time, consider their past behavior and what you know about them, then answer the following questions from their point of view: How do they feel about you? What is their goal/agenda? How far might they go to achieve it?

"Scar hates me," Tony said, when he did the exercise, "and he probably feels resentment, and jealousy too. His goal is obvious—he wants to be the top trader. And he's willing to scheme, manipulate, sabotage, bully, and harass me to get there. Jason's agenda is to blame me for his poor performance so he doesn't get fired."

"I agree," I said to Tony. "Right now, Jason is still performing poorly, and Scar is still behind you in the rankings. So, how likely are they to let things go back to normal?"

Tony groaned. I hated being the bearer of bad news, but that's the goal of the exercise—to raise awareness of potential threats so you can catch them and respond. My next session with Tony was a week later. I knew there was something wrong the moment I saw his face.

"I've been summoned to a meeting with human resources," he said, his voice uncharacteristically strained. "Jason filed a complaint against me for creating a hostile work environment. He claims I've been trying to sabotage his career since he started, that he's been so humiliated and traumatized by me that it's affected his mental health and made it impossible for him to do his job well." Tony took a deep breath. "They're opening an official investigation."

So, that was why Scar had called the team meeting—to set Tony up and make him look like a bully in front of the team in order to give more validity to an official complaint. I realized that Tony was wrong. Scar wasn't just trying to become the top trader; he wanted to get rid of Tony, to ruin his entire career.

Tony was deeply upset by the complaint, which raised a new concern— he was likely to bring that stress home with him. Most of us do when our work is causing us excessive tension, pressure, or worry. Reducing stress at the source by upping our error-management game, overcoming our blind spots, and minimizing repetitive mistakes on the job is important to our overall functioning and emotional health at work. But what happens after work matters just as much.

FAMILIAR PATTERNS

When we're going through periods of high stress at work, it's critical to use our evenings and weekends to recover from the strain of the workday. Unfortunately, dozens of studies have shown that what most of us do in order to recover from the workday is marginally effective at best. Many of us don't even think recovery is necessary.

CHAPTER SIX

Tuesday Evening

Poor Rest and Recuperation—
How to Recover from the Workday

"I'M GOING TO GET fired," Liam, a corporate lawyer in his thirties, announced as he sat down on the couch. He had recently moved to the suburbs with his wife, his two preschool-aged children, and his anxiety disorder. Liam took off his tweed cap, straightened his back, and cupped his hands on his lap like it was 1930s Austria and he was interviewing for a job with Captain Von Trapp.

"The deal I'm working on is on indefinite hold, and I'm already low on hours," Liam explained. "If I don't hit 2,400 by the end of the year, they won't consider me for the partner track, and I'll have to leave the firm." He sighed. "We shouldn't have bought the house. We won't be able to cover the mortgage if I lose my job. I spent the whole night worried about losing our home and the kids having to sleep in the back of the car. I avoided my boss all morning just in case he had bad news to tell me."

"Did any of that strike you as anxiety and catastrophic thinking?" I asked.

"You don't understand. My boss was acting weird when he passed me after lunch yesterday. Couldn't meet my eye. Didn't even nod hello."

"Um-hm," I said.

"Give me one other reason he would look at me like that and not say anything."

"Gas."

"What?"

"It was after lunch; he could have been gassy. Or his kid just got into a fight at school. His mother broke a hip. He forgot his anniversary. Toothache. Should I go on?"

"No," Liam said stiffly. "You're right. I missed it again."

Liam had been doing a decent job of catching catastrophic thoughts and labeling them as "anxiety," but increased pressures at work were making him slip back into bad habits. One of them was permitting anxious thoughts. The other was trying to avoid situations that made him anxious, like bumping into his boss. I reminded him that anxiety makes us overestimate the likelihood of worst-case scenarios and that avoiding his boss would make him more anxious, not less.

"Avoidance always makes anxiety worse," I said, "because, while *you* know that what you were trying to avoid was your anxiety, *your unconscious* will think that what you avoided was getting fired (the worst-case scenario). It will then conclude that your boss firing you could not be *that* unlikely because, *Look, it almost happened.* Only your canny avoidance saved you. That will make you even more anxious about seeing your boss. Avoidance always supersizes anxiety. And as you know, anxiety is also a big driver of ruminations."

"Yes," Liam nodded, "it is."

Spending the evening ruminating about being homeless didn't just stoke Liam's anxiety and make him miserable, it also prevented him from doing something that we all need to do when our work is demanding and pressured—use the off hours to get a break from the stress of the day in order to allow our psychological and physiological systems to recover.

The idea that he needed to *recover* from his workday took Liam aback. "Seriously? That seems quaint. Indulgent even. I'm coming home from an office, not a war zone."

"Perhaps," I acknowledged, "but being under high stress all day and fighting for your professional life impacts you in many of the same ways that being under fire would."

Indeed, there's nothing quaint about the toxic cultures, bias, bullying, and harassment that pervade so much of the current work culture. Nor is it indulgent to mitigate the damage done by unreasonable quotas like Liam's 2,400 billable hours, hostile coworkers like Sally's co-lead and Tony's colleague Scar, uncaring bosses like Priya's, or any of the other threats and stresses that afflict so many workers. In fact, the hundreds of studies examining the impact work stress has on our health and well-being led experts to conclude that recovering physically, mentally, and emotionally in the off hours was a *physiological necessity.* Unfortunately, that same research found that the more stress and strain we feel by the end of the workday, the more likely we will be to choose *ineffective* recovery strategies once we get home. Our mental and emotional fatigue will then carry over to the next day and make us even more vulnerable to those same stresses and strains—cue the 67% of workers who have symptoms of burnout.

If you're thinking, *Not me! I always rest and relax after work, so I'm doing well in the recovery department*—hold that thought. I used to think so too until I realized that we're all stuck in a time warp.

Industrial Era Solutions for Information Age Problems

Until the twentieth century, the vast majority of jobs involved many hours of manual labor. Workers went home with sweat-stained clothes, aching muscles, and a strong desire to recline. The need for physical recovery was as obvious as was the solution—rest and relaxation. Over the past 150 years, the way we work has changed dramatically. Our approach to recovery, not so much.

Most industrial age workers had scant free time because their workday was so long. The little leisure time remaining after they completed their home duties was dedicated to resting and relaxing. Today, most jobs aren't physically laborious but mentally and emotionally so. Recovering from mental and emotional drain requires very different techniques than recovering from physical drain does. Yet, we still spend our evenings reclining on couches and beds as if we had just spent sixteen hours dipping fabrics into dye vats.

Consider too that when our nineteenth-century counterparts got home from work, they wanted to spend their scant leisure time doing the opposite of what they had been doing all day—reclining instead of standing, resting instead of moving heavy loads. The majority of us now spend our workday sitting and looking at screens. What do we do to recover from our screen-heavy workday? We sit and look at screens again. For hours. A 2024 survey found that the global average for screen time for television and gaming alone (without social media or other uses) was over four hours *per evening*. That's why you wake up tired many mornings. Rest and relaxation prevent your mental batteries from further drain, but they won't recharge them effectively.

The good news is that we have far more leisure time than our nineteenth-century counterparts did (except perhaps for parents, caretakers, small business owners, and some others). We could, in theory, use that time to recover more effectively. Relaxing after the workday is worthwhile, but rest is just one of the components necessary for an effective recovery. Another is recharging—engaging in physical, social, or creative pursuits of the kind that are hard to do while reclining.

But one aspect of the post-pandemic workplace makes it difficult for many of us (and almost impossible for some) to rest and recharge effectively—we no longer know when our workday ends.

Our UNENDING Workday

Most people define the end of their workday as the hour at which they leave work or close their laptop at home. In other words, when they're no longer expected to be available (in person or virtually) to coworkers and managers. But that's not when our workday ends.

Our workday only ends when we stop thinking about work.

What matters is not when we leave work physically but when we leave work psychologically—when we feel mentally detached from our job and our duties. If we're thinking about work at home or responding to emails, we are psychologically still at work.

Some people are cool with being psychologically tethered to work after hours because they've integrated their personal lives into their jobs. They socialize with friends from work, spend their evenings and weekends with clients or colleagues, and they're happy doing so. *Integrators* whose work and personal life are fused in such ways also need to mentally detach from work. They can do so by inhabiting different mindsets than during regular work hours, for example, by giving space to other aspects of their personality like humor, playfulness, and curiosity or by leaning in to the social, friendship, and recreational aspects of their after-work pursuits (e.g., sharing feelings, hopes, or memories with one another, or doing activities together that create shared meaningful experiences).

Separators, who prefer to keep their work and personal lives distinct, need to mentally detach by feeling that they are psychologically *away from work* and *present in their home or personal life*. Failing to detach from work, whether you are a separator or integrator, will significantly impair your efforts to recover.

Recovery efforts aside, failing to mentally detach from work is associated with fewer positive emotions after hours (e.g., joy or happiness) and more negative ones (e.g., irritability), more sleep disturbances, feeling less refreshed and being less creative and productive at work the next day, poorer well-being, and a slew of other negative outcomes. Further, as we'll see in Chapter 9, detaching from work will not only help you prevent these outcomes, it will help reduce tension and conflict at home, and it can benefit your loved ones' emotional health too.

Detaching is therefore critical, but as dozens of studies have found (feel free to sing along with the familiar chorus)—*the more stress and pressure you experience during the workday, the harder it will be to detach from work after hours.*

To properly switch off, you need to signal your brain that it's time to unwind from the workday and manage interferences that could drag you back into work mode.

The Power of Rituals

In 2022, artificial intelligence burst onto the world stage via large language models such as ChatGPT. Large language models were a breakthrough because they were trained to predict *what comes next*. Interestingly, recent theories in neuroscience have proposed that conscious experience arises from the dynamic interplay between our brain's predictions of *what comes next* and the sensory input it receives. Our brain can make such predictions because it excels at spotting patterns.

Training our brain to anticipate *what comes next* after our workday will make it easier for us to detach from work. Many of us already have a routine we perform at the end of the workday (e.g., listen to a specific playlist while driving home), which is great. The question is whether your routine is sufficiently effective—whether you truly switch off and are focused on whatever you're doing or whether work thoughts still intrude. Many people I speak to who have a routine still struggle to switch off on many nights. Perhaps because their routines include only one or two steps (e.g., listening to music while commuting), and that might not be enough to get their brains to shift gears from work-related stress to recovery.

When talking about how to shift from work to home, I prefer the term *ritual* to *routine* because rituals tend to be imbued with meaning and are more often associated with transitions (e.g., grieving or graduations). Rituals have also been found to reduce anxiety and to block out emotional "noise."

"There are several factors to consider when creating your ritual," I explained to Liam. "First, it should be one you can repeat at the end of every workday, whether you work from home or in person. Second, it should include as many of your senses as possible."

Studies of the brain's ability to identify patterns found that adding a second sense improved pattern recognition by 15% and that the more senses were involved, the quicker pattern recognition occurred.

"Music is extremely emotionally evocative, so create playlists that help you prepare for whatever you'll be doing. Have one that relaxes you if you will be resting, energizes you if you're going to the gym, or puts you in a romantic mood if the kids are sleeping at your in-laws."

Liam looked up. "That covers sound. Next?"

"Sight," I responded. "Use lighting to create the mood you want. It's worth installing dimmers or getting lamps for quick adjustments. Scent is important too."

Sally, the single working mother who was into optimization, incorporated a specific scent into her transition ritual. "My daughter has two favorite stuffed animals: a hedgehog and a rabbit. Every morning, she chooses one and gives me the other. I take it with me to work, and before I leave, I close myself in a bathroom stall, stick my face in it, and inhale deeply. Nothing gets me into mommy mode quicker than a whiff of my angel."

"Scents evoke not just emotions but memories," I explained to Liam. "Scented candles, diffusers, a specific perfume or cologne, can help put you in a different mental space."

"Got it," Liam responded in clipped tones. It reminded me that I had never seen Liam in a "different mental space." He always came straight from the office, still in fight-or-flight mode, his manner serious and businesslike throughout. I decided to try mild humor to see if doing so would help him loosen up and be able to access his feelings more easily.

"You're in the suburbs," I continued, "simply stepping outside or opening a window can bring in calming, refreshing scents. I'm in Manhattan." I smiled. "The scents that waft in when I open a window are rarely refreshing."

Not even a hint of amusement on Liam's face. I realized that I had never seen him smile. We had not worked together for that long, but there were clearly entire aspects of his personality that I had yet to encounter.

"Lastly, there's touch," I continued. "Clothing is both tactile and visual—the look and feel of clothes on our body have a surprisingly powerful impact on our mood and mindset. One study split the participants between two rooms and had them do a boring, detailed task. One of the rooms was significantly colder than the other and had a white lab coat hanging on the door. The participants in the cold room were told they could wear the white lab coat if they felt chilly. The people who wore the white lab coat made a lot fewer mistakes on the task than those who did not because the lab coat made them, unconsciously, feel like scientists, and scientists are known for attention to detail. So, change clothes when you get home from work, and if you work from home, designate some of your clothes as 'work clothes' and change to your regular clothes when you finish working."

Liam nodded. "I do that already."

"Great. At the end of the ritual, announce that you are now starting your evening or weekend. Saying that aloud, to yourself or to your family, adds intention and accountability. Blocking out evenings and weekends in your calendar and labeling them as 'movie night,' 'kid's recital,' or simply 'personal/family time' is also helpful."

"Some days are brutal, though," Liam said, "I know I'll have trouble switching off, even with a ritual. Is there a nuclear option? Something I can do to get my thoughts off work on the really bad days?"

"Yes, but you might not like it."

Exercise Your Right to Detach

One activity has been found extremely effective at helping people detach from work—cardiovascular exercise. In a recent study, 74 employees reported how much time they spent on mild, moderate, or strenuous physical exercise over 10 days. All forms of cardiovascular exercise helped the participants detach from work and were associated with better recovery from the stress of the workday. But only *strenuous exercise* had strong results across the board. Mild and moderate exercise are great, but you can still think clearly enough to surf from one rumination to another. When you're going all out and huffing and puffing, it's much harder to keep a train of thought going, and the endorphins your brain releases will lift your mood too.

"Would a few minutes of jumping jacks work?" Liam asked.

"That depends on your fitness level. You'll have to experiment to find out how many of them you would need to do," I responded.

"But isn't a ritual pointless for someone with my kind of job?" Liam asked glumly. "I get dozens of emails every evening. Some I have to respond to, some not, and I can't know until I read them. How do I detach if I have to check emails every few minutes?"

Switching Off in the Always On Workplace

A recent Pew research survey found that over 50% of all workers are expected to respond to emails after hours. Those numbers go up to 60% for workers with college degrees and 70% for those with graduate degrees. An Academy of Management study found that workers spend an average of eight hours a week reading and responding to messages after hours—the equivalent of a full day's work.

The expectation that workers respond to emails after hours exploded in the late 2000s when smartphones rendered us reachable no matter where we were, but COVID shot it into overdrive. The pandemic shattered the psychological barrier between home and work. Whatever awkwardness or hesitation managers felt about troubling an employee at home disappeared. The result was that instead of the office feeling like a second home, home now felt like a second office. The blurring of this critical psychological boundary and the ensuing constant drip of emails has enabled work to hijack our personal and leisure time even after the return to in-person work.

After-hours emails don't just interfere with what you're doing, they interfere with how you *feel* about what you're doing. The distinction matters. Researchers found that *what* you do to rest and relax after hours matters less than the *experience* you have doing it. To get the most out of your downtime, you have to experience a sense of autonomy—to feel that you, not your job, control your free time.

"You can't control the flow of after-hours work emails," I agreed with Liam.

"But you can control how you deal with them. There is a technique you can use to respond to emails and still maintain autonomy so that you can quickly re-detach once you're done."

Red Light, Green Light: The Email-Management Exercise

To maintain autonomy while dealing with email, you need to signal to your brain that you are in control at each step. "Define whatever your plans are that evening or weekend as the *main event*," I explained to Liam. "It could be dinner, watching a show, or time with the kids. Then determine when it would be least disruptive to have a short intermission. Like before dessert, between episodes, or if your kid takes a bathroom break."

Liam figured he could get by with taking a single break during the weeknights because he got home late and two breaks per weekend day.

"Start by giving the green light to the activity you're doing and alerting others to when you'll be taking a break. For example, if you're watching a show with your wife, let her know that you'll need fifteen minutes to check emails after the first episode." Next is the yellow light. Its purpose is to reinforce your sense of control, so it comes before you take a break to do the emails. Acknowledge the activity you just did and state your intention to resume shortly. For example, *Great episode. I'll be back in fifteen minutes to watch the next one.* Or, *Loved the casserole, can't wait for dessert.* The red light is when you do the emails. It should be brief, so only do the work you must so you can stick to the schedule you specified. When you finish, indicate the green light by announcing that you're resuming the activity: *Intermission is over, let's watch another episode.*

If it isn't appropriate to announce your schedule to others, do so silently to yourself. But don't skip that ingredient—it tells your brain that you're in charge of your schedule, which is critical for experiencing autonomy. Since the mere sight of your phone can trigger associations to work (even if it is face down), put your phone away when you are in *green-light mode.*

Detaching from work has another benefit—it will make it easier to get restorative sleep, especially if we have an effective bedtime routine to help us wind down. Getting good sleep is the foundation for physical and psychological health. It's associated with better long-term health and well-being, better mood, increased productivity, resilience to stress, enhanced learning and memory, less illness and disease, and still more benefits. Poor sleep, on the other hand, increases our vulnerability to work pressures such that the mental strain we feel will be greater than it would have been otherwise. When our job is intense and demanding, prioritizing sleep is truly critical.

When I asked Liam about his sleep, he stiffened. "We don't need to talk about that."

"I ask because anxiety often comes with sleep disturbances."

"I do stuff for that, so it's fine," he insisted, eager to change the subject.

"May I ask what *stuff* you do?" I asked casually.

Liam looked embarrassed for a moment, then said, "Our five-year-old was having trouble falling asleep when he started preschool this year, so his teacher gave him a coloring book and blow bubbles. He colors for fifteen minutes, gets into bed, we do story time, and then he blows bubbles slowly for five minutes. Works like magic. I was tossing and turning, so I decided to try it." He looked down at his lap. "It helps. I don't know what that says about me, but it does."

"It doesn't say anything about you," I responded. "Blowing bubbles is just a way to get kids to slow their breathing and calm themselves. It does the same for adults. And coloring is very meditative. That's why coloring books aimed at adults are so popular."

Liam blinked at me. "They make coloring books for adults?"

"Mandalas, geometric patterns, nature scenes. What have you been coloring?"

"Dinosaurs, trucks, and Captain Underpants," he said, embarrassed.

"Captain Underpants with the big tighty-whities? Interesting use of white space," I said deadpan. And then it happened—Liam smiled. It was like looking at an entirely different person. It reminded me that I had no idea what Liam did for fun, what made him laugh, what he was like with his kids and his wife, or what he'd been like before he became a lawyer.

That was a problem for numerous reasons, not the least of which was that the second prong of effective recovery from the workday is to recharge and rejuvenate—to refill your mental and emotional batteries by accessing those parts of yourself you don't get to express during the workday and doing things that make you feel like you. Liam's life had been dominated by law school and his work for many years. I wondered if he even remembered what *feeling like him* even meant.

Self-Recovery: How to Recharge After Work

Work often takes over our lives so thoroughly that we lose touch with critical aspects of our identity—who we used to be before we started this job or career.

"Who were you before you became a lawyer?" I asked. Liam seemed taken aback by the question, so I explained: "Your work occupies so much of your mental real estate." Liam nodded. "And your wife and kids take up most of what's left." Nod. "That doesn't leave much room for you—for your passions, your interests, your friends—things I assume were more present in your life before you became a lawyer and had a family." Nod. "How was that Liam different than the Liam I know today?"

Liam swallowed, then straightened his back. "That was another life."

"Do you miss that other life?"

"I try not to think about it."

"Because it reminds you how much of yourself you've lost?" Liam winced and nodded.

The wince was important. It meant those parts of himself were still meaningful to him, even if they were in deep hibernation. He wouldn't have been pained if they weren't. To recover effectively, he would need to wake up those dormant aspects of his self and access them regularly. Resting by itself will not restore our bandwidth. We need to recharge by doing the things that revitalize us personally, even if they require effort.

The good news is that you don't need to devote the time you used to in order to access those feelings. If you're athletic, a quick workout at the end of the day might tire you physically, but it will recharge you mentally. If you're a maker, artist, or writer, spending even 10 minutes on a project can nourish that part of your identity. If you're an actor, dancer, singer, or musician, practicing your craft for just a few minutes a day will keep you feeling like one. If you're an extrovert who recharges by being around people, have a quick meet-up with a friend after work. If you're an introvert who needs quiet time to recharge, ask your partner or family for a few minutes of alone time when you get home so you can decompress.

When you feel drained at the end of the workday, gearing up for an activity might be the last thing you feel like doing, but recharging activities typically restore more energy than they consume. They will leave you feeling revitalized, empowered, and grateful that you didn't give in to the undeniable allure of your couch.

Accessing important parts of your identity and expressing meaningful aspects of your personality is essential for emotional and mental well-being. Allowing them to wither is psychologically costly, and it will increase your risk of burnout, depression, or both. During my first seven years in the United States, the combined demands of work and school meant that entire aspects of my personal identity received no outlet. At some point, I even stopped missing them—an unofficial symptom of burnout to which we don't pay enough attention. When you're burnt out, you don't just feel cynical and numb about your work, you feel cynical and numb about your life and all its missing ingredients. You get so used to doing without those parts of your "self" that it could take getting hit by a proverbial truck to wake you up and force a change.

Though in my case, it was a Honda.

The Car That Knocked Sense into Me

A year after my early career burnout, I decided to take a 10-day vacation to visit my twin brother. It was the most time off work I'd ever taken. My second day there, I waited for the light to change at a crosswalk, stepped onto the crossing—and got hit by a car making the turn. I lay on the ground, dazed, as a worried crowd gathered around me. The driver got out of his car, yelled at me for not looking where I was going, and tried to leave the scene. I was too dazed to respond, but the crowd around me made sure he stayed until the police arrived. A visit to the emergency room yielded a diagnosis of bruised ribs. I was grateful that I'd escaped more serious injury.

The rest of my "vacation" was spent recuperating on my brother's couch. I was in therapy with an amazing psychologist at the time. When I got home and told her about the trip, she said, "You're barely out of burnout, and that vacation did nothing for you. You need to take another one, a restorative one, and you need to take it now."

The idea of taking yet another week off from my fledgling practice seemed clinically and fiscally irresponsible. My brother was quick to point out that not taking the vacation would be psychologically irresponsible. I eventually agreed and decided to sightsee in Europe for a week. At least, that was the intention. I ended up spending the entire time working on an idea I had for a screenplay (I had majored in both film and psychology in college, so it was something I knew how to do). I sat in parks and cafés and wrote for eight hours a day. I saw none of the sights, yet somehow came back feeling energized and recharged.

Also confused.

Resting on a couch for 10 days hadn't put a dent in my mental exhaustion; why would writing full-time for a week totally rejuvenate me? Part of the answer was that I enjoyed writing, but more importantly, writing put me in a state of *flow*. Flow is a psychological state of deep concentration in which you're so immersed and focused on what you're doing that you lose track of time. To achieve flow, the task has to be moderately difficult (we tend to be most engaged when a task is neither too easy nor too hard), and there has to be a feedback loop in which we see our progress (e.g., filling a notebook with screenplay notes). Despite being a state of deep concentration, flow leaves us feeling vital and refreshed. That's what made my vacation so restorative.

My affair with writing was not just a summer romance; I was eager to keep it up when I got back. But given how many hours I worked and how little free time I had, there simply wasn't room in my life for something as time-intensive as writing a screenplay. I promised myself that once I could afford to work only five days a week instead of six, I would make time to return to it.

"You're doing it again," my brother quickly pointed out, "prioritizing fiscal responsibility over your psychological needs. That's definitely a blind spot for you. You're not a starving graduate student anymore. If you keep thinking like one, you'll burn out again in a hurry." At least, I think it was my brother who said that. It could have been my therapist. Their feedback was distressingly similar. I made some time to write here and there at first, noticed that I was happier on those days, and decided to make time to write every day—even just for a few minutes. I still do.

It hasn't been easy to keep up. Work makes it so difficult to hold on to our passions that many cherished activities and aspects of our identity fall by the wayside.

Amputating Aspects of Your Identity One by One

It happens to most of us. Careers get more demanding as we move up the ladder, as do our responsibilities and workloads. Something has to give, so we stop going to our book club, we let our gym membership lapse, or we only put the baby to sleep on weekends. The more demanding our job becomes, the more interests, people, and moments we let go. Before we know it, little of "us" remains.

Meanwhile, we're too busy managing the demands and pressures of work to notice how differently life feels, how differently *we* feel. The things that used to bring us joy, satisfaction, meaning, and connection slowly recede from memory. We go from being a multidimensional person with a full life to a two-dimensional version of ourself whose existence revolves almost entirely around work.

"If reflecting on who you were before you started law school makes you sad," I told Liam, "it means those missing aspects of your former self represent a meaningful loss." He nodded, indicating he was open to the conversation.

"Tell me about a moment in time before law school, when you were happiest."

Liam took a deep breath. "When I met my wife. Last year of college."

"Where did you meet?"

"Improv show."

"You sat next to each other?"

He shook his head. "Wife was in the audience. I was performing."

My jaw almost dropped. Liam did improv in college? Liam was a kind-hearted, hardworking, good person, but he was so . . . constipated. His posture and body language were stiff, his speech was clipped, he did everything by the book.

Improv required the absolute opposite mentality. You needed flexibility to go with whatever scenario you were given, no matter how ridiculous or silly. You had to be agile, to adapt to the unexpected twists and turns castmates threw at one another, nimble enough to go from serious to funny, from suggestive to outrageous, from subtle to over-the-top, and you had to do it instantaneously. Liam had never displayed a hint of those qualities.

Which told me how deeply buried they were.

Liam had completely lost touch with that version of himself. If he hadn't, some of the "old him" would have leaked out in our discussions. But he had clearly compartmentalized those feelings long ago—retained the memory of the events themselves but buried the emotions that accompanied them. Simply recounting those years wouldn't be enough to reawaken them. But I knew what would.

Tripping Down Memory Lane

Compartmentalizing is a coping mechanism that usually happens automatically and outside our awareness. We compartmentalize our emotions when the feelings associated with certain events are distressing in some way, or when they are happy but remind us of what we've lost (like for Liam). Some of us are more skilled at compartmentalization and do it both automatically (unconsciously) and deliberately, while others might struggle to do it effectively in either modality.

To reconnect to his feelings, Liam would need to reactivate them anew. Simply recounting them wouldn't suffice; he would have to visualize them so vividly and viscerally, he would practically relive them—the rush of hearing the audience roar with laughter, the excitement of not knowing what his fellow performers would do next, the satisfaction and pride of a well-earned standing ovation, the thrill of catching his wife's eye in the audience, the joy of making her laugh.

"I want to hear the full love story," I said to him. "Start at the very beginning."

"My love story with my wife?"

"Your love story with improv. Tell me about the first time you got a big laugh."

Liam's lip twitched upward. "Second week of improv club. We were doing shopping scenes. My friend Case was a pushy mattress salesperson, and I was a newly divorced dad with erectile dysfunction and a limited budget."

Liam's rigid posture eased as he described the setup. "The pair before us killed, so we were amped." In all forms of comedy, it's far better to follow an act that *killed*, or got big laughs, because the audience is primed to laugh. Bombing (not getting laughs) makes the audience tense and uncomfortable, which makes it much harder to get a laugh out of them if you go next.

"Case was throwing aggressive sales tactics at me, so I had to keep coming up with objections." Liam acted out the gestures as he narrated. "Case pointed to an imaginary bed and announced, *Our flagship model made from space age foam! Yes, that's right—this mattress has a memory!*" Liam, pretending to be panicked, said, "I don't want anything with a memory in my *bedroom*! I want to be able to say to my date, *Sorry, this never happened before* without my mattress going, *Whaddaya mean? It happened last Tuesday!*"

I laughed. The joke was funny, but watching Liam commit to the act-out was priceless. He beamed with mischievous joy. I wanted him to stay in that space, so I said, "That was week two. I'm sure you only got better from there."

He nodded enthusiastically. "With improv, you're constantly learning and improving." He was quiet for a moment, then his smile faded.

"How do you feel right now?" I asked.

"Like I just saw an old friend who can no longer be in my life."

I understood why he thought that to be true. Liam had no time to join a troupe or practice regularly, so he believed there wasn't room in his current life for improv.

"Good friends are hard to find," I said to him, "both literal friends and figurative ones like improv. When you make one, you should do everything you can to keep them. You won't be able to engage with the person or the activity as much as you used to, but you can still have them in your life. Liam, you can still do improv every day, you can still express those wonderful parts of yourself. You just can't do it on a stage, at least not regularly."

"Then where can I do it?"

"At home. You know, when my brother's daughters were young, they would tell him what character they wanted him to be when he woke them up in the morning. At first, it was all about Disney princesses, but then they started to make it more challenging. He had to be a dragon, a dog, a balloon, even a wall."

Liam's eyes lit up. "I could do that with *my* kids."

"And with your wife. She fell in love with an improv actor. She probably misses that goofy, funny side of you as much as you do." Immersing himself in improv for just a few minutes a day and bringing joy and laughter to his family would rejuvenate him. It would also allow him to access his happy memories without experiencing the pain of loss or nostalgia.

Giving air to any aspects of your personality and identity that you miss would do the same for you. Even briefly inhabiting those parts of yourself could help bring out those sides of you more often and give you the experience of being a fuller, more well-rounded person. Liam was lucky to have a clear passion that defined meaningful aspects of his personality. I was too (writing), as was Tony (weight lifting). But many don't have a clear passion or interest. Sally lost her parents when she was eighteen and worked to support herself even before the birth of her daughter. She didn't have an obvious pursuit to rekindle.

If you struggle to identify activities that could be recharging and revitalizing, you might need to do a little excavating.

A Visit to Your Identity's Lost-and-Found Department

Sally had little time to devote to extracurriculars, but she had agreed to pay more attention to her personal needs once her first project launched. So, I insisted she do so.

"The goal of the exercise is to identify both people and pursuits that brought out aspects of your personality that you once enjoyed but no longer get much expression," I said to her. "You need to make two lists. One contains the activities, hobbies, interests, and pastimes you once enjoyed, however long ago that was—even childhood. The other contains the people who brought out unique or valuable aspects of your personality. That means anyone in your life who made you feel adventurous or daring, who inspired your creative side, who you felt comfortable being wacky or silly with, who connected you to your spiritual side, or who made you feel empowered. For each activity or person, indicate the aspects of your character they helped bring out.

"The next part is a thought exercise," I continued. "Think of a memory for each activity or person that evoked those specific aspects of your personality, and note the feelings that come up."

Sally nodded. "And use those feelings to decide which ones I want to bring back."

"Exactly. The last step is to brainstorm ways to integrate those people, activities, or aspects of yourself into your current life, even in small ways. If the person who made you feel optimistic and empowered is no longer relevant, then how can you introduce those feelings into your life in other ways?"

"I used to do kickboxing," Sally said. "It made me feel strong and safe, and it was a good workout. I don't have time for a class, but maybe I could get a punching or speed bag." She smiled. "It would be fun to go a few rounds."

"You're going to put a printout of your co-lead's face on it, aren't you?"

"Absolutely not!" she objected. She smiled and said, "Paper would tear. I'll make a decal."

The more aspects of your identity you can revive, the more options for recharging activities you will have from which to choose, and the more restorative your leisure time will be, little of it as you may have.

But what if you have no free time at all? Some professions, industries, and companies require individuals to work such extreme hours (up to 120 hours per week), they have no time to relax or recharge. For those who tend to periodically overwork, the question is not whether extreme overworking is damaging to your well-being—it is—but how much damage you might be sustaining as a result.

CHAPTER SEVEN

Wednesday Morning

Overwork—How to Know When You've Had
Too Much of a Bad Thing

WEDNESDAY IS OTHERWISE KNOWN as hump day, a term that origi-nated in the 1950s. The idea was that you just need to "get over the hump," and it would be downhill to the weekend from there. These days, the last two days of the workweek rarely feel like a downhill skate, and the weekend isn't exactly a work-free oasis either. A recent survey found that 68% of people do some work over the weekend. Overworking has become acceptable, common, and, too often, extreme.

"I'm in a bind," Carlos, a data scientist in his thirties, said when I asked him what brought him to therapy. "I have a startup with my partner, Ilya, so I work a *lot*. We're over a year in, and founders always work seventeen-seven for the first couple of years—seventeen hours a day, seven days a week, with no breaks. We're not growing fast enough, so we're on calls all day with clients in separate rooms, and since I cover the West Coast, I go to bed later than Ilya. I thought working together would bring us closer, but we barely see each other. Ilya always says startups require sacrifices, but I've been feeling lonely, and it's affecting my work."

I too was in a bind. Loneliness was a valid and important concern because it can pose a serious threat to our emotional and physical health, especially when it becomes chronic. But Carlos faced a bigger and more immediate threat—extreme overworking—however, he did not put that issue on our agenda because he believed it was normal for founders to work 120 hours a week.

It is not. Working 120 hours a week for a full year with no breaks is neither common nor sustainable. Carlos and Ilya thought it was because famous billionaires claimed to have done so themselves—for example, the US founder who slept on the floor of his factory for a year or the Chinese founder who touted the *996 Workweek* (working from 9 AM to 9 PM six days a week, or 72 hours per week) until it was ruled illegal in 2021. I don't doubt they worked hard, but they also had personal assistants, chefs, housekeepers, drivers, trainers, and massage therapists at their disposal. Most of us do not.

Carlos did not recognize those distinctions, though. Worse, his interpretation of the 120-hour founder-workweek was literal. He and Ilya had not taken a single day off since they started their company over a year ago, not even holidays. That wasn't just unwise, it was dangerous.

The Price of Overwork

Working excessively entails significant risks to health and well-being. Studies found that working over 55 hours a week was associated with a 30% greater likelihood of stroke, increased risk for heart attacks and cardiovascular disease, Type II diabetes, depression, and anxiety. It can also predispose you to cigarette smoking, excessive drinking, unhealthy food choices, and a slew of other harmful effects.

In Japan, where workers have historically demonstrated high loyalty to their company, there are names for the ultimate price some workers pay for overworking: *karoshi*, which translates to death from overwork, most often by sudden heart attack or stroke, and *karojisatsu*, which refers to death by suicide from overwork. Karoshi deaths garner much media attention in Japan, and they have rekindled a national discussion about overwork, as well as government action to limit the number of hours employees work per week.

The standard workweek is considered to be between 35–40 hours per week in many countries. Where the boundary of *over*working lies is far less clear. Karoshi is defined as the "sudden death of any employee who works on average at least 65 hours per week for more than 4 weeks, or averages 60 hours per week or more for at least 8 weeks." Most researchers place the cutoff between working hard and overworking at about 55–60 hours per week.

That said, the impact of overwork depends on the person, their circumstances, and the intensity and duration of overwork. Yet, the risks to health and well-being of overwork are so convincing that in 2024, Australia passed a *Right to Disconnect* law that allows workers to refuse unreasonable work demands, including having to respond to emails after hours. Employers who punish workers for asserting those rights risk fines. Hopefully, workers down under will see a big change, but I remain skeptical. I've worked with employees of many companies that had rules against overwork and were even lured by them during job interviews. But the moment they onboarded, it became clear that not responding to emails after hours or taking time off would put their advancement, bonuses, and even their jobs in jeopardy. The bait-and-switch tactics some companies employ are brazen. In one case, the company offered unlimited vacation days, which sounded great, only once you got there, you discovered that there was one *minor* condition—you have to attend all your meetings virtually while you're away, even if you are on your honeymoon. And they say romance is dead.

Carlos was using a virtual background, but whenever he shifted in his seat, I got a glimpse of the room behind him. There were papers everywhere, clothes on the floor, and dead plants on the bookcase. His personal appearance matched his surroundings—unshaved, hair uncombed, dark circles under his eyes, and a gaunt, exhausted look that made him seem 10 years older than the handsome, put-together man in his profile picture taken only a year earlier. When someone I work with is out of touch with the extent to which they're putting their mental and physical health at risk, expressions of concern and measured words of caution rarely have an impact. To get Carlos to recognize how dangerous his and Ilya's work habits were, I would have to shake him.

"You've both been working seventeen hours a day, seven days a week, for a year," I asked, "without taking a single break?"

"Sure," he nodded as if it were obvious. "We have a startup, we have to.

But I do take breaks. I go for a long walk every Sunday. At least an hour. Rain or shine."

"One hundred and twenty hours a week," I noted. "That's twice the number of hours prisoners in Russian gulags and North Korean labor camps work."

Carlos blinked at me, slightly confused as to where I was going.

"And it's eighty-five percent less outdoor time than maximum security inmates get when they're in solitary confinement," I continued, "which, functionally, you both are."

Carlos recoiled. "You're saying we live like prisoners?"

"No. That would be a step up." I asked more gently, "Do you *feel* like a prisoner?"

He swallowed and turned away. He looked close to tears. His coping mechanisms were probably as exhausted as he was. Carlos's functioning at work was already impaired. If he and Ilya kept going at their current pace, their ability to function productively would continue to decline, and that could endanger their entire business. They were already endangering their individual health and well-being, and their marriage, or what was left of it.

Their one advantage was that their extreme overwork was self-imposed, which meant that, in theory, they had the power to modify their work habits. Most overworked employees do not.

The Rise of Overwork

In a 2024 survey, 44% of respondents said they had to work a second job or side gig because of unlivable minimum wages. Of those, almost half spent 10–20 extra hours a week on their second job, and 12% spent over 31 additional hours per week on their second job.

Entire professions, industries, and companies have normalized overwork despite the dangers it poses to their employees (e.g., truckers, small business owners, hospital and health care professionals, software engineers, and startups). Working parents and caretakers can spend almost all their waking hours "on duty" in one way or another. Seasons (e.g., tax season for accountants or the holidays for retailors) and circumstances (e.g., starting a new business, losing a critical employee) also foster massive overwork.

Historically, business owners only improve working conditions when laws, regulations, or unions force them to do so. During the Industrial Revolution, 12- to 16-hour workdays were the norm, women received only 50% of the pay men did, and children received only a tenth. In some industries, laborers rarely lived past the age of 25. It took that level of injustice and catastrophic health impacts to spur change. The rise of labor unions in the twentieth century brought additional protections for workers and bolstered the middle class, but things have definitely slipped since then, especially in the United States. In the 1950s, one in three workers was in a union. Today, that number is one in ten. The United States is the only country in the world that has neither a policy for legally mandated leave nor a federal policy for sick leave, which means you probably go to work even when you are unwell or when you have hours of caretaking duties to do once you get home. Overwork infects every level of employment, from frontline workers to the C-suite, from gig workers to the self-employed.

Until 50 years ago, people suffering from alcohol addiction used to be portrayed in popular culture as amusing and lovable (e.g., W. C. Fields in *My Little Chickadee* [1940]; Dudley Moore in *Arthur* [1981]) rather than as sufferers who need help. In today's popular culture, overworkers are also portrayed in misleading ways—inspiring, charismatic, and mentally tough (e.g., *Steve Jobs* (2015); Joy Mangano in *Joy* [2015]). Such misleading representations cast a false sheen of normalcy, respectability, and sustainability upon a dangerous practice.

The Romanticization and Bias of Overwork

Overwork has become so embedded in our workplace culture that leaders and managers frequently reward and even romanticize it. Instead of recognizing how stressed and oppressed their workforce is, employers applaud the brave employees who sacrifice so much to help the "team" succeed. If overwork led to a better product than more humane working hours did, managers' appreciation of such "devotion" might be understandable.

But does it?

Scientists put that question to the test. In one experiment, managers were tasked with evaluating two groups who had identical performances but differed in how many hours they worked in order to achieve them. Workers who completed their work within their basic work hours were evaluated as being less committed and less competent than workers who overworked to achieve exactly the same result. In other words, employees who were more competent and efficient were judged less favorably than those who were slower but made up for it by overworking. Which of them would you want on your team?

In this and other experiments, managers' appreciation of overwork was not just misguided and wrong, it was biased too. Men who overworked were evaluated as being more committed and more competent than women who overworked and produced the same work product. Here is yet another bias that women face in the workplace in addition to unequal pay, lack of representation at senior levels, being seen as unlikable for displaying the same leadership behaviors that are perceived as desirable in men, having their competence and judgment questioned, even in areas of expertise, being spoken over in meetings, and too many others to mention.

Based on projections that were made before the abolishment of Diversity, Equity, and Inclusion (DEI) initiatives and programs in 2025, gender parity would only be achieved in 60 years, meaning few of today's women workers will benefit from it. Without such programs, it will take even longer. Bias does not disadvantage people in minor ways—it turns the hills they have to climb into mountains. For example, Black women are exposed to even worse bias than white women or other women of color are. In 2024, for every 100 men promoted to managers, 89 white women were promoted, but only 54 Black women were.

Bias in the workplace is a subject about which volumes have and should be written, and although it is beyond the scope of this book, it is essential to keep the following in mind: bias makes any job far more stressful and damaging to your emotional health and well-being than it would be otherwise. It is systemic (e.g., promotion rates for Black women), misguided (e.g., biased managers who judge efficient women as less competent than inefficient men), and pervasive, not to mention grossly unfair. Bias at work causes significant additional stress, which means overwork could exhaust you more quickly and severely.

Overworking hijacks your life quite literally in that it leaves you little time to have one. Some people can still thrive despite overworking, provided they have regular daily downtime to reset their stress response and to take breaks and vacations. But Carlos and Ilya took no breaks at all. Consequently, to survive their extreme overwork, they had to regulate their feelings in equally extreme ways.

When You're Buried by Work, Your Feelings Become Buried Too

Carlos and Ilya had moved to the East Coast because that's where most of their client base was and where Ilya's family lived. Carlos left behind two older parents, with whom he was very close, who promised to come and visit him every few months. Unfortunately, his mother's health declined soon after he and Ilya left, and since Carlos couldn't take any time off, he hadn't seen them since. It was the longest he had ever been away from them.

"Ilya gets stressed-out when I bring up going to go see them," Carlos said, "so I stopped bringing it up."

"Does Ilya see his family?" I asked.

"They bring dinner over every Saturday, and we eat together for forty-five minutes. Ilya's strict about the time. He gets tense if we're away from work longer than that."

"Wait, Ilya sees his family every week, but you can't even discuss seeing yours?"

"He's just doing what's best for the company," Carlos insisted. "When he was at his previous startup, he didn't see his parents for two years straight. He knows it's hard for me, but we knew we'd have to make sacrifices."

"How do you feel about not seeing your folks, especially given your mom's poor health?"

"I try not to think about it because there's nothing I can do."

To survive overwork, many of us bury our emotions because touching them is too painful and we have to keep working regardless. Over time, we can lose touch with our feelings such that we don't realize how miserable we actually are.

Numbing ourselves in this way is useful as a survival mechanism, but it comes with a price. Emotional pain, like physical pain, serves an important function—it lets us know when something is harming us. Without that warning system, we can keep doing the harmful thing until the damage becomes too great to ignore.

"Let's think about it together," I insisted. "How do you feel about missing your parents?"

"Terrible. But Ilya would have a fit if I—"

"Carlos," I interrupted, "every time I ask you about your feelings, you tell me about Ilya's. It's important to consider your partner's needs, but when you bring them into your thinking too quickly, it keeps you from getting in touch with yours. We can address Ilya's feelings in a moment, but let's understand yours first. Once you have a clear idea of how you feel and what you want, you can add Ilya's perspective to the equation, but not before. What would it be like for you to see your parents for a weekend?"

Carlos smiled. "It would be amazing. But I can't be away for an entire weekend."

"There's Ilya's voice again. You keep going into his head instead of staying in yours. Close your eyes for a moment, imagine you're visiting your parents, and describe what that looks like."

"We're chatting in their living room. I'm in the armchair, legs dangling over the armrest like when I was a teenager. They're smiling, telling me how much they've missed me." He swallowed and blinked away a tear.

"That's a lovely scene, Carlos. But you're telling me about your parents' feelings. Do you notice how hard it is for you to focus on your own?" He nodded. "Try again. Tell me what a visit would be like for *you*."

"It would be . . ." He lowered his head, his shoulders shaking.

"This is why you keep going to other people's feelings," I said softly as he cried. "You've been in pain for a while, so much pain that it's easier to deal with Ilya's and your parents' feelings than to touch your own."

Carlos nodded, weeping silently. In my clinical experience, silent weeping is a habit that often starts in childhood, in situations in which, for any number of reasons, it wasn't safe for the person to express sadness or distress. Carlos grew up in a small, highly religious, and conservative town. He had to hide being gay for most of his life or risk being shunned by the community and, potentially, even his parents. When he came out to them in college, they were devastated and shocked, but they searched for ways to reconcile their religious beliefs and values with their love for their son and were eventually able to accept Carlos fully while remaining strong in their faith.

Carlos was now an adult, but he was still hiding his tears. "I see your anguish, Carlos," I said. "I see how hard you try to bury it, how you hide it from Ilya, from your parents. I'm glad you're not hiding it from me."

He took a deep breath and wiped his eyes. "My parents are dying for me to come, but Ilya's been so against it."

"If you gave your needs as much weight as you give Ilya's and your parents', things might be different."

"True," Carlos nodded. "We might be divorced."

"Is there so little room for your feelings in the marriage that expressing them would lead to divorce?"

"I don't know."

"Maybe it's time to find out."

Our next session was a week later. "I had the conversation," Carlos announced, "and it didn't lead to divorce."

"I'm glad to hear," I said with a smile.

"It led to the emergency room." I stopped smiling.

"Ilya got so freaked out when I brought up seeing my folks, he thought he was having a heart attack. We went to the ER, but the doctors said it was a panic attack and sent us home."

Panic attacks can be extremely scary. Your heart beats so fast, it's easy to think you might be having a coronary event. A substantial portion of emergency room visits for non-cardiac chest pain turn out to be panic attacks. That said, going to the ER was the correct choice. If you ever think you're having a heart attack, you should always go straight to the emergency room. Heart attacks and strokes are too lethal to take chances. In busy ERs, even a stab or gunshot wound victim might be asked to wait if someone comes in with a suspected heart attack.

Once they got home from the ER, Ilya was open to discussing Carlos visiting his parents. They agreed that Carlos would go for a two-day weekend and work while he was there, but only eight hours a day instead of seventeen. We scheduled our next session for after he got back. My one worry was that instead of reinforcing how important it was for Carlos to work less, it would do the opposite and make him overwork to make up for the time he was away.

How We Become Addicted to Overworking

Overworking has an addictive quality. Once we see how much we can get done, going back to regular productivity makes us feel unproductive and inadequate, which makes us want to keep overworking.

Indeed, trying to get a break from overwork often makes it worse. The demands and pressures of our job mount, and we struggle to keep up with our workload. Lured by the promise of that intoxicating *caught-up* feeling, we work into the evening or spend the entire weekend trying to get ahead, eager to lighten our workload and experience a peaceful, worry-free night. Except that dozens of studies show that the more we overwork, the more compromised our functioning will be the next day (e.g., poorer attention, impaired executive functioning) and that restoring our abilities fully can take several days. By then, the gains we made have faded, we no longer feel caught up, and the suffocating stress and pressure we were trying to escape come charging back. Desperate to get another taste of being caught up, we stay up even later so that this time, we can truly get ahead. That compromises us even more the subsequent days, so we fall behind again.

Another factor that makes it difficult to break free from overwork is that our managers and coworkers have gotten used to our work product, so any efforts we make to cut back can actually make us look like we're slacking off. Any promises we made to ourselves about getting home earlier or enjoying weekends with our family quickly go the way of the dodo. But, while scientists are making efforts to bring the dodo back from extinction, corporations and employers are making little efforts to render overwork extinct.

The one upside of overwork is that it can make a simple weekend away seem like a ten-day vacation. "I feel a hundred times better!" Carlos announced when he got back from his parents. Not to me he didn't. He still had dark circles under his eyes and a haggard look, but the fact that he *felt* more rested and refreshed was important. He gushed about how great it was to see his parents and to be in his childhood home.

His demeanor changed when I asked how things were with Ilya.

"Bad," Carlos said. "He got anxious and pulled an all-nighter while I was away. He said it was to make up for my being *on vacation*. I'm getting really worried for him. I told him that working all night when he had been in the ER just days earlier was incredibly irresponsible. He told me that my going away was far more irresponsible."

Overwork is often confused with devotion and loyalty. Many employers see it as such, and those attitudes filter down to leaders and managers and into the culture at large. Psychologists, on the other hand, even those like me who occasionally overwork themselves, view chronic and extreme overwork very differently.

Self-Care or Self-Neglect?

The barometer researchers use to define overwork is the average number of hours worked per week. That might be useful for looking at large groups of people, but on a case-by-case basis, it's useless. Our tolerance for overwork (as all our tolerances) is highly individual and situational. How many hours we work per day or week isn't necessarily indicative of how we're holding up. What matters isn't the number of hours we work but the extent to which our mental and physical well-being are compromised.

Self-care always declines when we overwork because we lack the time and bandwidth to maintain the various practices and habits we would otherwise. The questions are how many of them have dropped off, to what extent have they declined, and what are we risking as a result. Some slips might be minor or insignificant, but others can be substantial and even alarming. In fact, there's a line beyond which drops in self-care are so serious, the person is considered to be suffering from self-*neglect*.

Self-neglect is a concept used primarily by social services to describe a mental or physical decline severe enough to qualify someone for assisted living or a home aide. Historically, the condition was associated primarily with people suffering from brain damage, those who became incapacitated, or the elderly. But today, many chronic overworkers end up compromising their self-care so substantially that they would qualify for special assistance if not for the fact that their "symptoms" are self-induced.

Sam Altman, the founder of OpenAI, admitted that when he was working on his previous startup, Loopt, he neglected his nutrition for so long that he got scurvy. Scurvy is a disease, caused by a lack of vitamin C, that killed more than two million sailors between the sixteenth and eighteenth centuries. It took bleeding gums, fatigue, and joint pain to alert Altman to the damage his self-neglect was causing.

During the pandemic, I worked with many who swore that their companies would collapse if they took a single day off. They then ended up getting COVID, were out of work for a couple of weeks, and . . . none of their companies collapsed. Another perceptual distortion that fuels extreme overwork is our belief that our companies and work products are more fragile than we are. The opposite is usually true. When I brought up self-neglect with Carlos, he looked worried—not for himself, but for Ilya. Ilya had been taking anti-anxiety medication but stopped cold when his prescription ran out because he didn't want to waste time seeing a doctor. He also made frequent trips to the bathroom because of stomach cramps, indicating potential gastrointestinal issues. Even more worrisome, he had occasional shortness of breath. Carlos begged him to get a checkup, but Ilya refused. "I don't know how to get through to him," Carlos lamented.

"You can't," I responded. "And more importantly, you have your own health and well-being to worry about. Your overworking has been just as extreme and as dangerous as his, and you haven't had a checkup in almost two years either. Make changes, set an example, model a more sustainable way of overworking. You have a startup; I'm not expecting you to put in a forty-hour workweek. But if Ilya sees you taking care of your needs, even minimally, while still putting in a serious effort at work, he might come around."

Overwork, even extreme overwork, can be necessary for some people, some of the time, and for others, much of the time. Any activity that involves greater risks, like overwork, should be accompanied by greater safety measures. For that reason, I developed a tool to monitor emotional and physical self-care—*The Overworking Self-Care Assessment*. It has a dual purpose: first, to help you catch when your self-care is beginning to slip—the line in your "stress gauge" above which stress becomes unmanageable and your self-care slips as a result. When it does, sometimes even a small adjustment can bring the pressures down to below that line (e.g., delegating an obnoxious task, reducing ruminating, improving your recovery). The second purpose is to warn you if your self-care has declined to the level of self-neglect. In that case, more substantial changes are warranted.

You can take the assessment here.

Overworking Self-Care Assessment Tool:

This questionnaire is not a scientific instrument. Its purpose is to detect changes in self-care over time and to encourage self-reflection. It should not be used for research or diagnostic purposes, and it should not substitute for a full professional evaluation. If you have concerns about self-care, self-neglect, stress, or burnout, consider seeing a health care professional.

Instructions: For each item, choose the response that best represents your typical frequency.

1. Personal Hygiene – Bathing/Showering

In the past seven days, how many times did you bathe or shower?

  1: Once or less
  2: Twice

3: Three times
4: Four times
5: Daily (7 times)

2. Clothing – Wearing Clean/Fresh Clothes

On how many of the past seven days did you wear clean, fresh clothes?

1: Once or less
2: Twice
3: Three times
4: Four times
5: Every day

3. Dental Care – Brushing Teeth

In the past seven days, how many times did you brush your teeth?

1: Less than 7 times
2: 7 times (about once a day)
3: 10 times (roughly 1.5 times a day)
4: 14 times (about twice a day)
5: 21 times or more (three times a day)

4. Grooming – Personal Appearance

On how many of the past seven days did you engage in your usual personal grooming routines (e.g., hair care, shaving, applying makeup if part of your routine)?

1: Once or less
2: Twice

3: Three times

4: Four times

5: Daily

5. Nutrition – Eating Healthy Meals

In how many of the past seven days did you eat at least two meals that you consider healthy and nutritious?

1: Once or less

2: Twice

3: Three times

4: Four times

5: Every day

6. Medication Management

In how many of the past seven days did you take your medications or follow your prescribed health regimen?

1: Once or less

2: Twice

3: Three times

4: Four times

5: Daily or Does Not Apply to me

7. Home Environment – Cleanliness & Organization

In how many of the past seven days did you spend time cleaning or organizing your living space?

1: Once or less

2: Twice

3: Three times

4: About once a week (≈4 times)

5: More than once a week (8 or more times)

8. Financial Management

In the past month, how many bills got paid late or not at all?

1: All of them

2: Most of them

3: A few of them

4: One

5: None

9. Medical Care – Routine Checkups

In the past 12 months, how many routine medical checkups or appointments have you attended?

1: None

2: One

3: Two

4: Three

5: Four or more

10. Physical Activity

In how many of the past seven days did you engage in physical activity (e.g., walking, exercising) for at least 30 minutes?

1: Once or less

2: Twice

3: Three times

4: Four times

5: Daily (7 days)

11. Social Engagement

In the past month, on how many days did you spend time catching up or socializing with friends, family, or community members (in person or virtually)?

1: None

2: Once

3: Twice

4: About once a week

5: Twice a week or more

12. Health Self-Monitoring

In the past month, how often did you note issues or changes in your physical or mental health (e.g., pay attention to physical aches or pains, big drops in mood or motivation, or loss of productive mindset)?

1: Never

2: Once, but I didn't do anything about it

3: More than once, but I didn't do anything about it

4: I think through why they happened and what I could do to bounce back

5: I monitor my well-being regularly and take action to get back on track when I see myself slip.

13. Sleep

In the past week, how many nights did you have trouble falling or staying asleep?

1: None
2: One
3: Two or three
4: Four or five
5: Six or seven

Self-Neglect Score: *Add up the numbers that precede each of your responses for items, 1, 3, 5, 6, 9, and 13 to get your score. Interpretation: Note that any questions that you rated 2 and below should be taken very seriously regardless of your total score.*

24–30: Adequate Self-Care
You generally maintain your self-care routines, with only occasional lapses.

18–23: Inadequate Self-Care—Mild Self-Neglect
Some areas of critical self-care require attention and improvement.

13–17: Moderate Self-Neglect
Critical areas of self-care are inadequate and require immediate attention.

6–12: Severe Self-Neglect
Your self-care has declined to the point of serious self-neglect. Urgent intervention is advised. Consider discussing your results with a health care or mental health care professional for further evaluation and support.

When Carlos completed the assessment, he was firmly in self-neglect territory. Anyone who works that many hours a week would be (unless you have a sizable staff to support you).

Given how extreme Carlos's overwork was, I suggested he reclaim at least 20 hours a week and use them for self-care and recovery. He hesitated. I pushed.

"How would you feel if Ilya agreed to convert two or three work hours a day into recovery and self-care?"

"I'd be delighted."

"Then you should be equally delighted to do it yourself."

Carlos agreed to drop to a 14-hour workday, which, while still extreme, was a significant improvement. It is an approach I call *Excess in Moderation*.

How to Make Dangerous Overworking Less Dangerous

Excess in Moderation and other "harm reduction" approaches are based on the premise that it's far more difficult to abolish risky behaviors entirely than it is to limit the damage they cause via moderation. The self-neglect score in the assessment focuses on areas in which self-neglect is more consequential (e.g., medical care, sleep, nutrition). Neglecting his nutrition put Sam Altman in a potentially life-threatening situation, and I personally know many people who suffered serious medical consequences due to overworking-induced self-neglect.

There was the C-suite executive who ignored a cough that turned out to be lung cancer, the schoolteacher who kept running low on diabetes medications and lost toes, the psychologist who ignored neck pain until he lost functioning in his entire left side and required multiple epidural shots into his spine and a year of physical therapy to recover. That last one was me, and it happened 20 years ago. The long recovery was a painful reminder of how hard it can be to get back to your previous level of health and functioning once it becomes compromised by self-neglect. Five years later, when writing my first book, I slipped into overworking again, neglected my self-care, and needed another round of epidural shots. That was when I developed the self-care assessment.

I have been epidural-free since, but only because I monitor my self-care and self-correct when I start to slip.

The Squeaky Wheel Gets the Axe

You might be waiting for me to lay out strategies for tackling overwork at its source by pushing back against your manager or company directly. However, as I explained in the Introduction, while some employers and managers might be open to complaints about overwork, others will very much not be, and doing so in those cases could even cost you your job. How to tell which response you're likely to encounter is complicated and made more so by the fact that even within the same company, two people can voice the same concern and get very different responses because of their rank, relationships, timing, individual managers, etc.

However, if you're determined to speak up regardless of the risks that speaking up can pose to your job and career, here are factors to consider: (1) *Culture*: Are your manager and company generally open to employees pushing back? Have you seen peers do so and get a positive response? (2) *Document*: Document the extent of your overwork as best you can—urgent emails at 11 PM, weekends in the office, denied vacation requests, etc. (3) *Gather Allies and Witnesses*: Any complaint becomes more powerful when it's voiced by more than one person. Can you get others to join you? Be advised that you are taking on additional risks by doing so because you can be seen as an instigator, and some coworkers might want to take distance in order to not be associated with you. (4) *Follow the Chain of Command*: Start with your manager. Ask for a meeting, and either come with solutions (e.g., I would like to offload this specific task or responsibility) or ask for advice (e.g., help me decide what to focus on because I can't do it all). If your manager can't help, consider going to human resources, but remember that their primary responsibility is toward the company, not you. (5) *Seek Counsel*: If you do complain and believe you are being retaliated against, consider getting advice from an employment lawyer. (6) *Create an Alternative*: If you do speak up, but nothing changes, Chapter 12 of this book will help you decide if it is time to start looking for a new job.

Before you take any of these steps, consider one thing you can do to reduce overworking that usually goes undetected by managers and even coworkers, especially if you are putting in over 60 to 70 hours a week.

Ten Percent Slackier

If you are putting in 12-hour days at the office, and certainly if you are working weekends too, one thing is likely to be true—there aren't eyes on you all the time. Unless you work in an electronically monitored industry like call centers, your manager and teammates are unlikely to know if you put in 10 hours of work on Saturday or eight, nor do they know what you are doing at any given moment when you're in the office. For that reason, many overworked employees I have worked with, at all levels, have been successful at pulling back 5% to 10% of their work time and converting it to personal or recovery time without their managers or teams being the wiser.

Two points of caution: (1) This strategy is for significant overworking; if you work a regular workweek, the likelihood that slacking off will get noticed is much greater. (2) Don't wait to get to the end of your rope to pull back. Your manager doesn't know how long your rope is, only you do. Getting close to the end of it is dangerous enough to your emotional health. The 10% pullback can be very effective, but to implement it well, you need to be able to catch the rising tide of work demands before it overwhelms you. Ideally, you would have an early warning system to alert you when your self-care starts to decline *before you reach self-neglect levels.*

As I said to Carlos, "You need to know your canaries."

Personalizing Your Early Warning System

For decades, canaries were used in coal mines as sentinels because of their sensitivity to carbon monoxide. Their job was to alert miners when levels of the gas became dangerous. Sadly, their only way to do that was by dying. By giving miners more time to evacuate, the little birds saved countless lives. We each have our own *canary in a coal mine*—that first sign of self-care decline that tells us when we're stepping onto that slippery slope. Your first sign of slippage is a critical intervention point because by correcting that one slip, you'll return to solid ground, whereas by ignoring it, you will inevitably slide down the slope.

To identify your personal canaries, complete the following Canary Finder exercise.

Canary Finder: *Review all 13 questions on the Self-Care Assessment on pages 114–119 and circle those you scored 3 or below. Make a note of the specific self-care activities that tend to decline first (e.g., I stop seeing friends, I skip showers, I push off checkups)—those are your canaries. Correct your canaries as soon as you catch them in order to avoid further slippage in self-care—by doing so you will be intervening at the point at which it is easiest to get back on track.*

My specific canaries have changed over the years, but their category has not—*home environment.* My current canary is the organization of my physical workspace (or lack thereof). I'm fortunate in that regard because messes are easy to spot, so it is a useful canary to have.

Other common self-neglect canaries are declines in maintaining your immediate environment (bed not made, dishes in sink, laundry piling up, broken light bulbs), personal care (fewer walks, skipped shaves, shorter workouts), grooming (middle-aged men with Rapunzel-length nose hair, missed hairdresser appointments), or social life (no date nights or dating, forgotten birthdays). The canaries of some workers might be in the more consequential categories of nutrition (eating more junk food, skipping meals, stress eating), substances (more drinking or smoking than usual), medical care (missing medications, skipping appointments), and trouble falling or staying asleep.

Regardless of what your canary is, correcting it won't be easy because, by definition, that first early warning sign will be small and therefore easy to dismiss or minimize. Focusing on that minor glitch when you already feel stressed will be the last thing you feel like doing. You will therefore have to remind yourself that it isn't the small habit you are fixing but the cascade of bad habits that will follow if you don't.

Canaries aside, the best way to counterbalance the strain of overwork and of work stress in general is to up your recovery game. Resting and recharging in the off hours are essential for maintaining adequate emotional health and the ability to stay on top of your duties at work and at home.

Recovery efforts can happen during the workday as well, but they rarely do because few of us pause to assess how we're feeling or to consider what we could do to revitalize when work feels like a roller coaster. But perhaps the biggest impediment to our practicing self-care during the workday is that, as recent studies have shown, when our work is overly stressful, our emotional intelligence plummets.

CHAPTER EIGHT

Thursday Morning

Faulty Emotional Intelligence: How to Avoid Foot-in-Mouth Disease

IF A TOUGH WORKWEEK can feel like a 26.2-mile marathon, Thursdays can feel like the 20-mile mark—the point at which runners often "hit the wall" and experience debilitating fatigue. When that happens, those last 6.2 miles can seem painfully long. Thursday mornings at work can feel just as daunting. You're already stressed and fatigued yet still have two full days to go. Your leg muscles won't cramp or give out, but one aspect of your functioning that might is just as critical—your emotional intelligence.

Our *Emotional Intelligence* (EI, also known as EQ) refers to our ability to understand our own emotions and manage them effectively, as well as to understand the emotions of the people around us and use those insights to manage our interactions and relationships with them productively. In the workplace, having high EI is associated with lower stress, increased productivity, greater well-being and job satisfaction, enhanced teamwork, stronger feelings of connection, and better conflict management—highly useful for both our professional aspirations and our emotional health.

Some people have naturally high EI, while others do not. Fortunately, EI is not just a trait but also a skill. Aspects of it can be improved with training and practice, regardless of our starting point. As is the case for most mental skills and capacities, our ability to use our emotional intelligence can be compromised by fatigue, stress, or pressure, or by specific contexts and situations. Researchers of EI in the workplace have recently shifted their focus away from studying workers' emotional intelligence levels to assessing how effectively they apply their emotional intelligence in various situations.

One recent study, "Emotionally Savvy Employees Fail to Enact Emotional Intelligence," looked at the effect of being ignored by colleagues and found that workers who had high EI struggled to apply their skills effectively on days when they felt ostracized by their coworkers. Other studies have found that when workers neglected to manage their own emotions (e.g., by calming themselves or lowering their stress levels), they were less likely to seek social support from colleagues or advice from managers when doing so could have benefited them. In other words, one EI fumble (not regulating their own emotions first) led to another (not seeking social support or advice).

Emotional intelligence failures in the workplace tend to manifest in three common ways: (1) failing to manage your own emotional state, (2) failing to use opportunities for recovery during the workday, and (3) failing to read the emotional states of colleagues or to consider their personal motivations and agendas. The damage done by EI stumbles is usually minor—a small meltdown here, a ruffled feather there. But when the stress at work is intense and ongoing and our exhaustion accumulates, our emotional intelligence can take a serious nosedive. As Sally found out, when it does—the consequences can be serious.

Never Go to Boss Angry

One of the reasons emotional intelligence failures in the workplace are so common is that we're unlikely to notice when our EI becomes compromised. Doing so would require us to pause whatever task we were doing, take our own emotional inventory, and realize things are amiss (see the exercise at the end of this chapter). That kind of emotional checkup could take less than a minute, yet few of us do it—especially when we're already stressed-out, which is when doing so would serve us most. We might be aware that we're feeling irritable, frustrated, depleted, or in a funk, but few of us are likely to translate that awareness into greater caution when interacting with coworkers. And yet, those moments are exactly when even the most emotionally intelligent of us can put their foot in their mouth and do damage.

Sally, the harried single mother, had been able to deliver her first product on time by working with her hostile co-lead's team while he was on vacation. Her second product launch had gone down to the wire as well, and again, she had to overwork to make up for her new co-lead's deficiencies. As she put it at the time, "He was extremely nice but also extremely disorganized and scattered." Now on her third product, Sally was again paired with a new co-lead. This one was also pleasant to deal with, but she posed an even bigger challenge than Sally's first co-lead; her team was very, very slow.

"Now I get why my predecessor never got his bonus," Sally said, looking frustrated. "Do you know what people call my new co-lead? Ms. Bottleneck. She's notorious for holding up projects. I'm about *moving fast and breaking things*, and this place is all *moving slow and faking things*."

I had never seen Sally so agitated, but after six months of brutal overwork, it wasn't surprising that she would be. She was physically exhausted and emotionally depleted, and her critical performance bonus was still six months and two product launches away.

"This launch is my biggest so far, so I need Ms. Bottleneck to mobilize her troops and put some pep in their step," Sally continued. "I tried bringing it up a few weeks ago, but she got prickly, so I changed my approach. I got myself into the right mindset and went to her office oozing collaborative vibes. I asked how her day was going and then *mildly* suggested that *maybe*, just *perhaps*, we could explore how her team could work *slightly* quicker. She shot me down immediately. Said she believed in doing things carefully and accurately and that she was proud of her team and did not tolerate criticisms of them." Sally huffed. "That team is going to cost me my bonus."

Sally faced a problem many high performers have in the workplace—expecting or wishing that others display a similar proficiency, effectiveness, and work ethic as they do and feeling deeply frustrated and resentful when they can't or won't do so.

Sally's co-lead, on the other hand, faced something many long-term institutional employees deal with—the arrival of new ambitious employees who, instead of taking a second to understand the culture and workflow, seek to disrupt it, improve it, or mold it to their own way of doing things—which the Ms. Bottlenecks of the workplace find equally annoying and frustrating.

Sally was aware of this dynamic, which was why she had planned her talk with her co-lead so carefully. "After I left Bottleneck's office, I hit a low point," she admitted. "I was getting deeper into debt every day because of the nanny, and if I don't get that bonus, I won't be able to pay it off. Everything felt incredibly unfair and hopeless, and I didn't know what else I could do to move the project along. So, I marched straight to my manager's office, laid out the situation, and asked for her help."

"Good," I said. "You've been a model employee and haven't asked her for anything so far. She has every reason in the world to help you."

"I know, right? Well, she didn't. She said Bottleneck didn't report to her, so there was nothing she could do about it. I asked her to at least talk to Bottleneck's manager, but she refused. She seemed put off that I even suggested it. I must have looked as frustrated as I felt because she told me to *calm down and learn to work with how things are done around here.*" Sally took a deep breath. "I smiled, somehow. Then I thanked her and got up to leave. I should have walked out, but I hesitated at the door."

Sally looked down and shook her head. "I totally lost it. I told her I was the best employee she would ever have, but that Bottleneck was going to cost me my bonus, and the job wasn't workable for me without it. I told her that, as my manager, it was her duty to help me find a solution to a totally unfair situation. I told her that if she didn't, she would be failing me and failing the company because they would lose a valuable and dedicated employee."

Every word Sally said was true. A good manager should be thrilled with an employee who had so much passion and drive. Of course, a good manager would not have responded with condescension and apathy to that employee's heartfelt request for help.

"I told her that Ms. Bottleneck had cost my predecessor his bonus," Sally continued, "that she should have intervened on his behalf, but that it wasn't too late to do it now for me."

"Okay," I said, trying to hide my growing sense of worry.

"Not done yet," Sally interrupted me. "You haven't heard the grand finale. I told her . . ." Sally sighed. "I told her to grow a pair."

I swallowed hard, not because of what Sally said—she had every right to be upset and angry—but because Sally's boss seemed to have no compassion for her, no appreciation for how much of an asset Sally was. She'd already provided zero value add to Sally; I was worried she would now make the mountain Sally had to climb to reach her bonus even harder to summit.

"I know," Sally nodded, "total cringe. I don't know what came over me."

"Exhaustion and truth," I said, "that's what came over you. You've been overworking and dealing with one frustration after another for six months without a break. And then the person who is supposed to be in your corner turns their back on you when you ask for their help and criticizes you for being motivated and driven. There's only so much a person can take."

Sally's outburst was an unfortunate example of emotional intelligence failure number one—neglecting to manage our emotions, in this case, before a critical conversation with her boss. What made it obviously exhaustion-related was how out of character it was for Sally. She always prepped for important meetings as she had with Ms. Bottleneck—defined her goals, reviewed her strategy, and cleared her head (regulated her emotions) so she could "ooze collaboration." But she had done none of those things before talking to her boss, nor had she taken a moment to assess her emotional state. Had she done so, she might have realized that she was out of sorts and taken a minute to calm herself.

If you're upset or distressed before an important meeting, conversation, or presentation (for any reason, even if it has nothing to do with work), take a moment to regulate your emotions beforehand. First, reframe the situation as an opportunity to address your concerns. Then determine the best (realistic) outcome you would like to achieve and work backward to figure out how to attain that outcome. In other words, go in with a clear head and a clear plan. If you don't, the likelihood of your emotions getting the best of you is high, as are the chances of you not getting the outcome you need. This type of emotional intelligence failure can easily cost you your job or career. Most workplaces are hierarchical organizations that require employees to treat higher-ups with respect and look poorly upon those who don't. (Of course, respect should be afforded to all employees regardless of seniority or rank for many reasons, including that when workers feel seen and respected, they are more loyal and productive.)

Sally was clearly blaming herself for the outburst. I hoped that understanding why she had acted as she did would help her go easier on herself and help her avoid it happening again. "Chronic stress and fatigue exhaust our coping mechanisms," I explained, "and that makes it easier to get dysregulated. When we get dysregulated, our emotional decision-making is likely to skip the frontal cortex—the area of our brain in charge of things like impulse control, good judgment, decision-making, and anticipating consequences."

"I definitely skipped *all* of that," Sally acknowledged.

"For good reason," I responded. "There's only so much injustice and unfairness a person can tolerate. Sally, you know how resilient you are; you know that you can take more than most. But you're human. You have your limits too."

The best way to avoid this kind of EI failure is to adopt the *five-minute-delay rule*. When you feel upset, frustrated, impatient, or out of sorts, take a few minutes to calm and center yourself so that you can regain control of your coping mechanisms and be more intentional in your emotional regulation. Otherwise, you risk giving someone a piece of your mind that you should keep to yourself. A few minutes of slow deep breathing, a mindful walk around the block in which you focus on the air coming in and out of your lungs, a check-in with a loved one to get social support, and other such efforts will help reduce your agitation. Remember, you do not need to be totally calm, you just need to lower the intensity of your emotions enough to allow you to access the wiser and more mature abilities that reside in your prefrontal cortex.

Sally needed to do damage control and she started with her manager. She took the time to compose a detailed and genuine apology in which she took full responsibility for her outburst. Her boss listened to what Sally had to say, but she remained aloof, apathetic, and entirely unsupportive. She thanked Sally but offered no indication that she'd forgiven her.

Luckily, Sally had better success with Ms. Bottleneck. She found out that her co-lead had a daughter and suggested they have a working lunch. She then used the opportunity to bond with her over their shared experiences as working mothers. "She was hesitant to discuss personal matters at first," Sally reported, "but she—her name's Janet—warmed up, and we even decided to make our lunch a weekly event." Janet didn't say anything about her teams' workflow, but to Sally's relief, their deliverables began arriving on schedule. When I saw Sally a month later, she reported that, despite the initial delays, it looked like they would be able to launch the product on schedule.

Sally was able to repair the rupture in her relationship with her coworker despite the stress and exhaustion she was dealing with. But the best way to avoid EI fails of any kind is to utilize opportunities to mitigate strain and fatigue both during the off hours and during the workday itself. The only thing that prevents most of us from doing the latter is that to take advantage of opportunities to recharge and refuel during the workday, we have to be able to spot them first.

Stress Blinds Us to Recharging Opportunities During the Workday

My fifth and last year of graduate school was the most grueling year of my professional life. I was working full-time in a New York City hospital (a requirement for graduation) and had to complete my doctoral dissertation—a multi-year research project—at the same time. I put in 50 hours a week at the hospital and spent nights and weekends working on my dissertation with no days off. The possibility that I wouldn't be able to finish my dissertation by the time my visa ran out at the end of the year loomed over me. If that happened, I would have to leave the country without completing my degree. It would be like running a full marathon only to be kicked off the course a few yards before the finish line.

As part of my duties, I was assigned to work in a locked psychiatric ward. Patients there were in the worst mental states possible—hearing voices, acting aggressively, and often needing to be physically restrained and placed in padded cells. It was a noisy and chaotic unit with constant screaming and "codes" that required all available staff members to drop what they were doing in order to assist with a violent patient.

Until that point, I had only done regular talk therapy with fully functional people whose problems did not prevent them from performing their duties in their jobs, homes, or schools. The prospect of working with people who were delusional and actively hallucinating felt intimidating and overwhelming, and I was eager to meet my supervisor and get her guidance. When I did, she told me she was pregnant, had no time for "an intern," and allowed me to ask only a single question. I went with the most urgent one: "Where is the staff bathroom?" She rolled her eyes and said in a patronizing voice, "I'm sure you can find it." I disliked her instantly.

The next morning, I was assigned my first patient—a Holocaust survivor in her late 80s who was in an extremely psychotic state. She exhibited severely confused thinking, paranoid delusions, and morbid hallucinations. My supervisor handed me her file in the hallway, told me to place her in isolation (she was agitated), and walked off. A nurse saw me escorting the patient, rushed over, and said, "The second she's in the padded room, get out and close the door quickly." I had no idea why this frail woman warranted my making such a hasty retreat, but I heeded the advice. I got her to the room, ran out, and closed the door—as lumps of feces pelted the glass observation window.

I stood there, imagining how unpleasant it would have been had the nurse not given me the heads-up. I realized that I had no idea how to function on this kind of unit, and I wouldn't be getting any help from my supervisor. Hospitals are hierarchical institutions, and supervisors usually have to be from within your profession. My supervisor was the only psychologist in the unit, so I decided to approach the head nurse and ask if she would be willing to supervise me (my first effort at role curation). She was surprised by my request, but she generously agreed. That turned out to be timely and fortunate because things only got more stressful for me on the unit.

The only treatment that worked for the Holocaust survivor was a series of electroconvulsive therapy sessions (ECT), to which I had to accompany her. After the third session, her mental state started to improve, and she was allowed to return to her room. When I showed up to take her to her fourth ECT session, she smiled at me for the first time and started to chat as we made our way down long hallways to the treatment room.

"You're my doctor?" I nodded. "You're going to help me?"

"I am." I smiled.

Her expression turned sour, "By taking me to be electrocuted?!"

"No, that's not what I . . ."

"Nazi!" She screamed. She looked around, trying to get the other patients' attention. "The Nazi doctor is trying to electrocute me!" She screamed those accusations all the way to the treatment room. My "Nazi walk of shame" went on for the next four treatments, after which her thinking cleared, and she was no longer psychotic (and in fact, quite sweet).

Every patient I was assigned on the unit was difficult in some way—which is why they were in a locked ward to begin with. Some threatened violence and promised to "get me on the outside," others cursed at me, spat on me, and one (a middle-aged man) bit my thumb so hard, it took three staff members to free my hand. I was in bandages for a week.

Each night, I got home, ate at my desk, and worked on my dissertation until I was too tired to continue. Two months into the internship, the sleep deprivation and exhaustion were so crushing, I had to face reality—I simply could not keep going at that pace for 10 more months. It was looking more and more like I wouldn't finish my dissertation in time, and I would have to leave the United States without my degree. I felt my dream of becoming a psychologist slipping away.

In today's workplace, many of us have moments in which the workload, pressure, and cumulative exhaustion bring us to a breaking point. What doesn't occur to us in those dark moments is that exhaustion and stress have compromised our emotional intelligence such that we can't manage our feelings effectively, which makes us even more susceptible to hopelessness and overwhelm. Getting more breaks and allowing our coping mechanisms to recover would insulate us against the stresses that are suffocating us. The problem is that because our EI is compromised, we're likely to overlook opportunities to rest and recharge during the workday itself (EI failure number two). Studies found that the more stress and strain we experience at work, the more benefit we could derive from short breaks during the workday—but the *less likely we will be to take them* or even notice them. This *oasis-blindness* prevents us from seeking or recognizing potential recovery opportunities.

My low point happened after my middle-aged patient turned my thumb into a chew toy. How could I possibly finish writing my novel-length dissertation in time if I could only type with one hand? On the verge of giving up, I reached out to my lifelong source of support—my twin brother. "I don't think I've ever been this exhausted and stressed," I said. "I was barely managing to keep up as it was, but now, with my hand bandaged, it's impossible."

"Do you get breaks during the day?" he asked. "Is there any downtime on the ward?"

"An hour here or there maybe, but I'm in a locked unit—I can't exactly run home and nap." My brother sighed heavily.

"What?" I demanded impatiently.

"Your psychology supervisor is only on the unit a few hours a week, right?"

"So?" I responded.

"You have access to her office, right?"

"So?"

"She's a therapist, right?"

"So?"

"Therapists have couches in their office, right?"

"Oh . . ."

The perfect napping setup had been staring me in the face this entire time, and I hadn't seen it. Over the years, I've worked with many whose foreheads were equally deserving of a self-administered smack. So many of us overlook opportunities to recover during the workday because we typically have only a few minutes to indulge them, and we assume that any recovery efforts we make will be ineffective at best and a waste of our already severely depleted resources at worst.

But we assume incorrectly.

The Macro Impact of Micro-Breaks

The short power naps I started to take on my supervisor's couch were a true game changer. They improved my energy levels, mood, and thinking and backed me away from impending burnout. Napping was seriously studied only years later, and the findings validated my experience. Naps of 10–15 minutes in the early afternoon were found to be the ideal length for restoring cognitive functioning and lowering stress. Longer naps, on the other hand, might leave you groggy and interfere with your sleep later that night.

Once I realized how refreshed I felt after a short nap, I began to experiment with adding other refueling stations to my day. I did push-ups and sit-ups after every nap, both to wake myself up and to get in a mini workout. I ate lunch in the adjacent park so I could sit among trees for 15 minutes, and I listened to music while I ate. Those small breaks boosted my energy levels as well as my productivity.

The research on taking short breaks during the workday is now substantial, and while all kinds of breaks have found experimental support (napping, exercise, nature, music, socializing and connecting, gaming, etc.), which of them would work best for you depends on who you are and the context of your situation. For example, different types of work can require different types of breaks. If you're working on something that requires deep focus, you might find one kind of break beneficial, but if you're doing rote work or thinking creatively, you might need another. Studies are clear about one thing, though—taking breaks is always better for fatigue, attention, and performance than not taking breaks.

Breaks that offer cognitive relaxation and help you detach from work for a few minutes were found to be most beneficial overall. Power napping at work isn't practical for most people, but there are other ways to combat fatigue. For example, low-intensity cardiovascular exercise like brisk walking for as little as three minutes has been found to lower stress, and exercising and stretching for a few minutes has been found to increase performance on work tasks. If you hate exercising, you might do better spending 10 minutes calling a loved one or taking a stroll in nature, which has been found to lower stress and the urge to ruminate.

Surfing social media was found to be less effective overall, especially if you're looking at what your friends are posting. None of them are likely to feature images of your besties at their desk, looking burnt out and despondent, and seeing them sipping mai tais on a beach will not reinvigorate you vicariously. What might put some skip in your step is funny videos of adorable puppies or kittens. Those kinds of Reels rack up millions of views for a reason—they are instantly absorbing and therefore likely to help you feel detached from work. I'm partial to Vizsla puppies myself, so it's a quick fix I go to regularly.

If you don't have 10 minutes, no problem. Micro-breaks of one to two minutes have been found to reduce fatigue and restore attention and vigor. For example, a few minutes of mindfulness meditation was found to increase executive functioning and improve emotional regulation. A quick chat with colleagues can boost general well-being as long as you share feelings, passions, or opinions and avoid small talk, because that will allow you to feel more connected to them, and connecting with others, even briefly, can recharge your physical and mental energy.

But not always.

The Safety Guide for Getting Social Support on the Job

Social support has been shown to lower stress, boost mood and emotional resilience, and offer a slew of other positive outcomes. However, as most of us know from personal experience, not every effort we make to seek social support leaves us feeling better. Indeed, studies have found that when stress at work compromises our emotional intelligence, our efforts to gain social support are more likely to leave us feeling worse. We might get into an argument with our colleague or, by talking to them, realize that our situation is even worse than we realized. Or we might approach the wrong colleague and feel judged, misunderstood, or criticized, or approach someone at the wrong time and get rebuffed off the bat.

Tony the trader needed all the social support he could get when he was under investigation for creating a hostile work environment. His nemesis, Scar, had manipulated Jason, a new and struggling employee, into blaming Tony for his poor performance. Scar then orchestrated a team meeting in which he set up Tony to look like he was ignoring Jason and staged a dramatic walkout with Jason to make the manufactured "insult" look even worse. Jason made his official complaint to human resources soon thereafter.

For Tony, a genuinely nice guy who had always had excellent relationships with his coworkers, the investigation was devastating. Although Jason's complaint and the ensuing investigation were supposed to be confidential, and all parties were forbidden to discuss it, I had no doubt that Scar would find a way to leak the details to the entire office. He was desperate to overtake Tony as the number one trader, and he was willing to sabotage Tony in any way in order to compromise his performance.

The idea of his coworkers knowing that human resources was investigating him for creating a hostile work environment was mortifying and humiliating for Tony, and not being able to discuss the situation and defend himself from whatever misinformation Scar spread made him feel even worse. Needless to say, he was anxious about going to the office the next morning. We spent the session working on his anxiety and thinking through who he could count on for support should he need it during the workday.

Tony left me an email during his lunch hour on Monday to let me know that he had followed my advice, and things had "gone okay at the office."

I was relieved to hear it. My relief did not last long. Tony reached out to me again that evening and asked for an emergency session. When his video came on, I was shocked by how distraught he looked.

"What happened?" I asked, worried.

"Do you remember my assistant, Daria, the aspiring fashion designer?"

I remembered her well. She was young and enthusiastic, and she loved Tony. When she designed a new outfit, she would proudly wear it to the office and solicit Tony's opinion. Since he knew nothing about design, he always responded with a big smile and a thumbs-up. Daria would curtsy and beam with delight. Six months earlier, she tearfully told Tony that she had decided to spend more time working on her designs and needed to drop to part-time. She knew he needed a full-time assistant and was sad to not work with him anymore. He was disappointed, but he urged HR to find her a role that she could do part-time, which they did.

"What about Daria?" I asked.

"I hadn't seen her in a while, but I ran into her yesterday, and she seemed as excited to see me as always. I couldn't even tell if she had heard anything about the complaint; it felt like old times. She was wearing a new outfit, so she did her traditional 360 to show it to me. I smiled and gave her a thumbs-up, and she giggled with delight as usual."

Tony swallowed hard, and his voice became raspy. "Neither of us noticed

Scar standing behind us. When I turned and saw him, he shot me a scathing look and walked off. That afternoon, I got another notice from HR. Daria had filed a complaint against me for sexual harassment." Tony could barely get the words out. "She claimed I objectified and belittled her by rating her appearance with my thumb, like I was," Tony read from his notes, "*an emperor in the Colosseum deciding the fate of an enslaved girl.*" Tony's lower lip trembled. "I wasn't judging her, I was giving her the same gesture of approval I always had, the one she wanted. And she was just as thrilled by it as she always had been."

I was stunned. "What would make her do that?"

Tony swallowed, "I never mentioned who she transferred to, did I?"

My heart sank. "Scar?"

Tony nodded. "He must have put her up to it. We were always so close; I never dreamed she would turn against me. I saw her as I was leaving the office. She was with Scar, but she waited for him to look away and mouthed *I'm so sorry*. She looked devastated. Scar must have put a ton of pressure on her to make her do that; her job must have been on the line. The poor woman must feel horrible. She doesn't deserve that—to be used like a pawn in his games."

I had never seen Tony look so haunted. "I spoke to a lawyer on the way home," he continued. "He said . . . he said I could lose my job. He said that even if I wasn't fired, the complaints could make it difficult for me to transfer to another company."

Tony's screen went dark. I could hear him crying. "I'm sorry," he sputtered from the dark screen, "I don't mean to upset you too. I'm sorry."

"You're not upsetting me, Tony. You never have to apologize for crying, especially with me. And you don't need to turn off your video. What would you do if this session were in person?"

"I'd cover my face with my hands."

"Then do that, but please keep the video on. I want you to see that I'm here with you and that I will be, no matter how much pain you're in."

Tony turned on his video. His head was down, shoulders heaving with sobs. His blind spot about office politics, his trusting nature, and the stress of Jason's complaint had combined to form the perfect storm of compromised emotional intelligence. Knowing that Daria worked for Scar should have made him cautious of any interaction with her. Scar didn't take Daria on out of the goodness of his heart—he obviously hoped to leverage her against Tony in some way. Yet, none of that crossed Tony's mind.

The consequences of Tony's mistake were potentially much greater than most emotional intelligence missteps when it comes to seeking support at work, but finding the right person to open up to in the workplace is always tricky. Your coworkers are likely to have their own thoughts and feelings about the issues that are troubling you and be far less objective than an outside friend or family member would be. And as Tony found out after his conversation with Daria, even work friends might have competing loyalties and agendas.

The Who, When, How, and What of Seeking Social Support

Liam, the lawyer who was a few months away from finally finding out if he was on the partner track, also needed to consider the competing agendas of his friends at work. He recognized that, as stressful it was to be in suspense about his professional future, seeking support from his cohort of sixth-year associates was problematic because they were all competing for the same few spots.

"I wish we could all just talk about it openly," Liam lamented, "but everyone is keeping to themselves. We've been tight for years, and we go to one another all the time, so I never developed that kind of relationship with anyone else in the firm, and now I don't know who else to trust."

"Trust is important, but that's not the only consideration," I responded. "The four elements you have to think through when seeking social support in any context are *who, when, how*, and *what*. When it comes to the *who*, trust is an important factor, but mostly for ruling people out. You also want to rule people in. Are they empathetic and compassionate? Can they express emotional validation well? Sharing your thoughts and feelings for fifteen minutes over lunch and getting only a *Sucks to be you* in response isn't going to feel cathartic."

Liam nodded. "I might need to do better on that front myself."

"Then keep that in mind. The *when* is about timing. It matters. Don't start a conversation when you see the person in the hallway. Ask if they have a few minutes to talk first. Don't approach someone if they seem rushed or stressed, and don't go to the same person repeatedly unless they come to you for support too, or you'll strain the relationship."

"Spread the joy," Liam responded.

"Exactly." I smiled. "The *how* is the trickiest part."

Studies found that getting support in the workplace can fail to provide true emotional recovery because of the kind of support we seek. We typically seek support when we're in a heightened emotional state and having big feelings, which signals the other person to favor empathy over helping us figure out the actual issue by providing insight or a broader perspective. Their compassion and validation are important, though, because the emotional and stress relief they provide can help restore our mental bandwidth. Feeling understood and supported has also been found to lower our risk of getting dysregulated and even to reduce unhealthy snacking and cravings for comfort food.

"Being able to know the *what*—the kind of support you need in moments of stress and strain—is also not simple," I told Liam. "It requires you to first identify what you're feeling in that moment so that you know what to ask for in order to address those feelings. For example, if you were feeling insecure, you would need them to boost your confidence. If you were anxious or fearful, you would need reassurance. If you were upset about being treated unfairly, you would need them to help soothe your resentment and calm your anger."

Most of us would not have the wherewithal to ask for those things in those situations for one simple reason: our feelings are nuanced and complicated, and our ability to label them accurately is poor, because few of us have ever been taught how to do so.

Those Who Cannot Be Named

When I ask my clients what they are feeling in the moment, they rarely mention more than one or two emotions, and those they do mention are not especially nuanced—variations of *good* (okay, cool, fine), *bad* (bummed, upset, angry, down), or *vague-in-betweens* (meh, so-so, whatever, shrug). While it's common for people to think of their feelings as happening in single strands—one emotion at a time—we actually experience our feelings in rich tapestries—many of them at once, each at different intensities, some pleasant, some not, all woven together.

I shared that with Liam and asked him to describe how he generally felt at work.

"I guess stressed and . . . tired?"

"I'm glad you named more than one feeling," I said. "Let's expand your emotional vocabulary by adding some more to the list. What about angry or irritated? How often do you feel those, and at what intensity?"

"Angry, not often. Irritated, a couple of times a day. Not too intensely, though."

"How about resentful or frustrated?" I inquired.

"More often. Sometimes high."

"Sad or lonely?"

"Some days. Medium intensity," Liam said.

"Anxious?"

"Only between panic attacks."

I smiled. Doing improv for his family had allowed Liam to begin expressing his humor in other parts of his life too, including therapy. Naming his feelings and thinking through what they might be telling him wasn't just a way for Liam to boost his emotional intelligence; it was also a potent form of emotional regulation.

Identifying our feelings and articulating them to others, especially when we can do so accurately, has a magical effect—it feels soothing and relieving. More importantly, it helps us recognize the kind of support we need so that we can convey that to the person we're seeking it from. For example, one study found that when we're feeling worried or regretful, receiving practical or problem-solving support is useful, but if we're feeling angry or sad, it's irritating. Anger and sadness usually set us up to prefer emotional validation and compassion, respectively.

Increasing our *emotional granularity* (our ability to distinguish one feeling from another) and *emotional literacy* (our ability to identify and understand our feelings) significantly boosts our general emotional intelligence. To that end, I've included a Work Feelings Chart at the close of this chapter that you can use to practice identifying your feelings at and about work. Using it when you're emotionally activated will help you figure out the different strands in your emotional tapestry, the kind of support you need, and which of your colleagues could best offer it.

Of course, colleagues aren't the only option for getting social support at work. Your friends and loved ones can be just as effective. Receiving support and validation from loved ones is an effective way to recover during the workday. It doesn't just refresh our energy and focus; it prevents our emotional intelligence from taking a dive and the fallout that could happen if it does. One consideration to keep in mind is that since you're at work, you'll be using your phone to connect with them. When seeking support and connection, not all forms of phone communication carry the same impact. Video calls tend to enable greater feelings of connection than phone calls or texting do.

Priya, the personal assistant, had a history of being overwhelmed by stress and then quitting, so I suggested she schedule a midday video call with her boyfriend during which she could vent to him and get support. He was happy to do it and eager to be there for her and help her manage the pressures and unpredictability of her job. I was glad Priya had found such a patient and supportive boyfriend. But I worried that whatever was going on with the partners at her new job was creating the kind of chronic stress that could impact not just her emotional health but her relationship as well.

Indeed, a large body of research has shown that when work pressures mount, our relationships with our partner, friends, and family rarely go unscathed.

Emotional Fluency Exercise

When you catch yourself in a moment of intense emotion, go through the Work Feelings Chart below. Write down at least 10 feelings you have and rate their intensity on a scale of 1 (low) to 10 (high). Expect to have a few of each intensity (high = 8–10, medium = 5–7, low = 1–4). Repeat the exercise regularly until you can list at least 10 feelings without having to refer to the chart.

Work Feelings Chart

Anxious	Shocked	Burnt Out	Pressured	Demotivated	Confused
Worried	Surprised	Strained	Bulldozed	Impotent	Uncertain
Apprehensive	Stunned	Stretched	Harassed	Demoralized	Doubtful
Fearful	Amazed	Exhausted	Pushed	Disengaged	Disillusioned
Concerned	Startled	Tired	Forced	Disappointed	Bored
Nervous	Astounded	Fatigued	Coerced	Dissatisfied	Discouraged
Troubled	Alarmed	Worn Out	Hassled	Disheartened	Baffled
Uneasy		Drained	Bullied	Thwarted	Puzzled
Bothered		Depleted	Intimidated	Disempowered	Bewildered
Distressed		Spent	Threatened		
Stressed		Weary	Frightened		
Overwhelmed			Oppressed		
			Persecuted		

Frustrated	Helpless	Insecure	Lonely	Guilty	Distrustful
Annoyed	Depressed	Doubtful	Isolated	Shameful	Betrayed
Irritated	Sad	Inadequate	Rejected	Embarrassed	Suspicious
Resentful	Hopeless	Unworthy	Ostracized	Regretful	Skeptical
Angry	Unhappy	Unseen	Shunned	Remorseful	Cynical
Used	Down	Unrecognized	Hurt	Uncomfortable	Doubtful
Agitated	Sorrowful	Self-Critical	Excluded	Mortified	Jaded
Irritable	Miserable		Discarded		Apprehensive
Prickly	Despondent		Abandoned		Wary
Infuriated			Snubbed		
Incensed			Insulted		
Outraged			Slighted		

Calm	Excited	Optimistic	Validated	Sensitive	
Satisfied	Engaged	Fulfilled	Grateful	Touchy	
Relieved	Motivated	Happy	Appreciated	Fragile	
Content	Empowered	Delighted	Valued	Delicate	
Peaceful	Energized	Elated	Supported	Weak	
Tranquil	Invigorated	Pleased	Trusting	Unprotected	
Serene	Eager	Overjoyed	Connected	Defenseless	
Relaxed	Enthusiastic	Hopeful	Respected	Exposed	
Rested	Confident	Euphoric	Assured		
Refreshed	Proud	Thrilled	Considered		
	Encouraged		Seen		
	Uplifted		Accepted		
	Inspired				
	Honored				
	Revitalized				
	Reinvigorated				

CHAPTER NINE

Thursday Evening

*Collateral Damage—How Your Job Impacts
Your Relationships*

IN MY SECOND YEAR of graduate school, a former head of the New York State Psychological Association gave us a talk. "How many of you are in relationships?" she asked our class of 10 people. Six hands went up. She nodded sagely. "A lot of you won't be by the time you graduate." A pep talk it wasn't. She went on to caution us about how demanding the program was and the negative impact it typically had on marriages.

A relatively new body of research has been studying how stress at work impacts our relationships at home. The findings indicate that similar relationship warnings should be issued to anyone who has a demanding job. As good as our intentions might be, when we finish the workday stressed and irritable, it's difficult to prevent our tension and bad mood from spilling onto the people around us.

Tensions and pressures at work can keep us in fight-or-flight mode for much of the workday. We then bring home our *combat-ready mindset* (another reason the work-to-home transition ritual is so important) and fail to recognize that our partner or friends are non-combatants. Shedding the fog of war—deliberately managing our mood and emotions so that we are less charged with irritability, preoccupation, and impatience when we reenter our personal lives—is therefore important. Because we typically overestimate our ability to contain work stresses and prevent loved ones from being impacted by them, I encourage the people I work with to solicit feedback from their partners about whether they succeed in keeping work tensions from invading the home. The responses typically range from a mild *I know you try, but it does leak out*, to *Are you delusional? The kids aren't in their rooms playing when you get in from work, they're hiding.*

Priya, the personal assistant, had been getting support from her boyfriend to deal with the recent escalation in tensions at her job. She and the other two personal assistants she worked with were entirely in the dark as to what was making their managers so secretive and overcritical, but something clearly was. As the situation dragged on, Priya's boyfriend rose to the occasion and provided increasing support. They did video calls during her lunch break, he sent her a constant stream of funny memes to boost her mood, and he listened to her unpack her day when she got home.

The secret was finally revealed months later when one of the partners called Priya and the two other assistants into a meeting and announced that they had sold the company to a large corporation and that new management was coming in. The five partners would remain in various capacities, but "cost-cutting changes were likely." The assistants exchanged worried glances. The first "costs" to be cut in such situations were usually people. Rumors circulated that the new company wanted to scale back to two personal assistants. Priya, Kev, and Jan would now have to compete against each other for the two positions while having to continue working closely together, and while dealing with the entire culture of the office becoming more corporate.

The changes and job uncertainty hit Priya hard, but they hit her relationship with her boyfriend even harder. According to her, he gradually went from being a source of support to being a source of stress. After living together for many months and establishing a calm and loving home life, their evenings and weekends now seemed laden with conflict.

"All he does is criticize me," Priya complained in our session. Her annoyance was palpable. "I try not to spill my drama when I get home, but he can't hold it in. He comes at me needy from the second I walk in. He totally doesn't get how brutal my day was."

I take my clients' narratives about their loved ones becoming "less supportive" with a grain of salt, especially when the person whose circumstances have changed is my client. Priya might have believed that she was trying to manage the tension and strain from her workday and that her boyfriend's attitude was the cause of their recent problems, but Priya was the one dealing with sudden job insecurity, and that is not a stressor we adapt to well.

Remember, our unconscious mind believes that work is our top priority, so it will consider any risk of losing a job to be an existential threat.

An Epidemic of Job Insecurity

A 2024 survey found that 55% of employees have job security concerns. For those in the IT sector, who fear the impact of artificial intelligence (AI), that number was 72%. A 2023 survey by the American Psychological Association found that almost 40% of all employees were worried about AI threatening their jobs, and over half of them felt like those stresses were having a negative impact on their mental health.

Having to work under the threat of job loss is challenging, especially when the threat is explicit and when, like Priya, you are competing against your colleagues for the survivor slots. Lawyers like Liam, who hope to become partners in their firms, go through years of intense work pressures, knowing that only 20% to 30% of them will eventually become partners and that it will take five to six years of hard work to find out if they are even on that track. Postdocs and academics face similar years of job insecurity—only 10% to 20% of them get tenure-track positions at academic institutions, and those who do then spend an average of seven years having to author a grueling number of papers to secure those positions—a gauntlet known as *publish or perish*.

Job insecurity is a profound stressor that has been found to contribute to poorer performance and significant damage to mental and physical health. It has even been shown to increase the risk of suicide attempts. The stress that job insecurity causes is so great, studies have found that the prospect of losing our livelihood causes even more damage to our mental health than actually losing a job does. In one study, the mental health and emotional well-being of people who feared losing their jobs was compared to workers who were recently laid off. Employed workers who felt threatened by layoffs showed more symptoms of depression, anxiety, sleep disturbances, worry, and exhaustion, and had more physical complaints (headaches, stomach, and back pain), than those who had been let go.

Uncertainty, whether about a job or any other aspect of life, creates intense feelings of dread, a feeling we do not tolerate well. In one experiment, subjects had the option to wait to receive a *mild* electric shock or to skip the wait and receive a much stronger shock immediately. Almost 30% of participants chose the stronger shock because they couldn't tolerate the dread of waiting for the milder one. Priya and her two colleagues had to deal with the dread of knowing that at any moment, they could be let go, while also being expected to make their best effort to impress the new management and keep their job. Unfortunately, as often happens in those situations, the uncertainty went on for months.

Most company leaders know how damaging the threat of layoffs is to their workforce's performance, motivation, mental health, and emotional well-being. Yet, while some try to minimize the uncertainty and dread, many handle layoffs in ways that make the situation even more stressful than it already is. Like Priya and her peers, workers often get little to no communication from decision-makers about their fate—no timeline, no reassurances, no compassion, and no leadership.

Leaders are often quick to mention the mental health services they offer employees via employee assistance programs and other online resources to help them deal with the pressures—but that does not absolve them of responsibility for imposing them. If the resources companies provided were accessible and beneficial, that would be one thing, but as recent reports by McKinsey indicated, 70% of employees have trouble accessing the mental health services their companies offer, and Gen Z employees like Priya are three times less likely to access them than baby boomers are.

Harsh Terminations

Terms like *layoffs* and *let go* might sound gentle, but the culling of employees is usually anything but. Such cuts often come in "rounds," which leaves those who survive the first fall of the axe to sweat it out until the second or third are complete. Because rounds usually take place months apart, employees never get a true break from the dread.

But what does even more damage is the manner in which the "breakup" itself goes down. Losing a job is hard enough, but how that news is delivered can be extremely harsh and humiliating. You wake up in the morning and discover that you can't log into your work email, or you get to work and your cardkey no longer opens the door, or you're escorted out of the building by security as if you were a criminal. "It didn't feel like I was being let go," a former employee at a social media app told me recently, "it felt like I was being terminated."

Workers who have had an ongoing relationship with their company for decades get dumped without a word of explanation, without any gratitude for their years of effort and devotion, without any opportunity to process the goodbye or to express their thoughts and feelings. Imagine if a person broke up with their spouse by suddenly blocking them from all communication and barring them from the home they'd shared for many years. Such a person would be considered heartless. Many of the surviving employees have similar feelings about their employers after witnessing harsh terminations, but since they're stuck working for them, they just have to swallow their feelings and keep grinding. They might feel traumatized and disillusioned, but they stay on regardless because termination horror stories are so common in today's workplace, they have no guarantee that their next relationship with an employer would be any different.

Leaders often have the misguided assumption that after a round of layoffs, their remaining employees' relief and gratitude will motivate them to regain their regular productivity. The opposite is true. One survey found that 74% of surviving employees experienced drops in productivity *after* layoffs were completed. As adaptable as we are, existential stresses like losing our livelihood are not ones we get used to over time. Studies have found that while we eventually adapt to unemployment, we don't adapt to job insecurity—our well-being just continues to decline. That finding shouldn't be surprising. Staying in any kind of emotionally abusive relationship erodes our well-being over time, especially one in which we're expected to keep making efforts despite the other party's lack of commitment.

I once asked a CEO (whose company was not doing layoffs at the time but had in the past) how he would feel if he really wanted to stay married and his spouse sent him an email saying, "I'm thinking I might break up with you in the near future. Bummer, I know. But keep working really hard at being a great partner. Who knows, I might keep you around." He said he would feel angry, resentful, and stressed. He also said that he would keep that in mind when his company next had to make job cuts.

I hope he does because clear, timely, and regular communications could make a big difference for employees, as could the attention of individual managers. Researchers found that when managers listened to the concerns and feelings of their subordinates with understanding and compassion, those workers exhibited smaller drops in well-being and fared better during periods of job insecurity than those whose managers did not demonstrate caring. I'm familiar with companies in which caring is a core value that gets reflected in every aspect of the culture. These are models that employers and managers could theoretically learn from, but few show any interest in doing so.

That is unfortunate, because when job insecurity and the stress it imposes on employees goes on for months, it doesn't just spill over into the home and impact our relationships with our loved ones, it can make our perceptions of them become more negative. It can even make us fall out of love with them.

How Work Stress Alienates Us from Our Partners

Two months after her company was purchased by a corporate entity, Priya's descriptions of her boyfriend continued to devolve, and her frustrations and dissatisfactions with the relationship continued to mount.

"He did it again last week," Priya complained in our session. "My day was a dumpster fire. Jan was on my back, micromanaging every little thing, Kev was super salty—everyone's losing it. I got home feeling totally dead inside and just wanted to chill. My boyfriend sees I'm wrecked and starts whining about how I didn't FaceTime him all day. Like I'm ghosting him or something. I was like, *Seriously? You're going to micromanage me too?* He walked away and didn't talk to me the rest of the night. He's so whiny lately, I hate it."

You might have had similar interactions with your loved ones after highly stressful days at work. They see that you're mentally depleted and preoccupied, yet they expect you to give them your attention anyway. You get no room to breathe, no time to decompress, no space to lick your workday wounds. You feel suffocated, but no matter how you try to convey the strain you're under, they just don't get it. If you've had such evenings, you know how justified your impatience and irritation can feel, how frustrating it can be to leave one pressure cooker only to enter another.

What might be less apparent to you is that your stress is causing you to misinterpret your loved one's intentions and diminish your compassion and empathy for them. In one recent study, participants were shown pictures of people's bodies and limbs in *obviously painful positions*. Stressed participants rated the positions as significantly less painful than their non-stressed counterparts. Over time, our muted empathy and compassion for our loved ones can foster a process of *emotional drifting* (a gradual process of decreased emotional connection, intimacy, and closeness) such that at some point, we begin to perceive their emotional distress as annoying and bothersome.

Priya's relationship trended in that direction. "He's constantly trying to suck up and pretend to care when he clearly resents my job," she said, frustrated. "Then he does his hurt-puppy act. It's such a turnoff; I can barely look at him."

Over the years, I've seen many such declines and noted four factors that contribute to them: (1) our depleted coping mechanisms, (2) our partner's reactions to how we come across when these mechanisms are depleted, (3) our mood confirmation bias, and (4) the cumulative effects of daily repetition. To break down how this dynamic unfolds, we need to dive more deeply into what happened between Priya and her boyfriend.

We already know that challenging days at work sap our coping mechanisms. As a result, we're more sensitive and reactive to mild provocations.

Imagine getting home feeling mentally and emotionally depleted. We might try to conserve our dwindling energy by lying low, staying quiet, or otherwise limiting contact with loved ones, so any efforts they make to engage are likely to strike us as intrusions on our much-needed peace. That's why Priya reacted to her boyfriend's attempts to engage with her with irritation and annoyance. She might have been able to move past that hiccup, but he then expressed dismay about her being out of touch with him all day. While that might seem like a minor complaint that shouldn't trigger a big reaction, it often does. When a loved one blames us for their distress, being able to contain their feelings without rebuffing them can be quite emotionally laborious. We first have to manage our own natural inclination to get defensive, and then we have to soothe their feelings as well. That can be hard to do when our coping mechanisms are operating at capacity, but when they are deflated by stress and fatigue, defensiveness will triumph and make it difficult for us to access our empathy.

Similar stress-and-fatigue-induced clashes play out in countless homes at the end of the workday. I've responded too sharply to the people around me a few times myself over the years and regretted it every time, sometimes the second the words left my mouth, at other times when I saw the hurt on the other person's face, and sometimes only once my coping mechanisms had recovered enough for me to accept the reality that I had behaved poorly. What makes our errors obvious, at least in level-headed hindsight, is that the incidents that provoke them usually involve entirely normal events, like your partner asking you to come to dinner, the kids running around, the baby crying, your roommate blasting music you otherwise enjoy, or even your parent coming in for a hug.

This brings us to the second factor that contributes to our seeing our loved one through a jaundiced lens. When we respond to them with chilly, harsh, or distancing behavior, we're likely to provoke a response that will make the situation worse. Let's look at the exchange Priya had with her boyfriend from his point of view.

When she initially asked for more support, he rose to the occasion. In addition to sending texts and memes during the day, he agreed to a daily lunchtime video call despite his own busy schedule. He then listened to her vent about work when she got home and tried to offer comfort and advice. All those things made him feel closer to her, as acts of kindness always do, and deepened his bond with her. When she began skipping their lunchtime video calls and being less communicative in the evenings, he must have felt confused. More importantly, the obvious decline in her communication must have hurt his feelings and made him anxious about whether her feelings for him were changing.

He did not approach her about these issues at first, probably because he knew how much stress she was dealing with and didn't want to add to it. Instead, he waited for her to reengage or to explain why she was acting more distant. But she didn't. At some point, he couldn't hide his hurt feelings, and he pointed out the change in her attitude. She responded by snapping at him. Realizing she was on edge, he figured the best he could do was to walk away so that he did not escalate the argument.

His mistake, if there was one, was to express his hurt feelings like many of us do, by voicing a complaint (*you didn't respond to any of my DMs or calls*) without mentioning how he felt in the situation (*when I DM you all day and you don't respond, I feel hurt*). As a general relationship rule, the formula *When you do _____ I feel _____* will usually make the other person more likely to hear your message and respond favorably because the emphasis is on how *you felt* rather than on what *they did wrong*.

Cue the third factor that promotes changes in our perceptions of our loved ones—Priya's response to her boyfriend's reactions.

Confirmation bias refers to our tendency to perceive, interpret, or recall information that confirms our preexisting beliefs while missing or misinterpreting information that contradicts those beliefs. Having our beliefs contradicted is always emotionally uncomfortable, which is why so many of us stick with news outlets that mirror our existing political beliefs and avoid those with alternative viewpoints. Our discomfort with contradictions is most noticeable when it comes to our assessment of a person's character. Our childhood sets us up to classify people into strict dichotomies of good or bad, hero or villain, and studies demonstrate that adults prefer unambiguous characters as well. Perhaps if we taught children to develop a tolerance for ambiguity, we might be able to hold more sophisticated and nuanced beliefs as adults, but alas, we do not.

This intolerance of ambiguity extends to our emotions. Our *emotional confirmation bias* predisposes us to perceive, interpret, and recall information that supports our current emotional state. In one study, participants had their arms submerged in either body temperature water (control group) or ice water (stressed group) for three minutes and were asked to rate faces with neutral expressions of surprise. Participants who had a greater reaction to stress, as measured by their cortisol levels, rated the surprised faces as being significantly more "negative."

When we get home feeling irritable and preoccupied, our mood can predispose us to misinterpret our loved one's actions as irritating when they were intended otherwise. Like Priya, we're likely to react with unwarranted impatience, annoyance, and even hostility. With our coping mechanisms fatigued, the emotional effort required to take responsibility and apologize is often too difficult to muster. So, we pivot to a less effortful solution— justifying our reactions after the fact. Indeed, Priya spent the rest of the evening ruminating about all the times her boyfriend had been needy, inconsiderate, and annoying. Of course, that darkened her mood further and made her question her feelings for him even more. That's why it can be so difficult to get out of a bad mood—our emotional confirmation bias sets us up to perceive the events and people around us in ways that reinforce the feelings we already have.

The worse our mood is when we get home, the more likely we are to overreact to our loved ones, and the harsher that overreaction is, the more villainous we will perceive them to be in order to justify it after the fact. When those dynamics rinse and repeat on a regular basis, it can shift our perceptions of the person themselves. When we perceive a loved one's bid for closeness or connection (e.g., wanting to talk, asking for a hug) as demanding and irritating, we register their *behavior* as inconsiderate or selfish. But when such incidents happen daily or regularly, there comes a point at which it is no longer their behavior that registers as needy and unsupportive but the *person themself.* That happens because of yet another bias we all have—our tendency to believe information to which we are exposed repeatedly, even if it's wrong. That's why misinformation is so dangerous and why social media has enabled so many outlandish conspiracy theories to spread. If we hear something enough times, we'll start to believe it, even if it contradicts our previous knowledge. The same is true of misinformation that's internally generated by our mood.

You might be thinking, *but what if my partner is selfish and annoying? What if my friends are demanding and needy? What if my kids do misbehave? Aren't my feelings justified then?* One way to answer those questions is to ask yourself if you've always felt that way or if it's a more recent development. Another is to consider why the other person might have changed. Even if you're convinced that they've changed, if you are the one who has been under stress at work, they might have changed in response to your stress.

To be clear, your feelings are always real, but they can be based on emotional bias, misperception, and misinterpreting others' intentions. In some cases, our unconscious mind will even distort our memories of specific events to bring them in line with our current emotional state. The time your friend was late to your birthday party because they hit traffic becomes a recollection about them not showing up for you. I explained these dynamics to Priya and asked her to reconsider whether she might have been seeing her boyfriend through a distorted prism of stress and exhaustion.

"Maybe," she responded. "I mean, that was just one fight. We had a way bigger one last night. I lost it and told him I wanted to break up. He started crying. I felt bad, so I told him I said it out of frustration and promised I wouldn't leave him. I won't, but I'm for sure taking a step back."

"You're quiet quitting your relationship?" I asked, dismayed.

"What? No," Priya objected.

"Priya, you just said that you're going to take a step back. That's what quiet quitting means. Don't you see the familiar pattern here?"

"What pattern?"

"You've been feeling stressed-out for months and for good reason; work has been really difficult. You get home exhausted every night and need time to decompress, but your boyfriend wants to connect, so you feel pressured to engage with him when you would rather be alone. Only you don't communicate your needs and feelings to him, so he keeps trying, which stresses you out more and more until you feel a strong impulse to quit the relationship entirely or disengage from it emotionally. Isn't that exactly what happened when the pressure peaked at your previous jobs—all eleven of them?"

She glared at me, then sighed and looked down. "Old habits exert a strong gravitational pull, especially when you're tired and stressed," I said softly. "But once you understand what's happening, you can choose alternative ways of responding, healthier ones."

If it sounds as though I was advocating for Priya's boyfriend, I was not; I was advocating for the relationship. I've seen too many good relationships go south when one or both of the partner's jobs became unreasonably stressful. When someone I work with tells me about an argument with their partner, and I believe they were in the wrong, I suggest that to them as gently as I can, even if it's hard for them to hear. Part of my job as a therapist is to hold up a mirror to the person so they can see themselves more clearly, and that includes things they might not like to see. I always lay out what the person was feeling at the time, as I did with Priya, as doing so makes it easier for them to feel self-compassion and not judge themselves too harshly.

"How do you feel about what I said?" I asked gently.

"Annoyed," Priya responded. "With you, with my boyfriend, with myself . . ." She was quiet for a moment. "He's a good person, and he loves me," she said eventually. "I know that. And I was happy with him. I know that too." She sighed. "You're right, I've been pushing him away. Why doesn't recognizing that change how I feel?"

"That's the problem with insight," I responded. "Our mind understands things quickly; our heart understands things slowly. We need to mind that gap. Your feelings will catch up."

"Will they, though? Part of me would love to close the gap and go back to how things were, but I feel so meh right now."

"There is something you can do to get back in touch with how you used to feel. An empathy exercise."

Repairing and Preventing Relationship Ruptures

To reconnect to warmer feelings for her boyfriend, Priya needed to reduce the frustration and irritation she felt toward him and access her compassion for him. You will need to do the same if you want to prevent work strain from driving a wedge between you and your loved one, or if you simply want to reconnect to the warmer feelings you used to have for them. The best way to do so is via an empathy exercise.

Empathy involves gaining an understanding of how the other person feels. "When you truly understand how someone feels and why," I said to Priya, "it's hard to remain resentful or angry toward them. It's like emotional alchemy in that way. Understanding dissolves anger. The reverse works too. Feeling truly understood by someone makes it hard to remain angry at them."

"But I already know how he felt," Priya said. "He felt ignored and hurt and frustrated."

I nodded. "That's how he felt during and after the fight, you're right. But what matters for this exercise is why he felt those things. And that starts earlier, with the expectations and feelings he had before you got home that collided with yours and caused the friction."

Priya could discern what her boyfriend was feeling once they were already in the fight because his words, facial expressions, body language, and behavior clearly showed his emotions. Figuring out how your loved one felt before the argument began, or how they were feeling before you even got home, is more complicated. Another cognitive bias we have is the belief that knowing someone extremely well gives us the power to divine how they would feel in any situation. It does not. The closer you are to someone, the harder it can be to truly see them because you have so much information to sift through. The empathy exercise helps you figure out what information to apply to the moment in which you find yourself.

The first part of the exercise is *the setup*: the goal is to gain insight into what your loved one's mindset, emotional state, and expectations were before you got home from work. The second is *the application*.

This is a visualization exercise, so it's best to close your eyes. Start by thinking through what the other person's day was like: (1) their stresses and pain points, including those that had nothing to do with you, (2) how they were feeling about your relationship, (3) what their mood was like, (4) what their needs were given the day they had, (5) what they hoped the evening would be like, and (6) what they expected from you as a result.

Once you have a clear picture of the setup, you can begin the second part of the exercise—apply the information as you replay the events from your loved one's point of view.

"He had an alright day at work," Priya said, her eyes closed. "He was probably worried about me—like, wondering how things were going between us and how I was feeling about him. He was probably looking forward to our video call at lunch, wanting that reassurance and connection. When I didn't call, he would have felt all hurt and disappointed, hoping we could hang when I got home."

"Very good," I said. "Now play out what happened once you got home—but through his eyes."

"He would have been hyped hearing me walk in but low-key hurt that I didn't seem happy to see him and even more crushed that I was acting like I wanted to bounce. When I got annoyed, he would have felt rejected and freaked out about whether I was planning to break up with him. Then bam, his worst fears hit, and I did, and it crushed him."

"Priya, that was amazing," I said. It was. Her perspective-taking abilities were excellent. I hoped they would make it easier for her to access her compassion.

"How do you feel about him right now?" I asked.

"Softer, I guess. Not like I used to, but better."

"Good. You can build on that."

"How?" she asked.

"By repeating the exercise. Add it to your work-to-home transition ritual, especially during periods of high stress at work."

"Okay, but what do I do tonight when I get home?"

"Talk to him," I responded. "Have a conversation about what's been going on. You have a good idea of his feelings, but he doesn't know about yours. Tell him about how suffocated you feel at work and how that's been impacting you. Let him know what you need—that you could use some time to yourself to decompress when you get home and that he should let you come to him."

Setting clear expectations with your partner, family, or friends about what you need when you get home (and being open to hearing what they need as well) will spare them from having to guess when and how they should engage with you. Asking them about their feelings, negotiating any differences in what your needs are, and making sure to revisit and update those understandings when circumstances change (e.g., when the pressure at work shifts in one direction or another) will help prevent future misunderstandings and tensions.

The empathy exercise is useful for another reason—it will help realign your tribal allegiances. We belong to many tribes (e.g., family, friends circle, work team, religious community, amateur sports team). After a day in the trenches at work, we're likely to still be in work-tribe mode when we get home. When we're in that mode, our loved ones can register as outsiders in our unconscious mind. Any expectation they have for us to display tribal affiliation (by engaging with them) before we have reoriented our tribal priorities could be seen as hostile (a demand to betray our loyalty to our work tribe) rather than welcoming. The empathy exercise reminds our unconscious processes that we're also a member of our home tribe so that efforts our family (or you) make to connect won't feel threatening.

The pressures of our work life do not just impact our relationships, they can damage our loved ones' emotional health directly. Numerous studies have shown that when the demands of our work are excessive, the strain we feel doesn't just make us displace our frustrations onto our loved ones and push them away; we actively undermine them and make their lives more difficult.

CHAPTER TEN

Thursday Night

Protecting the Home Front—
How to Set Boundaries with Work

WHEN SOMEONE I WORK with is going through an especially challenging time in their job, I make sure to inquire about how things are going with their partner, family, or friends. I do so because of the extensive body of research indicating that the more intense the demands of your job are, the more likely they are to conflict or interfere with your duties at home, making you have to choose one over the other.

You get home too exhausted to help with dinner or the kids' homework, too irritable to enjoy date night with your partner, or so tense and preoccupied that everyone stays away from you. Over time, your loved ones will feel that you're prioritizing work over them, not just because you're shirking your responsibilities at home, but because you seem so focused on work when you're at home.

Most people bristle at the suggestion that their work matters to them more than their loved ones do. In a 2023 survey, 73% of people said their family took priority over their jobs. Other studies found that people who prioritized family over work were happier than those who did not. That should put the question to rest except for one caveat: there is a gap between our *stated priorities*—what we believe matters to us most—and our *lived priorities*—the choices we actually make on a daily basis.

Consider the following scenario: Your boss, who decides the amount of your yearly bonus, invites you to a work dinner that conflicts with your kid's recital. Do you accept the invitation? When 500 workers were asked the same question, two-thirds of them—66%—said they would choose the work dinner. Indeed, surveys found that in the United States, employees spend less than 60 minutes of focused and meaningful time per day with their family and even less time with their friends.

The demands of our jobs don't just impact our relationships, they affect our loved ones' well-being and emotional health directly (known as *crossover effects*). One of the more unfortunate findings from this body of research is that when we feel tense and strained from work, we make life more difficult for our loved ones in various ways—including actively undermining them in the home, and we're often entirely unaware that we're doing it.

How Your Work Stress Makes Their *Life Harder*

Tony had two complaints lodged against him at work: one by Jason, the new trader who accused Tony of creating a hostile work environment, and the other by Daria, Tony's ex-assistant, who filed a complaint against him for sexual harassment. Both complaints were orchestrated by Tony's archrival, Scar, who resorted to plotting and scheming to get ahead when he was unable to overtake Tony as the top performer in their group. The idea of his coworkers thinking he was a bully and a sexual predator made Tony literally nauseous and caused him immense dread. He admitted that he wasn't handling the stress well, so I asked how things were going at home.

"Good. My wife knows everything that happened, and she's been super supportive. She sees how worried and upset I am when I get home, how much the situation's been weighing on me over these past couple of months. She's been giving me space to think and figure things out. She's been an angel."

A few days later, the angel in question wrote an email to Tony and copied me on it. It arrived exactly one minute before my session with him—enough time for us to see it but not enough for us to read it. She clearly wanted us to do so together in the session. The subject line was *Your Wife and Kids Are Suffering Too*. Tony's wife knew that I couldn't respond to her email because of privacy laws, but she was worried about Tony's mental health and wanted him to read the letter with a safety net present (me). I asked Tony to read it aloud.

Tony,

I'm worried for you. I'm worried for us. I also know how hard you are on yourself, so I wanted you to read this with your therapist present. I hope you will discuss with him what changes you can make because something needs to change and soon. I know you're going through it right now, but we're going through it with you. B*** [their five-year-old] is back to wetting the bed, and M*** [their ten-year-old] is refusing to have playdates come to the house. They pick up your mood, Tony. They register your tension, worry, brooding, and irritability. When you're around them, you're either checked out or miserable.

You have to start pulling your weight at home. You can't just leave everything up to me. You haven't asked me how I'm doing since this mess started, and I can't remember the last time you kissed me. You snap at me all the time, even in front of the kids. I feel like your punching bag. When I tell B*** he's not allowed to do something, he runs to you because you say yes to everything without checking with me. You're not showing up as a dad, and you're not showing up as a husband. You're dealing with a lot and I know you're trying, but you need to try harder.

Our home used to be a sanctuary, the place we shut out the world and felt safe as a family. It doesn't feel like that now. I need you to make it feel like that again.

I love you. We'll be okay.
H***

Tony sobbed so heavily as he read the letter that it took him several attempts to get through it. Every time he took a break to wipe his eyes, he said, "Sorry,

I don't mean to upset you too," despite my reassurances that he didn't need to apologize for crying.

He finished the letter and took a minute to compose himself. "I've been hurting my family," he said, his lower lip trembling. "I feel so bad for doing that."

"I understand why you feel bad, Tony, but guilt is a luxury you can't afford at the moment." He looked at me, confused. "When you focus on your guilt, you're thinking about you," I explained. "Your wife is asking you to think about *them*, what *they* need."

He stifled a sob. "I don't know what they need."

"She just told you. In her email." I said more softly, "This is why you have to resist the temptation to sit with the guilt. Guilt draws your attention to your feelings and away from the feelings of the people you're feeling bad about in the first place."

He nodded and reread the letter. "Sanctuary," he said once he finished. "That's what they need. That's going to be my mantra. I need to show up as a husband and as a father. I need to make home feel like a safe space, for all of us."

Tony's wife's email described many of the common ways work stress can lead us to undermine our partner at home. We leave them with most of the work, ignore their needs, sabotage their parenting efforts, and generally infect the home with stress. This tends to happen regardless of gender, although some studies found that men's work stress impacted their women partners more than women's work stress impacted their men partners, and other studies found that women's work demands can interfere with their duties at home more than men's do. Surveys by the Bureau of Labor Statistics found that women do far more housework and perform more parenting duties than men. Given they have more duties to juggle than men, it makes sense that work demands would impede them more. And, despite women carrying a greater proportion of responsibilities in the home, men spend more time on leisure than women do. Fairness would be best achieved by a couple having regular discussions about their division of labor so they can make adjustments as necessary.

Crossover effects can accumulate over time. When they do, the impact can be dramatic. Some studies found that when workers experienced high stress over sustained periods, their spouses began developing symptoms of burnout. To protect our loved ones and limit the negative impact of work stresses and intrusions, we need to set boundaries around our home life and, more importantly, we then have to maintain the boundaries we set.

Why Efforts to Set Boundaries Often Fail

Carlos, who founded a startup with his husband, Ilya, finally recognized that their extreme overwork—120 hours per week—was endangering both their health and their marriage. He told Ilya that he would be cutting his work hours to 90 per week and begged his husband to do the same. Ilya refused and accused Carlos of turning his back on their company.

"He's kind of been treating me like an employee all along, but it's gotten worse since we had that conversation," Carlos reported in our session. "One of the changes I made is that I take a nightly walk after dinner. It checks the boxes for fresh air and exercise; I get to check in on my parents and catch up with my friends back in the Midwest."

The combination of brisk walking and socializing had the added benefit of helping Carlos detach from work so that his mental and physiological systems got a break from high activation.

"The first night I told Ilya I was going for my walk, he didn't turn around from his computer, but he did say, 'Enjoy,' which I know wasn't easy for him," Carlos reported. "Fifteen minutes later, I got a text about an *urgent* work matter. Then he called with a *time-sensitive* question about one of our customers."

"Were the issues actually urgent and time-sensitive?" I asked.

"Slightly, but they could have waited an hour. I realized I needed to set a boundary, so I told him I was trying to get a mental health break and that he should wait until I got back to discuss work issues."

Carlos had the right idea but he was skipping important steps. "Let's review how to set boundaries," I said to him.

Boundary-setting has four steps and one overarching principle, and each of those needs to be thought through ahead of time.

1. Clarity: State exactly what would constitute a violation. Carlos did that part well—*I need a break from the stress, so no work messages during my walks.*

2. Explanation: Carlos did that well too. He told Ilya that he needed that time to recharge and recover.

3. Consequences: Specify how you will respond if they violate the boundary. This step is one many people skip or do poorly, and it's one you'll need to tweak because it's hard to cover every eventuality ahead of time. Carlos told Ilya that he wouldn't answer work-related messages until he got home, but as we will see, his messaging required updating.

4. Maintaining the Boundary—Enforcement: This step is the most important one and the one that most people have trouble executing well—hence the substantial fail rate. Setting a boundary alerts the person to your needs, but that alone won't get them to change their behavior; maintaining the boundary will. And that means enforcing it *every time it gets violated.*

5. Respect. A respectful approach is critical when setting boundaries. To understand why, consider what it's like to be on the other side of the exchange.

Being told that you have violated someone's boundary, especially if that person is close, is quite unpleasant. They're telling you that you did something that harmed them or made them so uncomfortable that they cannot tolerate it again. That is a lot to take in, and it's natural to feel defensive, embarrassed, blindsided, and even angry. Framing things calmly and respectfully, both when setting the limit and especially when maintaining it, will help minimize defensiveness and allow the other person to focus on the message itself.

You should also listen to any objections or concerns the other person raises; they might bring up factors you hadn't considered but should. If they do, discuss their concern with them and assess whether you might need to adjust your boundaries or consequences accordingly.

Carlos told Ilya that he would not respond to calls and texts while he was on his walk, as there were no emergencies that couldn't wait an hour, and that he would deal with work issues once he got home. Ilya huffed, but the next day, Carlos enjoyed an interruption-free walk.

"It felt so refreshing," he said in our next session. "I had great chats with people back home, I enjoyed the fresh air, and I even stopped to smell the roses—literally."

I was thrilled to hear it.

"The next day," Carlos continued, "Ilya called me five minutes after I left the apartment. I didn't answer. He called again and then a third time. I was worried, so I picked up. He apologized for the intrusion and said that a customer was upset and needed answers. It couldn't wait because we can't afford to lose any customers. I was already on the phone, so hanging up would have felt childish, and it only took a second, so I gave him the answer he needed. The day after he called again, but I didn't answer. He called back. Five times. And left me three texts. I didn't respond. I thought he finally got the message, but yesterday he called three times." Carlos sighed, "Boundary-setting isn't working. Ilya can't do it."

That's the conclusion many people reach when the other person repeatedly violates the boundary, but it's almost always incorrect. Carlos's mistake wasn't that he answered the phone after Ilya called three times—given Ilya's previous visit to the ER, it could have been an emergency. His mistake was not ending the call once he realized the call was work-related.

"Ilya keeps testing your boundary," I explained to him, "and you should expect him to. Adults always test new boundaries just like children do. They're trying to assess how firm the boundary is and how serious you are about maintaining it. Once they see that you're committed, their efforts to test it will decrease sharply. That's why it's crucial to maintain the boundary *every time* it gets tested or violated by sticking to the specific response you had laid out in step three."

"*Literally* every time?" Carlos asked.

"Literally. It's a high bar, but a critical one. If you don't do that, they'll keep testing the boundary. That will make you think that they refuse to respect your boundary when, in fact, you failed to maintain it."

If setting boundaries sounds emotionally grueling and mentally taxing—bingo. It is both of those things. But the investment is worthwhile. The upfront costs in terms of energy and vigilance are significant, but the violations will decrease sharply if you're consistent in maintaining the boundary and applying the consequences you specified. Once you hold the line, the long-term rewards are substantial. You won't have to waste energy on dealing with the offensive behavior, a chronic source of tension between you and the other person will be removed, and your relationship can even get stronger as a result.

"So be more consistent," Carlos concluded.

"No, be *totally* consistent."

The Difference Between 95% and 100% Consistency

If you've ever been to a casino with slot machines, you might have noticed that people sit there for hours, putting money into one machine after another until it runs out. They do it because every so often, the machine goes *ding-ding-ding* and you win a chunk of money. That releases dopamine, a neurotransmitter associated with reward, excitement, and pleasure. Hoping for another hit of cash and dopamine, they keep inserting money into the machine until there is no money left.

Known as a *variable reward schedule*, intermittent reinforcement has been found to be an extremely potent way to make behaviors persist in both animals and people. If the machine never paid out, no one would use it. If it paid out on a regular schedule, people would game it and only put in money when they knew a payout was due. But because they can't tell when the reward will come, they keep trying until it does.

When you maintain a boundary consistently, you're like a slot machine that never pays out. The other person will put in lots of money at first, but they will quickly realize that you're standing firm, so there's no reason to keep trying. But if every once in a while, you give in, they will keep up the behavior because they know that at some point, *ding-ding-ding*.

Total consistency eliminates behaviors. A variable reward schedule reinforces them.

Carlos's mistakes were ones we all make when setting boundaries—namely, giving in during vulnerable moments. You're tired and you don't feel like having an argument, so you let the violation slide. Or the other person has clearly been making efforts, so you think that maybe you don't have to be so "rigid" this time. Or they've gotten upset each time you maintained the boundary, and you hate confrontation or feeling guilty, so you give them a pass just that once.

Doing those things won't just set you back, it will inflame the situation.

The other person will then think, *Wait, you didn't object that I did/said the thing you said wasn't cool? You mean, it was cool for me to do/say it this time? Then why are you making up all these rules? Why are you making me jump through hoops if you don't mind it that much?* Your inconsistency will not just motivate the other person to keep testing your boundary, it will frustrate and annoy them when you go back to maintaining it.

"What you have to do now is update the consequences," I explained to Carlos. "Let Ilya know that you made a mistake in responding to his messages and that you will not do so from here on. He'll test you quite a bit at first to see whether *this time* you're as determined as you say you are. When he does, stick to the consequences you specified."

Setting Boundaries at Work

In the workplace, there are far more rules, guidelines, and hierarchies than in our personal lives, so the dynamics are slightly different. The four steps and the principle of respect are the same when setting boundaries at work, but the factors you need to consider and your delivery might not be. For example, if the boundary you're setting is with someone who reports to you, give them an opportunity to ask questions and seek clarification. You should expect subordinates to test the boundary infrequently if at all, as doing so would be going against their manager's directives. If they do violate the boundary, ask them to explain why that happened and how they plan to avoid doing so going forward.

When setting boundaries with colleagues, you will need to consider the culture of the workplace. You will be on much firmer ground if what you ask for conforms to the standard way of doing things in your company. Regardless, consider setting boundaries only when it is absolutely necessary to do so because it will be unpleasant for your colleague, and they might hold it against you. If appropriate, you can use the *It's not you, it's me* framing to make your message more palatable (e.g., I lose my train of thought when you interrupt, please let me finish before speaking over me).

When setting boundaries with a boss, you should be even more cautious and consider whether they would be open to such pushback at all. If you do proceed, the boundary should be framed as a request and not a demand. If your boss doesn't push back when you set the boundary, great, but you will need to maintain the boundary with similar delicacy.

One of the more common boundaries people need to set in the workplace involves microaggressions and inconsiderate behavior (e.g., mispronouncing your name, overtalking, taking up half the mini fridge when 20 people share it). Use caution here too, of course, but if you do plan to speak up: (1) Use "I statements" that emphasize how you feel, and avoid making accusations. For example, *I feel disrespected when you speak over me*, not *You are being disrespectful.* (2) Ask for specific changes. For example, *I would appreciate it if your feedback focused on my performance and behavior without making remarks about my personality.* And (3) Be collaborative. For example, *I recognize that we have different communication styles, but I need our interactions to feel respectful. Can we work together on this?*

One of the boundaries that gets violated most by our employers and companies concerns our personal and leisure time. If you're expected to be available after hours, you should use the *Red Light, Green Light* exercise from Chapter 6 to stay detached and respond when it's best for you to do so. If someone asks you why it took you an hour to reply to their email, draw a boundary around having to offer an explanation at all. Whether you were dealing with a sick kid, getting a massage, attending a play, or having an intimate moment with your partner isn't something you need to share. Simply say, *Sorry, I was busy.*

Speaking of which, Carlos and Ilya hadn't been "busy" since his visit home, something he attributed to the critical period their business was going through as much as to the tensions between them. But it soon became clear that more than their sex life was suffering; their entire relationship was in a deep freeze. Ilya's mood, self-esteem, and general outlook were all dictated by the company's fortunes. The psychological distinction between his professional identity and his personal identity was becoming blurred, such that his personal identity was becoming fused with their startup.

I, the Company

When you spend most of your waking hours and invest most of your mental capital at work, you can begin to identify with your company. The same is true when you're gunning for a promotion or a bonus, trying to reach sales and other targets, or striving to rank highly in your group. Your dedication might even cause you to change your pronouns so that "I work for a high-end novelty company" becomes "We make designer whoopee cushions."

Identifying with your company isn't necessarily pathological or problematic. It's expected in some companies and culturally appropriate in others. In Japan, for example, workers are more likely to spend their entire careers at a single company. When you started the business or were among its first employees, or when you have a significant stake in it or feel strongly aligned with its mission or purpose, your loyalty to your workplace can skew your emotions in unpredictable ways.

The day before Carlos was supposed to leave for his second visit to his parents, an in-person meeting with a potential new customer appeared on his calendar for that Saturday. Annoyed, Carlos asked Ilya to reschedule it. Ilya shot back that Carlos should reschedule his visit home instead. Carlos refused.

"Ilya totally lost it," Carlos told me in our session. "He started yelling, *You would throw away the most important meeting we ever had because you can't delay your trip home by one week? How can you be so selfish? And stupid! That's just stupid!*"

Carlos, boundaries freshly in mind, said, "Don't talk to me like that, or I'll walk away."

"I'll save you the trouble!" Ilya snapped and walked out.

"When I got back from the visit," Carlos continued, "all Ilya's stuff was gone. He moved in with his parents while I was away. He says he wants a divorce." Carlos, still in shock, winced as he said it. "I've been crying on and off since I got back, but I'm still working fourteen hours a day. Ilya hasn't slowed down either. We can't; all our assets are tied up in the company. He won't take my calls or go to couples therapy. He emails me, but only about work. The man I married is in there somewhere, but I don't know how to reach him." Carlos sobbed silently. "I don't know how to get him back."

Ilya was obviously not thinking clearly or considering consequences. If he were, it would have occurred to him that he and Carlos were already drowning from the pressures of running their startup. The stress associated with getting a divorce and the time they would have to dedicate to lawyers and negotiations could easily bring them to a level of burnout at which it was no longer possible for them to keep up with the demands of operating their startup, and they would be forced to close it.

Overidentifying with one's employer has all kinds of harmful effects, such as exhaustion and burnout, neglect of personal life, greater conflict in the workplace, and impaired emotional health. It can also impact our ethics and morals. But it isn't just overidentification that puts us at risk for ethical slippage. Many aspects of work can make us act against our own ethical standards, potentially costing us our careers and even our freedom.

CHAPTER ELEVEN

Friday Morning

Toxic Warfare—How to Recalibrate Your Moral Compass

THE PHRASE *THANK GOD* *it's Friday* isn't really about Fridays; it's about the weekend. Or rather, it is about how the cumulative stresses and pressures of the workweek make us yearn for a break. And we need one. Studies show that the number of errors we make at work peaks on Fridays. Not surprisingly, our productivity reaches its lowest levels of the week on Fridays as well.

Stress and exhaustion wear down our ethics too. New research has been studying what happens to our moral compasses in the workplace, and the findings are alarming. The demands and pressures of our jobs can make us view behavior we had considered to be objectionable as more reasonable when we see our coworkers engaging in it. In time, we can become detached from the ethical anchors that kept our conduct in check, and we're likely to be unaware of the extent to which our moral compass has drifted.

My first exposure to this phenomenon happened very early in my career.

Therapists Gone Wild

After I completed my PhD, I joined a group of therapists that was training with a master clinician who was known for his ability to capture the essence of complex cases in a single brilliant sentence. Each week, one of the trainees brought a case from our practices for a live consultation with our teacher, while the rest of us observed through a one-way mirror.

That week, the case involved a 14-year-old boy who had just returned home after a lengthy psychiatric hospitalization. The parents worried that he was still too "crazy" for them to handle and were considering putting him in a long-term facility. When the family's regular therapist presented the case (before the family arrived), it became clear that the boy was not "crazy." He had never exhibited any delusions, hallucinations, or disordered thinking; he was just very poorly behaved. The family then arrived, and the master therapist entered the consultation room and took the armchair facing the couch. The parents took the couch facing him. Their son wheeled a stool near the therapist and sat facing his parents, making it clear where he felt more comfortable.

The therapist looked the boy up and down, turned to the parents, and said, "So, is he crazy or are you incompetent?"

The parents gasped. We gasped behind the mirror too. This terse question communicated the essence of the case: *You, parents, might lack the skills to discipline your son, but that doesn't mean he belongs in a mental hospital.* Before either parent could respond, the boy pointed at them and smirked with delight, "Incompetent! You're incompetent!" The therapist kept his gaze on the parents, waiting to see how they would respond to their son's taunt. They did not. They turned to the therapist and waited to see what *he* would do. The boy saw this, laughed, and continued to taunt his parents, singing, "Incompetent, incompetent! Silent and incompetent!"

Our teacher urged the parents to respond, "*As* he does this, you do nothing?"

The boy immediately turned to the therapist, "You said ass! You said ass!"

The therapist ignored the boy and asked the parents how they typically responded to his misbehavior. The boy, unhappy with being ignored, turned his attentions to our teacher and imitated his gestures while loudly singing, "Ass, ass, you said ass!"

The therapist continued to ignore the boy and again asked the embarrassed parents how they typically responded to the boy's misbehavior. The boy saw he wasn't getting a response from the therapist and moved closer, hovering just behind his shoulder. As the therapist spoke to the parents, the boy spread his arms behind him, shimmied his shoulders, and sang right into the therapist's ear, "Incompetent ass! Incompetent ass!"

Behind the mirror, we were horrified to see our venerated teacher being mocked.

And then it happened.

The boy's hand brushed our teacher's arm slightly, barely touching the sleeve of his jacket. But he was too busy singing, "Incompetent ass! Incompetent ass!" to notice. The therapist did notice. Annoyed at being touched, our teacher instinctively slammed his arm backward. His forearm smacked the boy hard in the chest. The boy flew off the stool and landed on the floor with a thud.

Silence. Both in the therapy room and behind the mirror.

The boy, unhurt, got up, moved the stool away from our teacher, and sat down, displaying a smirk of bravado to cover for his bruised ego.

Stunned by seeing our teacher strike a client, I looked at my colleagues behind the mirror and whispered, "Wow. He hit him."

One of them immediately responded, "Yeah, but the kid hit him first."

"The kid barely touched him," I objected.

"Yes, but he made contact first," another colleague insisted, as if a touch justified a wallop strong enough to knock the boy onto his back. The justifications continued. "It worked, though; the boy's quiet now," another colleague said, as if the smack had been an intentional intervention. It was not. It was simple irritability and poor impulse control from our teacher.

My colleagues' rush to excuse the master therapist's misconduct was more surprising to me than the wallop itself had been. I had just spent months in a locked psychiatric ward working with aggressive and violent patients who constantly needed to be restrained, and I never witnessed a single staff member strike a patient in retaliation. Hitting a patient, especially a child with mental health issues, clearly violated our ethical and professional guidelines.

The boy's irritating provocations caused our teacher to lose his temper, but my colleagues' respect and admiration for him made every one of them excuse his conduct. After the session, our teacher immediately took responsibility for the incident and apologized for his behavior. Even then, two of my colleagues continued to justify his actions—efforts he quickly shut down. It was a stark lesson in how easily charismatic leaders can set our moral compasses adrift.

Unethical leadership is just one of the factors that corrupt our ethics in the workplace. There are others, some of which operate much more insidiously.

The Proliferation of Unethical Behavior in the Workplace

Unethical behavior refers to conduct that doesn't conform to basic social norms or expectations, which covers quite a lot of ground. Striking someone with enough physical force to knock them off their seat is a true anomaly in psychotherapy settings, but it is much less unusual in the current workplace. In a 2023 survey, 12% of employees admitted to experiencing physical threats or actual violence in the workplace over the past year.

The most common form of unethical behavior in the workplace is incivility. Being disrespectful, rude, insulting, or condescending might sound like a mild offense to some, but consider that interpersonal slights tend to produce significant emotional pain and distress, impair productivity, and are huge drivers of post-work rumination, which interferes with our ability to switch off. Some studies estimated that 96% of employees experience incivility in the workplace, which means the conduct has basically been normalized and sanctioned despite the disruptions it causes.

The statistics regarding more severe unethical conduct in the workplace vary substantially, so I'll use the more conservative estimates published by the American Psychological Association. Surveys in 2023 and 2024 found that 24% of workers have experienced verbal abuse, 30% have experienced bullying, 22% have experienced sexual harassment, 30% have experienced or witnessed racism, and all those numbers have been trending up dramatically. Unfortunately, women, people of color, and members of the LGBTQ+ communities are far more likely to encounter those kinds of behaviors, and those numbers too are trending upward. Add in the 19% of employees whose company cultures are toxic, and it's clear that unethical behavior is rampant in the current workplace.

A single unethical leader can infect an entire company, damaging the emotional health and the productivity of hundreds or thousands of employees and inflicting collateral damage on their families. But the problem isn't just that a few bad apples are having an outsized impact; something else is happening as well. The stresses and pressures of the current workplace are corrupting our values, turning good apples bad, and making many employees act outside their own ethical boundaries.

To understand how this happens and how you can mitigate it if it is happening to you or around you, let's examine the people we have already met who have shown unethical behavior of various kinds—my clients' coworkers.

How Bad Actors Convince Themselves They're Good People

Tony's life was upended when Scar pressured other employees to lodge complaints against him. Scar's handiwork in both complaints was obvious, as was his pattern of using vulnerable employees to pursue his agenda. Jason had been performing poorly and was happy to have someone to blame (Tony), and Daria had been working for Scar and feared losing her job if she refused Scar's directive to file a complaint against Tony.

There are Scars in almost every organization—people who manipulate, bully, harass, scheme, and lie to get ahead. They move up the ladder by manipulating those they can, climbing over those they cannot, and elbowing off anyone who is in their way. They do all this while presenting an entirely different image to anyone who could be of use to them, currently or in the future. The discrepancy between their carefully curated public image and their conniving, unethical behavior behind the scenes is often profound.

I've rarely had Scars as clients, perhaps because my reputation as an advocate of emotional health in the workplace renders me an unattractive option for them. However, I have had to work with Scars in some of my other endeavors, and I've been on the receiving end of their schemes. While my training allowed me to spot such people early, and although I know how best to handle them, dealing with them was always stressful and exhausting. I had to be constantly

vigilant, call out inappropriate or hostile behavior regularly, and set and maintain boundaries repeatedly. Every time I called out the person on their conduct
or reminded them of a boundary I had previously set, they responded with
feigned surprise, as if they had never heard such a thing before, even when I
had told them myself many times. In each case, they continued to scheme and
behave unethically. I exited such situations as soon as my obligations allowed.

The reasons the Scars of the workplace react with surprise when they're confronted is that most of them don't think of themselves as unethical. They excuse
their underhanded behavior with justifications that are just convincing enough
for them to maintain their self-perception as mostly decent people. Those who
are skilled at deceiving others are just as skilled at deceiving themselves.

Scar was trying to ruin Tony's entire career—a devastating blow that would
not just shatter Tony's professional life but harm his family too. The justifications he probably used to shirk accountability were the same chestnuts most
people use to rationalize unethical behaviors: *I was screwed over in my last
job—now it's my turn to catch a break* (I'm just correcting a past wrong), *If Tony
can't take the heat, he should get out of the kitchen* (everyone does it), *Tony's fake
good-guy act isn't fooling me—he deserves what he's getting* (turning the victim
into the victimizer), *Tony's been at the top for too long—it's time somebody else
got a chance* (I'm doing it for the common good), and *Jason is the one who filed
the complaint, not me* (externalizing blame).

Most Scars aren't occasional victimizers but serial ones. They're opportun-
ists who constantly seek to gain advantage for themselves and inflict damage
on others. As such, I feared Tony's struggles would not be over no matter the
outcome of the investigations. Even if he kept his job, which was in serious
question, Scar would find other ways to continue his campaign against him.

Tony sent me an email saying that human resources had completed the
investigation and asked to meet with him. I saw him soon afterward.

"Well?" I asked. "What happened? How did it go?"

"They accepted my counterargument that Jason was struggling from the
get-go and using me as an excuse," Tony reported. "The head of HR recognized
that Jason's performance did not decline after we came back to the office, which
was when my supposed campaign against him kicked into high gear. She also

acknowledged that I had no reason to pick on him and that I had always been given the highest rating for being strongly supportive of my coworkers. So, she dismissed his complaint."

"Phew," I responded. "That's great news."

"Daria's complaint was the bigger issue," Tony continued. "From what I understood—and I'm reading between the lines here—she tried to do damage control. She couldn't take back what she said in her original filing, but she insisted that she felt totally safe around me and that she wouldn't hesitate to work with me again. That changed the picture entirely. They probably suspect that Scar pressured her into making the complaint, but since she couldn't deny the original allegation without putting herself in hot water—it stays on my record. I have to sit through a sexual harassment webinar, which could be a problem if I ever wanted to change jobs and move to another shop. I don't, though, so I should be fine." Tony exhaled. "I just want things to go back to normal."

I nodded and smiled. I didn't want to deny Tony his relief, but again, I doubted that things would go back to normal. Scar would start plotting his next move as soon as he learned of the outcome, if he hadn't already. I hoped Tony would be able to use the calm before the next storm to recover from his intense stress and to continue repairing his relationships at home.

Self-serving, unethical behaviors like Scar's are common because of the financial and career advantages they confer. However, there are other forms of unethical behavior that aren't motivated by direct financial gain. These kinds of unethical behaviors don't directly benefit the employee who engages in them, and they can even put that employee at significant risk. What makes their proliferation remarkable is that this kind of unethical behavior benefits only the company, not the employee.

When Acting Unethically Feels Like a Job Well Done

A 2024 survey documented that 38% of workers say they would act unethically if asked by a manager to do so. Other surveys estimate that 10% to 20% of workers might act unethically in ways that *solely benefited their manager or company*. Such behaviors range from mild offenses like lying to clients to actual felonies. Some of these violations are bewilderingly brazen. In 2015, several Volkswagen executives were indicted for rigging the emission controls on 500,000 vehicles sold in the United States. One of them even served several years in jail. A year later, 5,000 Wells Fargo employees lost their jobs for opening millions of fraudulent accounts without their customers' authorization. They did so in order to meet unreasonable sales quotas.

Researchers found that one of the main culprits leading to these kinds of unethical behaviors is overidentifying with an employer. Workers who felt strongly connected to their employer, its brand, or its mission perceived unethical and even illegal acts as dutiful displays of loyalty and corporate good citizenship (going above and beyond their own responsibilities to contribute to the success of their colleagues, team, or company).

Identifying with or admiring a charismatic leader who acts unethically can create a similarly slippery slope. Seeing a respected figure behave unethically can put us into cognitive dissonance—an emotionally uncomfortable clash of beliefs and behavior. To resolve the inner tension cognitive dissonance creates, we can either downgrade our regard for the leader or excuse or justify their unethical behavior, as my fellow trainees did with our teacher. When employees do the latter, they are at risk of violating their own ethical standards going forward because they have reclassified unethical behavior as acceptable.

Taken together, these examples, along with the growing prevalence of incivility, bullying, harassment, bias, and toxic cultures, paint a bleak picture of moral decline in the workplace. And yet, those incidents represent only half the story.

The other half hides in plain sight because of another bias—we are far more likely to notice abuse than we are to notice neglect.

The Neglect of Neglect

When we hear that a child was removed from their parents' home by the authorities, we assume it's because there was abuse of some kind or accusations to that effect. We assume incorrectly. A recent report by the US Administration for Children and Families stated that only a third of children are removed from their homes for abuse. Two-thirds are removed for neglect. Our attentions are similarly lopsided when it comes to the workplace. We pay far more attention to aggression, hostility, bullying, harassment, and bias than to neglect by employers and managers.

Neglect in the workplace generally manifests in one of two ways: emotional or professional. *Emotional neglect* occurs when the emotional needs and experiences of employees are ignored. For example, when managers fail to act when their subordinates are bullied, harassed, ostracized, or treated unfairly. *Professional neglect* occurs when the professional development needs of the employee are ignored or thwarted.

We notice abuse far more than we do neglect because abuse is dramatic and attention-grabbing. When you experience or even witness it, you know it. Neglect, on the other hand, is about what *doesn't* happen; it's about subtle patterns of behavior, not remarkable moments, and that makes it far less noticeable.

We tend to assume that abuse gets more attention because it causes more harm. One study compared the impact of harassment in the workplace to ostracism (shunning) and found that employees considered ostracism to be more acceptable and less psychologically damaging than harassment. They were wrong. Shunning is significantly more damaging to employee well-being than harassment, and it causes significantly greater employee turnover.

Sally, the working mother who desperately needed the year-end bonus her company offered, was forced to overwork to the point of burnout as a direct result of managerial neglect. Her first co-lead was hostile and incompetent, and her third, Janet (a.k.a. Ms. Bottleneck), was known for being late on all her projects. Sally's manager knew the other teams' deficiencies were likely to cost Sally her bonus because the same thing happened to Sally's predecessor. Yet she made the bonus sound perfectly attainable in Sally's job interview. Then, when Sally went to her for help, she refused to intervene on her behalf. It was blatant professional and emotional neglect.

In fact, neglect pervaded Sally's entire company; systemic problems were ignored, broken processes never got fixed, and there was little accountability at any managerial level.

Managers often justify neglect in the same ways others justify abuse: They *deny responsibility* (it's not my problem), *blame the victim* (if she can't figure it out, that's on her), *minimize consequences* (she knew bonuses are not guaranteed, so she'll have to manage without it), or *externalize blame* (that's just how things work around here).

Neglect is also common when employees are facing job insecurity. Priya, the personal assistant, had new bosses who allowed the threat of layoffs to hover over her and her colleagues for months, creating stress and strain for all three. They didn't set any kind of timeline or communicate any expectations or criteria, and they remained apathetic to the toll it was taking on their employees.

Liam faced job insecurity too, as do all lawyers who aspire to the partner track. Liam was a sixth-year associate, so he knew he would find out if he was on the partner track at his annual review. At the review, his boss got right to the point. Liam was not on track to become a partner. His boss delivered the news gently and constructively. He assumed Liam would start looking for a new firm as soon as possible, but he was welcome to stay on if he chose. I was disappointed for Liam but glad to hear that his boss had handled things humanely and compassionately. Many do not.

Tony's boss wasn't purposefully cruel, but his neglect created consequences for Tony that were. He refused to intervene when Tony first went to him with concerns about Scar, and he allowed Scar to call a team meeting to deal with the tensions between Jason and Tony even though they were entirely manufactured by Scar himself (as Tony had told him). He also ignored the fact that Jason had filed his complaint with human resources without bringing his concerns to him first, which was how such processes were supposed to go. Once the complaint was filed, Tony's boss should have stepped in and actively managed the tensions spreading throughout his team, but he remained absent and uninvolved.

I've worked with people whose careers and lives were totally ruined by managerial and institutional neglect. I've also seen competent, engaged, and loyal workers suffer dramatic declines in mental health and physical well-being due to blatant professional and emotional neglect by their bosses and companies. Neglect in the workplace can be just as cruel and just as damaging as abuse.

Still, the absence of ethics in the current workplace cannot be explained by bad apples and neglectful bosses alone. Something else is happening that is enabling our own ethical standards to become corrupted.

How Our Moral Compass Loses Calibration

The process that distances us from our ethical core, makes it easier for us to engage in unethical behaviors, and shields us from the guilt, shame, and self-recrimination we would otherwise feel is called *moral disengagement*. Carlos had experienced this process firsthand in his previous job.

A home services company had lured him away from his data science job by offering him a sales position that promised huge performance bonuses. It was only once Carlos began his new job that he discovered the company used a winner-takes-all system that pitted employees against one another and encouraged questionable sales tactics. He resisted using such tactics at first, but his standards soon started to slip, and he began going down a path of moral disengagement himself.

Carlos began his sales job with his moral compass intact. He'd always been a hard worker, but the targets set by the company were so unreasonable he quickly found himself falling behind his colleagues. Curious as to how they were outperforming him, he noticed that they used more aggressive and less transparent sales tactics than he did. He had stayed away from such strategies because he considered them unfair—they misled customers and pressured them into acquiring services they did not need. But after seeing his colleagues earning higher commissions with that approach, his resolve wavered.

Stopping short of adopting the questionable tactics outright, Carlos slightly embellished the benefits of the company's products. He reassured himself that, compared to others, he was still performing ethically. Known as *cognitive restructuring*, we employ various mental gymnastics to justify mild excursions into unethical territory in order to retain our view of ourselves as moral people. Cognitive restructuring lets us redefine our moral boundary—*if I'm not as bad as them, I'm still good.*

Carlos's manager turned a blind eye to such practices, which Carlos took as a tacit endorsement of his colleagues' methods. Indeed, another problem with managerial neglect is how easily it can be misinterpreted as unspoken approval of unethical conduct. Seeing so many people around him using sketchy tactics reinforced a *diffusion of responsibility*—a psychological phenomenon in which the presence of other offenders spreads the perception of responsibility across the group, thus diminishing individual accountability.

As Carlos's unethical behavior became normalized in his own mind, his colleagues continued their own escalating process of moral disengagement. The last step in the process is *dehumanization*, when others are no longer considered fully human but merely a means to an end. Some of Carlos's colleagues openly mocked their clients' gullibility, viewing them as sales quotas instead of as people. Hearing their callousness and dehumanizing references shocked Carlos so much that he woke from his ethical stupor and realized he had to leave. Ilya had been eager to start his own company, so it was the perfect time for them to take a risk, leave their respective jobs, and create their startup.

Unethical leaders, toxic corporate cultures, and unreasonable performance pressures are major contributing factors to moral disengagement in the workplace, but they aren't the only ones. Stress, mental fatigue, and physical exhaustion weaken our inner resolve and predispose us to giving in to those pressures. Tension and conflict within the home do the same because they compromise our recovery and add to our stress.

If you're wondering whether your own ethical standards might have slipped, review the various justifications listed in this chapter. Do any of them sound familiar? If so, revisit the situations that elicited them and evaluate them with ethical considerations more prominently in mind. Perhaps there are things you could have done differently. Regardless, you might still want to take steps to prevent future moral slippage (or to correct slippage that has already occurred). Here's how:

Gaining Traction on Slippery Slopes

The aspect of our psychology that determines the importance we place on behaving ethically is called our *moral identity*. Generally speaking, the stronger our sense of moral identity, the less vulnerable we'll be to unethical lapses. The concept of moral identity isn't new, but how it functions in the workplace has only been explored recently. One of the first questions researchers asked was whether *priming* moral identity—putting it in the front of our minds—could reduce unethical behavior. Priming is frequently used in psychological research because it's easy to do. You merely remind the person of what you want to prime—in this case, their sense of morality. You can do so either overtly (e.g., by instructing people to write about a time they acted morally) or subtly (e.g., having their desk face images of Mother Teresa, Gandhi, and Nelson Mandela).

In one series of studies, researchers primed moral identity by using a rather heavy-handed approach: asking the subjects to name the Ten Commandments. I guess the fire department nixed their request for a burning bush. They found that priming did not help subjects withstand the lure of financial gain in a meaningful way, which wasn't surprising. Priming doesn't strengthen our basic moral identity; it just makes ethical considerations more prominent in our decision-making. To actually strengthen our moral identity, we need a different approach.

Our identity has many aspects—moral, professional, religious, sexual, spouse, parent, friend, amateur chef, etc. Any aspect of our identity can be strengthened by going through a process of exploration and self-examination in which we think through our feelings, beliefs, and experiences, and consider what these parts of our selves mean to us. Our professional identity includes our beliefs about ethical conduct in our profession and where the limits of ethical behavior lie. However, most of those things remain unarticulated because few of us take the time to think them through carefully.

With that in mind, I developed an exercise to help my clients create their own *professional creed*. Its purpose is to help you define your ethical boundaries ahead of time and create a plan for defending them.

Start by listing the various roles you have and the professional relationships they involve. For Carlos, that would have been things like sales and account management, internal relationships with team members and managers, and external relationships with clients, customers, or vendors. If you have people reporting to you, you would add manager, mentor, leader, and any other roles specific to your situation.

Once you have the list, go through each role and articulate the ethical guidelines you should follow. For example, if he were still in his previous job, Carlos might have mentioned transparency and accuracy when describing the pros and cons of their products, avoiding pressure or scare tactics, and treating clients and coworkers fairly and respectfully.

Next, you have to identify the kinds of actions and inactions (addressing neglect is important too) that might be required of you but which would conflict with your guidelines. For Carlos, that would have been using pressure tactics with clients or exaggerating the qualities of the product to secure more deals. You also want to list the pressures you'll face, like your boss insisting you up your numbers, seeing others use unethical tactics to do better than you, or the resentment you'll feel when you stick to your morals but fall behind as a result.

The last step is to plan how you'll deal with challenging situations by applying the following formula.

If [PERSONS/SITUATION] pressures me to [UNETHICAL ACT OR INACTION], I will [ACTION TO RESIST THAT MINIMIZES JEOPARDY TO YOUR JOB]. For example: *If I see my boss bullying a coworker and feel pressured to ignore it so I can keep my boss's favor, I will check in on my coworker discreetly, offer them support, and offer to be a witness if they choose to take official action.*

Having a clearly articulated professional creed can certainly help us retain our moral footing, but the pressures to slide can still be significant. That's why standing our moral ground is truly a noble act—*because* it comes at a heavy price. If it didn't, we'd have much less abuse and neglect in the workplace. Sticking to our ethical guns can mean forgoing financial gains, harming our social standing at work, as well as missing out on professional recognition or opportunities for advancement.

The one tactic that can counterbalance such losses is a deep sense of self-satisfaction—the kind you feel after accomplishing something truly meaningful and challenging—because resisting the lure of ethical corruption and doing what you believe is right when everyone around you is not, is, in fact, truly challenging.

Therefore, it will be even more effective to tweak your formula to: If [PERSONS/SITUATION] pressures me to [UNETHICAL ACT OR INAC-TION], I will *feel truly proud and satisfied* if I [ACTION TO RESIST THAT MINIMIZES JEOPARDY TO YOUR JOB].

Authentic pride boosts feelings of agency, control, mastery, self-satisfaction, empowerment, and self-worth. But when your workplace suffers from an unethical work environment, a toxic culture, or abusive or neglectful supervisors, or if you face unreasonable work demands, job insecurity, and unhealthy expectations to chronically overwork, you are likely, at some point, to consider leaving.

CHAPTER TWELVE

Friday Evening

Battle Fatigue—How to Know If It's Time to Leave

DURING THE GREAT RESIGNATION that accompanied the pandemic, 3% of the entire workforce quit their jobs every month. But while the surge of quitting has since dropped to pre-pandemic rates, the surge of misery in the workplace has not. If you're among the legions of unhappy and unfulfilled workers, the insights and tools we've covered so far should help you reduce stress and rumination, eliminate self-undermining behavior, improve your recovery, reclaim your leisure time, reconnect to neglected aspects of your identity, protect your relationships, and recalibrate your moral compass.

But that might not be enough. If you are still miserable, you are likely to be debating whether it is time to move on. Leaving a job involves many of the same complexities and considerations that leaving a long-term romantic relationship does. In both situations, the desire to leave triggers a process of evaluation and contemplation that can take months and even years because of the planning and strategic thinking required—factors such as your financial situation, where you are in your career, how close you are to retirement, or the impact on your family. There are still other considerations to keep in mind as you go through this process.

The first is: *Think several steps ahead so that you don't make impulsive moves.* Priya had failed to adhere to this principle eleven times in her short career, thereby contributing more than her share to the national quit rates. After surviving in her current role for 20 months (three times longer than any of her previous roles), she now needed only four more months to qualify for senior PA positions. But several months of job insecurity had left her feeling mentally and emotionally drained. She struggled to maintain concentration throughout the workday and to regulate her emotions effectively. I worried that she could slip into bad habits and quit right before the finish line.

When Your Career Goes Sideways

Priya already had over seven years of experience as a personal assistant, but her quitting streak kept her on the lowest rung of her career ladder. The sole advantage she gained by remaining at a junior level was that it was easier to find a new job each time she quit. The pyramidal structure of job availability (many entry-level positions, fewer senior ones) dictates that the more advanced you are in your career, the more steps ahead you'll need to plan if you want to find a new job because your options will be more limited. It also takes longer to find the right position. This means that if you need to find another job in a hurry, you might end up having to make a lateral move or even take a step down in compensation, title, or work-life balance.

Lateral moves can be necessary and justified at times, especially if opportunities for advancement in your current position are limited, but the move should not be a mere placeholder. Lateral moves can and should set you up to advance in your next role or provide opportunities for acquiring skills and experience that will make you a more attractive candidate for moving up. Otherwise, by going sideways, you will just be going . . . sideways.

"I almost quit, like, twenty times this morning," Priya admitted in our session. "Don't worry, I won't. I can make it another four months. But they'd better not let me go before then. That would be straight-up tragic."

Two months later, Priya's new bosses did a straight-up tragic move and let her go—eight weeks shy of the critical two-year mark. She didn't seem as upset as I expected her to be when she told me the news. "I was uberbummed at first," she said, "but then I decided to explain my situation and ask them to defer their decision for two months."

"Excellent move. Did they?"

"Nope. But then my amazing boyfriend suggested I ask Jan if she could persuade them. So, I asked, and she said she would talk to them."

"Another excellent move. Did they agree?"

"Nope," Priya responded. "But that made me realize that having to start over and put in another two years was not happening. I couldn't deal. I was desperate, so I went back in and begged them to just put me on leave without pay for two months. And they agreed!"

"Priya, that's brilliant."

She nodded in appreciation. "The downside—I won't be able to collect unemployment, but my dad's friend said he would hook me up with a senior PA role as soon as I hit the two-year benchmark, so I don't even have to look for a new job. I'll just waitress at the coffee shop near our apartment for a couple of months."

This was great news, and it was reassuring to hear Priya refer to her boyfriend in glowing terms again. Her father's friend also helped her fulfill the second consideration to keep in mind when deciding whether to stay in your current role: *Don't leave one job before finding another.* Being currently employed makes us look better to prospective employers, but more importantly, it's better for us psychologically. Unemployment and job searches are rough—the uncertainty and rejection can harm our mood, confidence, and motivation. The longer the search goes on, the more financially and emotionally stressful it becomes, the more demoralized we might become. By staying employed while we search for our next gig, we avoid both financial stress and self-doubt because our current job continues to tell us that we're employable.

There are exceptions to any rule, though. One of them is when the emotional and mental toll of staying in our current role is simply too great to bear.

From Tribe Member to Outsider

Tony's kindness to his coworkers and the good relationships it enabled had always made him feel like he belonged—that he was a valued member of his work tribe. As social animals, we all have a basic need to belong. Studies have demonstrated that a feeling of belonging in the workplace increases job satisfaction and productivity and that the connection and safety we feel in such situations boost our emotional health and well-being. Some companies recognize the win-win of enhancing feelings of belonging for their employees and weave those priorities into their culture. For example, at CY, a call center with Christian, Jewish, and Moslem employees, the holidays of all three religions are celebrated by the entire company. Teams decorate their workspaces, share traditional dishes, and also invite coworkers to family celebrations at home. CY even practices "social onboarding"—for example, by team members sharing their own onboarding experiences with the new employee as a bonding exercise.

CY is an exception; most companies do little to support employees' feelings of belonging. However, you can address those needs yourself regardless of how long you've been in your role. Invite a coworker to lunch, for a walk, or for drinks after work. Circulate a card for colleagues to sign when coworkers have a birthday, learn the traditional greetings associated with your coworkers' holidays and traditions (e.g., *Eid Mubarak* for Eid al-Fitr at the end of Ramadan), and follow up with colleagues who are going through family or health challenges. Creating closer bonds with coworkers takes effort, but it will make you feel more connected to them, which will boost your performance and job satisfaction.

On the other hand, lacking belonging and feeling like an outsider is intensely distressing and painful. Therefore, when debating whether to leave, you should consider more than just your role and career prospects. The third consideration is *Give thought to who you work <u>with</u> and <u>for</u>. How connected you feel to your coworkers can determine your quality of life at work more than your actual role or compensation does.* Studies have determined that feeling shunned or ignored at work creates such significant emotional pain that you will struggle to concentrate and perform your duties as well as you would otherwise, and that the impairment will be greater if your manager is indifferent to your distress (i.e., neglectful).

With the investigation over, Tony hoped the vibe in the office would be calmer and he would no longer be a focus of gossip. "Seeing that I'm still here should reassure any skeptics that I did nothing terrible, so they'll get that it's time to move on." The first person he saw the next morning was Daria.

"Daria came to my office to apologize again. I told her I understood why she did it, and I wasn't angry. She seemed really relieved, so that made me feel good. My assistant and two male colleagues seemed glad to see me too. But it was downhill from there."

Tony swallowed hard. "Everyone else avoided me. I asked two buddies on the desk if they wanted to grab lunch. They looked uncomfortable and made an obvious excuse. It was clear they didn't want to be seen with me. Other than Daria and my assistant, every single woman avoided me. One woman I've worked with for years literally turned away when I said hello to her."

Tony assumed Scar had leaked information about the complaints, and the office rumor mill had embellished the offenses. I was pretty sure Scar had embellished them to begin with. Making matters worse, a senior VP from another division shook his head as Tony passed him in the hall, indicating the rumors had spread far beyond Tony's department.

"I was afraid to leave my office," Tony said. "It felt like everyone would be lining the halls and chanting, *Shame! Shame! Shame!*"

The reception Tony received made him feel like a pariah, and he was on the verge of tears the entire day. I hoped the reactions would die down as the week went on, but they did not. By week two, Tony was struggling to maintain his focus during trading hours and second-guessing his decisions.

"It feels like being behind enemy lines, like I could be ambushed at any moment. It's upsetting, and depressing, and oppressive, and I'm making bad trades because of it."

Studies of how rumors and scandals permeate organizations have found that when they spread, it takes managerial intervention to quash them. I suggested to Tony that he speak with his boss for that reason. Unsurprisingly, his boss did not want to "get involved in office gossip," keeping his streak of managerial neglect alive and well. By week three, Tony's functioning continued to decline, and he began to exhibit symptoms of anxiety and depression.

"I can't stand being there anymore," he said with a shudder. "I wake up with a lump in my throat every morning. I dread walking into the building. I have to be on constant alert in case someone gives me a look or says something hostile to me or walks away from me." He groaned and rubbed his face. "I wish I could leave, but I can't. Any shop I approached would ask if I've ever had disciplinary action taken against me. I won't even get an interview. I'm trapped." He shook his head in despair.

Tony's breaking point came the following Friday. He decided to leave work as soon as the markets closed at 4 PM so he could avoid the rush of people walking out at 5 PM and the stares and glares that would follow. A young woman he didn't know was in the elevator when the doors opened on his floor. He smiled and said good afternoon. The woman looked up, saw him, gasped, and quickly ran out, even though that wasn't her floor. "She looked like she had just come face-to-face with a rapist," Tony sputtered before breaking into tears. He took a loud, shaky breath. "I'm done. I'm leaving."

"But Tony, your career . . ."

"It's over." He covered his face with his hands and sobbed.

It was as enraging as it was heartbreaking. Tony's boss had sat idly by while Scar's lies, schemes, and manipulations cost Tony his career. It was wildly unfair that Scar, the abuser, would be rewarded by becoming the top trader on the desk, and Tony's boss, whose incompetent management and cruel neglect caused the entire situation to escalate, would go unscathed and guilt-free.

Being ostracized at work can make even the best job feel intolerable. But strong feelings of belonging can have a downside too—they can make it hard to leave a job that no longer serves us well.

Getting Stuck at Work

Three months after Liam learned that he wasn't on the partner track at his law firm, he had yet to start looking for a new job. Many employees end up remaining in their positions for months and even years after they decide to leave. This happens in part due to tribal affiliation. Feeling like an outsider will make any job painful and stressful and make you want to flee, but feeling like you belong will do the opposite.

Researchers call this phenomenon *job embeddedness*, and there are three factors that contribute to it. (1) *Links*: ties that bind you to your coworkers or to the company; (2) *Fit*: how comfortable and well-matched you are to the organization and/or its values, mission, culture, or operating style; and (3) *Sacrifice*: the tangible and intangible benefits you would lose by leaving.

I suggested to Liam that we explore what might be delaying his job search. "What would you miss most if you left the firm?" I asked him.

"The doughnuts in the break room. Lemon glaze. Delish." He was only partially joking. Perks like doughnuts in the break room might seem trivial, but they contribute to embeddedness because they create feelings of comfort and familiarity.

Our relationships with colleagues keep us stuck considerably more than perks do. Liam had two colleagues with whom he socialized in and out of the office. They took the same train, their spouses got along, and they were his main sources of social support on the job. Liam's firm was also a good fit for his interests and values, which is why he joined them in the first place. He generally found the cases he worked on interesting, and he enjoyed learning from the partners he supported.

Those losses aside, leaving would mean having to face the same challenges every new job entailed—adapting to an entirely new interpersonal and political landscape, having to learn new managers' moods, expectations, and idiosyncrasies, and having to make new friends. Those factors can contribute to feelings of inertia as well.

"To get unstuck you have to identify the factors that are keeping you stuck and weaken the gravitational pull of each of them," I told Liam. "You're very comfortable at work. Make yourself uncomfortable; introduce friction. Bring your own doughnut to work, so it will no longer register as a perk. Focus more on small annoyances, inconveniences, and disagreements. Once it's safe to share that you're looking, talk to your close friends, discuss how you can stay connected after you leave, and make a plan for meeting up with them again before you leave."

Indeed, the next consideration, the fourth one, when deciding whether to leave your job is: *Create a friendship maintenance plan.* Doing so will weaken any hesitancy you have about leaving your work tribe.

Liam took our talk to heart and started his search. But he stopped after only a couple of weeks. "I was catching up with members of my cohort who started their new jobs already," he explained. "This is their last chance to make partner, so they're busting their behinds to prove themselves. It's weird, but these past few months have been the happiest I've ever been at work. The pressure's off. I'm feeling less stressed. And I've been getting home earlier much more often. So, I decided to stay. I won't become wealthy like some of the partners in my firm, but I'll be able to pay the mortgage and send my kids to college. And I'll have a much better quality of life. My competitive side is dying to prove that I can make partner somewhere. But the price isn't worth it. Not to me or to my family."

I smiled broadly. On his own, Liam had arrived at Consideration Five: *Work-life balance matters as much as compensation.* Partners in corporate law firms usually work just as hard as their associates, if not harder. Liam's priorities were his family and quality of life. His decision was both sound and wise. What enabled him to make it was that after finding out he was not on the partner track, he didn't demonstrate any resentment or animosity toward the partners he worked with (which wasn't easy, given they were the ones who made the decision); he wanted to maintain their positive regard in case their paths crossed in the future. That decision ended up serving him extremely well when it came time to negotiate the terms on which he would remain at the firm.

Professional relationships don't necessarily end when we leave a workplace. We might encounter coworkers and bosses again over the course of our careers. As such, every exit interview presents an opportunity to make fans or enemies and to curate our reputation in our industry. Leaving on a good note might only pay dividends years down the road but we lose little by doing so, and interpersonal investments of that kind sometimes pay off in unexpected ways.

Burned Bridges Can't Be Crossed

Sally's relentless determination and severe overwork had already put her into burn-out, but somehow, despite constant challenges, she'd been able to launch all her products on schedule. She now had only one product left to launch before her bonus would be determined. Unfortunately, her co-lead on this last critical project was . . .

"Eric!" Sally groaned. "The same incompetent co-lead I had for my first product. We're only two weeks in, and we're already behind schedule. He's still angry with me for managing his team behind his back when we first worked together, so I've been all sweetness and light, but he's not having any of it. The man is as stubborn as a rock."

A geologist friend of mine had just visited from out of town, and something we talked about was still fresh in my mind. "Do you know how geologists split large rocks?" I asked.

"No," Sally responded, looking confused by the question.

"They find its natural plane of weakness and apply controlled force to that exact spot. You need to find his vulnerability. Is there anyone he looks up to or manages up to?"

She nodded. "Our new senior vice president. He's working her like crazy. Last quarter, he complained about how overworked he and his team were, and told her he needs to hire more people. There's a hiring freeze, so he knew the SVP would say no. When she did, he promised to do everything in his power to limit the delay to no more than a few weeks. Then, he got it in only one week late and got accolades from the SVP despite missing the deadline."

"Clever," I commented. "Okay, she's his plane of weakness. Any ideas?"

Sally thought for a moment. "Maybe. It might not work, but I have nothing to lose."

On their next call with the SVP, Sally waited for her co-lead to complain about being short-staffed and then interrupted him before he could mention any delays. "I apologize for jumping in," she said to the SVP, "but my colleague is being too modest. His team is definitely short-staffed, but they've totally rallied. His leadership and dedication and the whole team's hard work have been remarkable. In fact, I just ran some projections, and we're on track to launch on time." She smiled at her co-lead, "Phenomenal job!"

Cornered, Eric smiled awkwardly. The SVP thanked Sally and praised Eric. Her co-lead fumed, but he said nothing.

"I felt such a relief after that meeting," Sally reported. "For the first time, I allowed myself to think about how life-changing the bonus would be, what it would mean for me and my daughter. I got emotional, so I went to the coed restrooms on that floor, took a long whiff of my daughter's stuffed animal—the hedgehog—and had a cry." Sally's expression hardened. "A couple of hours later, the SVP reached out and asked me to come to her office. I assumed she wanted to thank me for praising my co-lead and showing good citizenship. She started by saying that Eric brought to her attention that I was remarkably productive and that my manager confirmed that I was indeed driven and tireless."

"That's great," I responded.

"No, she said it like it was a bad thing, like Eric and my boss had expressed concern."

"Concern *about* you?" I asked, confused.

"Concern *for* me. They told her they thought I was on drugs and that they suspected either cocaine or methamphetamine. According to them, that was why I was so tireless and how I got so much done. Drugs."

I was stunned. "How did you respond?"

"I told her they were right about my productivity and energy, and I added that I had a strong work ethic. Then I asked her what made them think that I was on drugs. She said they had each heard me snorting and sniffing in the coed bathroom on multiple occasions. She said she would refer me to our employee assistance program for treatment."

"Treatment for sniffing a rabbit and a hedgehog," I smiled.

"My little angel's stuffed animals," Sally said with a nod.

"What did you do?"

"I burst out laughing. I couldn't help it. The SVP was all like, *You think this is funny? Are you high right now?* She had a picture of her kids on her desk, so I asked her if she missed them when she was at work. She said she did. I took out Hedgehog and placed it on my lap. I told her that I had never done drugs, but that

I doubted cocaine could be better than the scent of my angel. Then I took a long sniff. She started smiling immediately. I told her I totally understood my boss and co-lead's concerns given the sniffing they heard and that I was ready to take a drug test immediately. She said that she believed me but that a drug test would help her put an end to my manager and co-lead's concerns. She apologized for the inconvenience, said she was impressed by me, and told me to keep up the good work."

Sally worked feverishly over the next six weeks to get her last product ready for launch. Two days before the deadline, she went over to her co-lead's office for their final meeting and found it empty. His entire team was absent. She checked her inbox and saw an email from him. It was addressed to her, their direct managers, and the SVP. It had an image of a positive COVID test attached. He claimed that he had potentially infected his entire team, so he sent them all home as a safety measure. As a result, they would be a couple of days late for the launch.

Sally hoped that delivering a single product two days past the deadline would not be held against her. She met with her manager two weeks later for her performance review. Her manager got right to the point. Sally would not be getting her bonus; maybe next year. Sally was devastated. She cried the entire weekend, pausing only to reassure her daughter that it was "just allergies."

When Sally told me what happened in our session, I was so upset at the injustice of it that I had to take a few moments to get my own feelings in check. She had already started looking for another job, but the mommy cliff was again proving to be a problem—the salaries made her ineligible for childcare benefits but were insufficient to cover a private nanny.

Sally showed up to our next session looking fresher than she had the entire year. "Ready for a surprising update?" she asked with a smile.

"Yes, please."

"Bottleneck," Sally said. "Of all people. Janet had my back. After the two projects we did together, she knew I deserved that bonus, and she was *rather displeased*, as she put it, that they didn't give it to me. So, she reached out to her network, told them she knew an excellent product manager, and asked if anyone was hiring. Someone she knew had an opening, but the title and position were a step above mine. Janet urged them to meet with me anyway. I spent all day there yesterday. I met her contact, his team, and their HR person."

Sally smiled broadly, "They offered me the position. I have to wait for my six-month review for the title to be official, but the salary that goes with the title—*that* I get now. And here's the crazy part. It's higher than what I would have made with the bonus! Can you believe it? I'm getting off the mommy cliff! I'll be able to pay back the credit card debt, we can move to a bigger apartment, I can finally have my own bedroom. I . . . wait, are you crying?"

"No," I sniffled, "It's just allergies."

On her last day, Sally gave Janet a generous thank-you gift and promised to stay in touch. She then stopped by her first co-lead's office. "I told Eric I owed him an apology for intervening with his team when he was on vacation," Sally said. "And for committing him to the second deadline without his permission. I said that I understood why he had reported the sniffing—what else was he to think? Then I wished him well and shook his hand." She smiled. "My dad taught me to always leave nice."

Sally had anticipated the sixth consideration to keep in mind when you're deciding whether to leave your job: *Don't burn bridges until you decide whether to leave, and if you do decide to leave, don't burn them then either.*

Sally's insistence on mending her relationships was astute both professionally and emotionally. By leaving with goodwill, she gave herself the freedom to walk away without lingering anger and resentment or the blitz of ruminations those feelings would have fostered. She also eliminated any awkwardness that could arise should she encounter her co-lead at professional events or future workplaces. Lastly, she minimized his motivation to badmouth her after she left.

How you leave a job matters. But in some situations, like the one Carlos found himself in, deciding whether to leave your job could impact far more than just your career.

When More Than Your Job Is at Stake

I once gave a talk to an organization that employed many foreign nationals who were in the United States on work visas, some with their entire families. In private conversations, I listened to one employee after another describe an emotionally abusive culture, how miserable they were in their jobs, and how powerless they were to do anything about it. If they quit, they would have to uproot their families in the middle of a school year, and if they spoke up about mistreatment, they risked getting fired.

Leaving a job can have additional consequences that greatly complicate the decision. Having to relocate is certainly one of them, as are factors such as noncompete agreements that would sideline you for many months, losing your health insurance (in the United States), or forgoing equity, stock options, and other financial losses. The stakes are even higher when you own the business or founded the startup, as your heavy emotional investment in the company can make leaving especially painful.

But when you work with your spouse, close friend(s), or family members, leaving can impact those relationships and even end them. For Carlos, quitting the company he founded with Ilya would have a dramatic effect on virtually every aspect of his life—most critically, his marriage and finances. Ilya would never forgive him if he left the startup, as Ilya wouldn't be able to manage it alone and it would force the business to shut down. Both of them would have to live with their parents and start over with no money, no savings, and no partner.

Carlos wrote to Ilya and told him he was thinking of leaving the company and moving back in with his parents until he found a new job. He didn't hear back from Ilya for two days. When he did, Ilya sounded different: less angry and more himself. He even agreed to come to the apartment to talk. Carlos hoped that the time apart had made Ilya reconsider the separation. But it soon became clear that Ilya wasn't there to save the marriage; he was there to save the company.

"I asked him point-blank if he was still in love with me," Carlos said. "He said he didn't know. He had been feeling unsure for a couple of years. That means when I was still in the sales job. I asked him why he suggested we start a company together if he had doubts about the relationship. He said he hoped starting the company would bring us closer together." Carlos sighed. "That hurt a lot. But at least it made things clear."

I urged Carlos to take a few days to rest and recharge before making a final decision. He was still exhausted, and it would be unwise to make such a critical move when he was mentally and emotionally depleted.

Exhaustion and burnout can make us feel jaded and cynical about our jobs and our professions. When we're seriously depleted, everything we do feels *blah*—neither exciting nor rewarding. When I got burnt out a year after opening my private practice, I felt so ambivalent about psychology that I worried I'd chosen the wrong profession. But once I recovered from the exhaustion, my love of psychology came bounding back.

The quickest way to recover is to take a vacation. However, as most of us know from experience, not all vacations are actually restorative. To help us recover effectively from the stresses and pressures of our jobs, our vacations need to include specific ingredients. Fortunately, scientists have been studying just what those ingredients are.

CHAPTER THIRTEEN

Saturday

The Stress Ceasefire—
How to Make Your Vacation Restorative

SATURDAY IS THE HAPPIEST day of the week for most people, peaking at 7:26 PM. That highly specific time was derived from a survey of 3,000 people whose happiness maxed out, on average, at that moment. Fair enough, Saturdays are when we're most likely to engage in leisure and socializing and enjoy the recovery benefits they offer. But when you've accumulated enough stress and exhaustion—a single fun evening will not restore you, no matter how giddy you feel at 7:26 PM.

What could is a vacation.

Ironically, vacations require effort—there's the planning, coordination, and negotiation with others, and taking time away from our job often necessitates working harder before we leave to clear our desk and after we get back to catch up. But the investment can yield significant returns. Studies have shown that the right vacation can boost our general health and well-being, foster creativity upon our return, reduce the harmful effects of chronic stress, decrease burnout, increase general life satisfaction, and even reduce the risks associated with cardio-vascular disease. In one study, men with cardiovascular disease were followed over nine years, and those who took frequent vacations had significantly lower risk of dying from coronary heart disease than those who didn't.

One of the primary takeaways from the science of restorative vacations is that vacations aren't a one-size-fits-all affair—they require personalization. To be restorative, the type of vacation we take should match what our needs are at that moment. What works for you might not work for someone else, and what worked for you in the past might not provide the same benefits now.

However, there's one thing everyone should do on every vacation: *detach from work.*

Work: The Mental Stowaway

We know that to recover effectively from the workday, we need to detach mentally and stop thinking about work. The same is true for vacations. We must minimize work intrusions, especially the kind that can foster ruminations. The challenge is that most of us, myself included, cannot be entirely off the grid when we go away; we need to check in with work on occasion and take care of certain matters.

Researchers have found that such intrusions almost entirely nullified the vacation's restorative qualities. However, we can mitigate those effects by using the same strategies that protect our recovery time in the evenings: minimize how much we work, do the work we must in a single chunk using the *Red Light, Green Light* exercise from Chapter 6, and get back into vacation mode as soon as possible. Carlos did exactly that each time he visited his parents. Despite working eight hours a day when he was there, the visits felt restorative for him because he worked in two four-hour chunks and kept his lunchtimes and evenings free to engage with his parents. Now, with a life-changing decision to make and exhaustion weighing him down, I urged him to take an actual work-free vacation so he could clear his head and gain perspective. Because his and Ilya's resources were tied up in their startup, he had little money to spend, so he decided to call in a favor from a college friend who now managed meditation retreats. The friend offered Carlos a big discount to attend an upcoming retreat, the kind in which you have to surrender your phone.

For Carlos, the prospect of not being reachable for a week was both tantalizing and terrifying. Despite the technology-free environment, it took him two days to stop ruminating about work. The first hours (or days) of a vacation are often spent battling our unconscious mind for the right to unwind. Using the rumination-busting tools from Chapter 3 to win that fight before you leave will make your time away more restorative.

The retreat helped Carlos recover physically and mentally and enabled him to reflect on his situation with a clearer mind. "This past year broke me," he said in what turned out to be our last session. "I need to heal, and I need to restart my life, and I can't do that with a husband who no longer loves me and a business that's slowly killing us."

The week after he got back, Carlos left the East Coast, moved back in with his parents, filed for divorce, and began a long journey of professional, financial, and emotional recovery. Ilya tried to keep their startup going, but his untreated panic disorder soon landed him in the emergency room for a third time, again convinced that he was having a heart attack. This time, the scare was enough to persuade him that he could not continue alone. He closed the company soon afterward.

Carlos sent me the update in an email. He was relieved to hear that Ilya had done the right thing for his health and that he could now fully close that chapter in his life. "The company took everything from me," he wrote. "I'll never allow a job to take over my life like that again."

Sally was as overworked and burnt out as Carlos and was just as much in need of a vacation. But her new boss needed her to start as soon as possible, and that left Sally with only a single weekend to recover from her brutal year. With little time and money—how could she possibly get a restorative break? Many workers face similar predicaments.

In the United States, companies typically offer their employees 10 paid vacation days per year—half of what most Europeans get. Making matters worse, almost half of all workers don't use all their vacation days, and as mentioned, there are plenty of US companies that unofficially penalize employees if they do. The subtle and often overt hostility employers display toward employee vacations can make us feel like we have to *earn* our break by getting ahead in our work before we leave in order to spare our colleagues inconvenience and to have less of a backlog when we return. The overly apologetic mindset we're expected to adopt, and the feeling that by *getting away* we are *getting away with something*, forces us to overwork before our vacation and makes it difficult to disconnect once we're on it. We then get to our vacation even more exhausted and spend the first few days like Carlos did—getting our mind to stop thinking about work instead of being fully present in whatever we're doing.

In some professions and workplaces, it's customary for colleagues to cover each other's workloads or shifts when they are away (e.g., doctors and nurses), which removes much of the need to get ahead before and catch up after. If such arrangements aren't part of the system in your job, you can explore the option of establishing them unofficially with your colleagues or teammates. If, like most people, you don't have that option, do your best to get ahead during the workday, but try to leave your evenings free so that you can prioritize rest and recovery.

Why We Should Rest Before Our Vacation

When I suggest resting *before* you go on vacation, I often get confused looks. *Isn't that what the vacation is for?* Focusing on rest and recharge in the evenings leading up to your vacation will not just make it easier for you to detach from work when you're away, it will help you deal with the gauntlet of getting away.

Travel is often stressful, and too many vacations start on a sour note because of it. Traveling with young children is always a challenge, and even if we're traveling solo or with adults, we have to deal with traffic, busy airports, flight delays, long lines, unfamiliar cities or countries, and the stresses and tensions our friends or family members bring along. Our coping mechanisms are likely to be somewhat deflated at that point, which will make us more reactive to the frustrations and annoyances we're likely to encounter en route. Therefore, to the extent possible, dedicate the days before your vacation to clearing your inbox during the workday and catching up on sleep, packing, and getting organized after hours.

Sally was basically running out the clock until her two weeks' notice were up, so she was able to do just that. Her challenge was figuring out how to fit multiple agendas into a single weekend. She hoped to squeeze in fun activities with her daughter, catch up on socializing, and do something for herself that felt exciting. That might seem like a lot for a single weekend, but mini vacations of 24 to 48 hours can be quite restorative if we plan them thoughtfully.

Experiences Count More Than Time

One of the misperceptions we have about vacations is that the more exhausted or stressed we are, the longer we'll need in order to recuperate. Another is that the more we spend on a vacation, the more we'll enjoy it and the more rejuvenating it will be. The benefits of vacations peak after about a week in many cases, which means that, in terms of cumulative restorative power, taking frequent shorter vacations will be more effective than taking fewer longer ones. In a similar vein, expensive vacations often come with the burden of higher expectations (to justify the cost), which can make us feel disappointed and frustrated if that high bar is not met.

Indeed, it's not how much money we spend that matters but what we spend it on. One of the more established research findings in the happiness literature is that *experiences* promote more happiness than *purchases* do. That's why our photo and media albums are more likely to feature images of beaches, parties, concerts, and adventures, and less likely to be dedicated to the air fryer we treated ourselves to last Christmas.

Sally curated her weekend vacation by dividing the days into three segments and planning an activity (experience) for each segment. The mornings and afternoons were devoted to doing things with her daughter, and the evenings, for her to go out and socialize (her nanny agreed to babysit).

"I'm taking my angel to the Bronx Zoo on Saturday morning and the botanical gardens in the afternoon," Sally said, vacation spreadsheet in hand.

"Saturday night, I'm going dancing with my girlfriends—so amped for that. And Sunday, I'm doing a ceramics class with my daughter in the morning, and a friend is driving us to an apple orchard in the afternoon. I'll close it out with my cousin—we're doing dinner at my favorite restaurant." Sally looked up from the spreadsheet, "Those are all fun activities, but how do I make them feel like true *experiences*?"

I smiled. "You triple-dip them."

I've long believed in and practiced *triple-dipping vacations*—getting three rounds of benefit and enjoyment out of a single holiday. You start the first round of dipping at least a week or two before you leave for vacation or before you start a staycation by deliberately building anticipation and excitement.

I suggested to Sally that she show her daughter images of the animals she'll see at the zoo and read their stories together from the website. That will make her daughter even more excited to see them because they'll be characters that she already knows, and it will make Sally look forward to taking her there and seeing her reactions to meeting them in person. I suggested the same approach for the botanical gardens. This principle also applies to adult activities like dancing. "Get amped about the outfit you're planning to wear, model a bunch of options for your daughter, and make an event out of getting dressed up and made up." To create excitement for the ceramics class, Sally went around the apartment with her daughter and decided with her where they would display whatever they made in the class. She also showed her daughter different apple recipes and discussed what they could make with the apples they picked, and she checked out the menu of her favorite restaurant to remind herself of the dishes she most looked forward to having.

Building excitement around specific moments or events ahead of time will elevate your entire experience and make the things you do feel more meaningful and impactful. That is true whether you are taking a mini-vacation or a lengthy one. Do keep your expectations realistic, though. Use the same guideline I recommend for the pictures my clients post on dating profiles: create as much appeal as possible while still leaving room for the real thing to seem even better. Include enticing details, but avoid spoiling the best parts. For example, you can get excited about visiting the Eiffel Tower without looking online at videos of the views or Eiffel's office at the top. The second round of dipping is the vacation itself. Try to be present and mindful so that you can take everything in fully and, by doing so, create more durable memories. To stoke your excitement and elevate the experience in the moment, say things to yourself or to those you're with like *I can't believe we're finally here*, or *I've wanted to do this for so long*, or *This is so exciting/amazing/special*, or *I'm so glad we get to share this together.*

During the vacation, you should also set up the third round of dipping that will take place once you get back home—reliving the good parts. Make sure to leave extra time at each station so that you can take pictures and videos that capture the experience—and make sure you appear in them too. However, don't focus on images at the expense of being present yourself. First engage in the experience, and then document it.

As mentioned, the restorative effects of vacations often fade within a few days, but you can stave off that decline by reviewing, editing, and organizing the pictures, videos, pamphlets, and other mementos you brought back. Consider printing booklets of them as keepsakes (there are quick and inexpensive options online). Then go over the media chronologically in order to relive the vacation and reconnect to how you felt when you were on it.

Documenting your experiences while you're on vacation is critical for another reason. Much of what we end up remembering from our vacations depends on the media we recorded at the time. That is why what and how much you document matters. *You are not just taking photographs when you are on vacation, you are curating your memories.*

By triple-dipping your breaks—extracting value from them before, during, and after—you can elevate peak moments into memorable experiences to savor for years to come. Packing six different experiences into her weekend vacation was the best way for fast-paced Sally to feel recharged and restored, especially since she was able to get to her vacation rested.

Priya had a very different approach toward her time off. "The only plan I want to have is to not have one." Priya was correct to insist on being unstructured because there is another aspect of our vacations that we need to personalize—feeling in control of our time.

Do What You Want

Sally associated a sense of control with meticulous planning. Priya's workdays were dominated by others telling her what to do. For her, control meant waking up each day with no agenda and having the freedom to decide what to do and when to do it. Feeling a sense of autonomy and control over how we spend our vacations has been found to make the time off feel more restful and revitalizing. The only other person Priya had to consider was her boyfriend. I suggested they each share their ideas for the kind of vacation they wanted and what, in principle, they wanted to do, and then negotiate from there. When two or more people are involved, it's important to address each person's needs as much as possible, even if it means splitting up at times and reuniting later.

If you're unsure about how structured or spontaneous your vacation should be, visualize waking up at your destination. Does the idea of having a set agenda make you feel pressured and obligated, or does it make you feel relieved that you don't have to figure out how to spend your day? You can also mix and match—have days or sections within them that are planned and others that are unstructured.

Priya and her boyfriend decided to rent a studio apartment in a beach town an hour away. "We spent the week sleeping late, cooking together, biking around, and watching shows," Priya reported. "My mom was like, *You call that a vacation? You did nothing!* I told her that she was right; we did absolutely nothing, and it was the best vacation I ever had."

Priya and Sally kept their vacations local, and they enjoyed them tremendously. But when you need to make important decisions or think more deeply about your life and direction, you might need to go farther from home.

Clarity Comes with Distance

Tony was on the verge of quitting his job, a move that would cost him his career because the complaints against him would make other employers hesitant to hire him. Given the intense stress he'd been under, I convinced him to first take a vacation. When you need to see your life in greater perspective, the most effective way to gain emotional and psychological distance is to go somewhere that is far and different, or that feels like it.

Tony's boss agreed to give him two weeks off. After discussing options with his wife, they decided to go to the theme parks in Florida because their kids had never been there.

It was a terrible idea.

"That's where you want to reflect on your life and career?" I asked him. "Sitting in a spinning teacup with kids screaming and vomiting all around you?"

"The vacation needs to be kid-friendly," Tony objected.

"It needs to be adult-friendly too. Those theme parks have places and activities that are exclusively for adults, but most parents end the day too tired to enjoy them."

Many hardworking parents make the same mistake—they craft their vacation around their children's needs and interests and neglect their own, even though they're the ones who need to recover. When planning a family vacation, you need to work backward. First, define everyone's needs, adults included, and then find places that have something for everyone. If you have young kids, find places that offer babysitting, so you can have some adult time.

"My wife's sister lives in Costa Rica," Tony said when I pushed him to think of an alternative. "She'd love for us to visit. If we got a place near her, she could watch the kids, and my wife and I could have time alone. It's beautiful there; it definitely feels different."

It sounded perfect. I saw Tony the day after he got back. He looked like the Tony of old—relaxed and calm with a warm smile. "I was an anti-ruminating *machine*," he reported. "I reframed and distracted like a champ—didn't allow myself to think about work until the second week. When I did, I started by doing the visualization exercise you recommended. I sat among the trees, closed my eyes, and imagined going to work when I got back. Know what happened? I started crying. Full on tears, right away—it felt *that* oppressive.

"My wife was watching me from the house. She wants me to quit and look for a new job. She knows that would mean a ninety percent pay cut, but she thinks the money isn't worth the cost to my mental health. Or hers."

"Ninety percent pay cut?" I asked. "That bad?"

Tony nodded. "I won't be able to stay in my industry, so I'd be starting at a much lower entry point wherever I land. It kills me to think about it, but my wife is right. I can't go back."

Tony did go back, but only to collect his things. Even though he quit voluntarily, he was ushered out by security in front of his entire office. "It was humiliating," he told me. "Scar and Jason made sure to be there and watch. The fact that they're still there and I'm not will take a long time to get over."

It took Tony almost a full year to find his next role, and as he expected, he had to take almost a 90% pay cut. Six months into the new job, I asked him if he ever missed being a trader. He answered without hesitation, "Every day."

Taking a Break from Your Work-Self

Unlike Tony, Liam remained at his firm. He was given a new role and encouraged to take a week off so that he could start fresh in his new position. He was able to take a break in a way that gave him not only a sense of control but of mastery. Spending some or even all your vacation learning, exploring, or diving deeper into your interests and passions can be highly rejuvenating, especially when doing so also strengthens meaningful aspects of your personal identity that don't get much stage time otherwise.

Liam was given a narrow window in which to take time off, and since his kids were in day camp and his wife couldn't get away from her own job, his options were to stay home for a week or to do something by himself. He chose the latter.

"Let me guess," I said in our session. "You're doing something related to improv."

Liam nodded. "I'm going to where my improv peeps will be gathering: the Edinburgh Festival Fringe." *The Fringe*, as it's known, takes place in Scotland annually. It is one of the largest arts festivals in the world, and it includes dozens of improv shows. Liam convinced two other amateur improv actors he knew to go with him. They rented an apartment together and planned to split their time between watching shows and working on a show of their own that they hoped to submit to the festival the following year.

If you have a passion, crafting a vacation around it is a great way to do something you enjoy while enhancing feelings of mastery. Those kinds of vacations are especially restorative because by engaging in your passions and interests, you will be inhabiting parts of your identity for days or weeks that you usually only get to visit briefly. During his week at the Fringe, Liam felt like an improv actor the entire time—not once did he feel like a lawyer.

Many years ago, when I got hit by a car on my first day of vacation, I spent my makeup vacation working on a screenplay. Only years later did I understand why that trip had been so restorative for me. The immersive nature of writing for a week allowed me to inhabit a different identity than "psychologist." For a week, I was living an entirely different life, that of a writer. That experience improved my writing skills, boosted my confidence, and fueled my passion for writing so much that I integrated it into my daily life and eventually became a published author.

Vacations that offer immersive experiences often feel like a break from our life, as if we're inhabiting another version of ourselves. Mindfulness or yoga retreats, surfing camp, language programs, cooking seminars, archaeology digs, wine appreciation tours, and bootcamps in photography, coding, or sports are all examples of vacations that can be both restorative and life-changing.

Vacations are a powerful tool for improving emotional health and well-being. Like all tools, we should use them wisely and carefully. They don't have to be of a single type; as we've discussed, mixing and matching works too. Activities for the kids in the morning and for the parents at night, hiking one day and museums the next, pool and spa the first half and biking tours the second, RV for the trip to the park and camping once you get there.

In today's workplace, it's more important than ever to recover effectively from the stresses we experience in our jobs. Having the freedom to rest and recharge, to connect to others, and to enhance aspects of our personal identity will give us the highly restorative break we need and deserve.

Bon Voyage

In the Introduction, I discussed how stress improves our functioning up to a point, but beyond that point, additional stress impairs functioning more and more dramatically. I believe the same thing is happening at scale; that stress and burnout have reached such high levels that *as a workforce* we are no longer able to manage them productively. For example, in March 2025, the number of TikTok employees taking mental health leave due to unsustainable work pressures was so substantial, it made headlines. In 2024, Glassdoor reported that mentions of burnout across all industries due to uncaring management had surged by 44% in just the past four years.

Few of us know exactly where our individual stress tipping point lies. Most people discover it like I did, by getting burnt out. The same thing is happening to us as a workforce. We have passed our collective tipping point, and we're getting increasingly burnt out.

It is on employers to show true leadership by taking responsibility and changing their cultures so that stress in the workplace drops back down to manageable and healthy levels. That does not mean eliminating work stress; it means dialing it back just enough to dip under the tipping point to where functioning is optimal. In 2024, Slack conducted an internal survey and found that only 38% of its employees felt comfortable taking breaks during the work-day. Efforts to encourage employees to take more breaks yielded a 21% increase in productivity and a 230% increase in employees' ability to manage stress. As a consequence, overall work satisfaction increased by 63%.

We cannot force our employers to enact effective change, and many of the variables and circumstances that make our jobs stressful are beyond our control. But what is in our control can still make a huge difference—how we manage ourselves psychologically both at work and outside of it. Our brain is complex, as are our conscious and unconscious processes. Knowing when to disengage our autopilot and take deliberate control, and how to conduct ourselves more wisely, healthily, compassionately, and productively once we do, will help us take back our lives and break free.

I sincerely hope the techniques in this book will help you reduce your work stress and lower your risk of burnout. The personalized toolbox you will create by practicing and tweaking the tools that are relevant to you can help you regain control of your thoughts, turn damaging coping mechanisms into healthy ones, reduce repetitive mistakes, boost your productivity, recover more effectively during and after work, reconnect to lost aspects of your identity, overwork less dangerously, enhance your emotional intelligence, protect your relationships and loved ones, prevent ethical slippage, and if all else fails, decide whether to look for another job.

The current workplace can be unhealthy, uncaring, and unrelenting. But by taking control of your mind, you can overcome the grind.

ACKNOWLEDGMENTS

WRITING A BOOK ABOUT overworking and work stress on top of my regular job required me to overwork at times, but the stress that should have come with doing so was much milder than it could have been because of the supportive, enthusiastic, and talented people I was fortunate to have around me.

My editor, Eamon Dolan, provided excellent guidance throughout the writing process and was a constant and reassuring presence. Eamon, your thoughtful, insightful notes and remarkable ability to pinpoint exactly why something works (or doesn't) made this journey infinitely smoother. Your openness to my ideas and rationales made me feel like I had a collaborative partner rather than just an editor. It has been a true pleasure to work with you—your stellar reputation is well-earned.

To my agent, Michelle Tessler—thank you for pushing me to write this book and for shepherding my career with such insight and mastery. To be the author of four books that have been translated into 30 languages and to be able to reach millions of people around the world is far beyond what I ever hoped to achieve as a writer.

My twin brother, Gil Winch, has always been first to read anything I write, whether an article, a joke, or a book. Gil, your brilliant advice and your helpful notes make anything I write better. Your support is always unconditional, your validation is always calming, and your wisdom always steers me in the right direction.

Given the expansive and varied research covered in this book, having the top student from the psychology department at Royal Holloway University—Shiri Winch—as my research assistant was a true privilege. Shiri, your dedication and humor made me laugh and smile, and your notes as a reader were as invaluable as your meticulous research.

A special thanks goes to Efrat Winch. Efi, you've influenced my thinking about workplace stress and burnout more profoundly than you probably realize. Your wisdom echoes not just throughout many sections of this book but also, thankfully, in my own head, often precisely when I need it most.

My deepest appreciation to the wonderful group of friends and colleagues who reviewed drafts, talked through ideas, helped me refine my message, or helped shape this book in some way: Behzad Zahiri, thank you for your extraordinary dedication and detailed, thoughtful notes on the manuscript. Asking a friend to devote so much time and effort is no small request, yet you delivered in grand style. I am also grateful to Tina Muir, Brea Tremblay, Raquel D'Apice, Ori Winch, Susan Zimmerman, Mike and Nick Fio (the Fio Bros), Tim Allen, Neil Laird, Roger Kawall, Anne Madden, Andres Ruzo, Kate Marvel, Anil Seth, Richard Leff, Ella Al Shamahi, Thalma Lobel, and Diana Fosha for your friendship and support.

To my wonderful readers, podcast listeners, and social media followers who've shared personal stories, reflections, and feedback via messages, comments, and emails—thank you for opening these windows into your inner worlds. While I wish I could personally respond to each of you, please know that your contributions motivate me daily. Your courage in facing today's unprecedented workplace stress and burnout reminds me why writing this book matters.

Finally, to the clients whose personal stories illuminate the pages of this book: your honesty, openness, and genuine resilience in the face of workplace challenges inspire me deeply. I've learned so much from each of you. Thank you for trusting me with your stories, for allowing me to be a part of your journey in life, and for being an important part of mine.

NOTES

Introduction: Sunday Evening

2   *Those were symptoms of burnout*: Sergio Edú-Valsania, Ana Laguía, and Juan A. Moriano, "Burnout: A Review of Theory and Measurement," *International Journal of Environmental Research and Public Health* 19, no. 3 (May 2022): 1780, https://doi.org/10.3390/ijerph19031780.

4   *43% of workers reported high stress, and 67% reported symptoms of burnout*: "2024 Work in America Poll," *American Psychological Association*, www.apa.org /pubs/reports/work-in-america/2024; American Psychological Association, *2024 Topline Data on Stress in America* (2024), www.apa.org/pubs/reports/stress -in-america/2024/2024-topline-data.pdf.

4   *thriving at work was also at an all-time low*: "Employee Life Evaluation Hits New Record Low," *Gallup*, November 18, 2024, www.gallup.com/workplace /653396/employee-life-evaluation-hits-new-record-low.aspx.

4   *Intense stress and burnout are serious conditions*: Edú-Valsania et al., "Burnout."

4   *excessive work demands cause us to make significantly more mistakes*: Arnold B. Bakker, Evangelia Demerouti, and Ana Sanz-Vergel, "Job Demands— Resources Theory: Ten Years Later," *Annual Review of Organizational Psychology and Organizational Behavior* 10 (January 2023): 25–53, https://doi.org /10.1146/annurev-orgpsych-120920-053933.

4   *and to unwittingly self-sabotage*: Arnold B. Bakker and Yiqing Wang, "Self-Undermining Behavior at Work: Evidence of Construct and Predictive Validity," *International Journal of Stress Management* 27, no. 3 (2020): 241–51, https://doi.org/10.1037/str0000150.

4 *Work also hijacks our emotional intelligence*: Keri A. Pekaar, Arnold B. Bakker, Dimitri van der Linden, Marise Born, and Heidi J. Sirén, "Managing Own and Others' Emotions: A Weekly Diary Study on the Enactment of Emotional Intelligence," *Journal of Vocational Behavior* 109 (December 2018): 137–51, https://doi.org/10.1016/j.jvb.2018.10.004.

4 *Work has even hijacked our moral code*: Alexander Newman, Huong Le, Andrea North-Samardzic, and Michael Cohen, "Moral Disengagement at Work: A Review and Research Agenda," *Journal of Business Ethics* 167, no. 3 (2020): 535–70, https://doi.org/10.1007/s10551-019-04173-0.

5 *38% of workers said they would act unethically*: Jim McCurry, "How Can Trust Survive Without Integrity?" *EY*, www.ey.com/en_gl/insights/forensic-integrity -services/global-integrity-report#.

5 *difficult days at work are often followed by arguments and conflict at home*: Jesse S. Michel, Lindsey M. Kotrba, Jacqueline K. Mitchelson, Malissa A. Clark, and Boris B. Baltes, "Antecedents of Work-Family Conflict: A Meta-Analytic Review," *Journal of Organizational Behavior* 32, no. 5 (2011): 689–725, https://doi.org/10.1002/job.695.

5 your partner *can develop symptoms of burnout*: Arnold B. Bakker, Evangelia Demerouti, and Maureen F. Dollard, "How Job Demands Affect Partners' Experience of Exhaustion: Integrating Work-Family Conflict and Crossover Theory," *Journal of Applied Psychology* 93, no. 4 (2008): 901–11, https://doi .org/10.1037/0021-9010.93.4.901.

5 *Work even hijacks our thoughts*: Dawn Querstret and Mark Cropley, "Exploring the Relationship Between Work-Related Rumination, Sleep Quality, and Work-Related Fatigue," *Journal of Occupational Health Psychology* 17, no. 3 (2012): 341–53, https://doi.org/10.1037/a0028552.

5 *we then are likely to wake up the next morning lacking vitality*: Sabine Sonnentag, "The Recovery Paradox: Portraying the Complex Interplay Between Job Stressors, Lack of Recovery, and Poor Well-Being," *Research in Organizational Behavior* 38 (2018), https://doi.org/10.1016/j.riob.2018.11.002.

5 *half of the adults who had cancer in the United States are diagnosed as a result of their annual checkup*: Qonita Rachmah, Tri Martiana, Mulyono Mulyono, "The Effectiveness of Nutrition and Health Intervention in Workplace Setting: A Systematic Review," *Journal of Public Health Research* 11, no. 1 (November 2021): 2312, https://doi.org/10.4081/jphr.2021.2312.

6 *23% of adults said they skipped their annual medical checkups*: Alison Roller, "Employees Skipping Preventive Care?" *HR Morning*, July 20, 2023, www .hrmorning.com/articles/employees-skipping-preventive-care/.

6 *high work stress makes us more likely to eat unhealthy foods and to skip exercising*: Bakker et al., "Job Demands."

6 *less likely to stay on top of basic tasks*: Bakker et al., "Job Demands."

6   *77% of workers reported that work stress was affecting their physical health*: Lyra Health, *2025 Workforce State of Mind Report* (2025), https://www.lyrahealth .com/2025-state-of-workforce-mental-health-report/.

6   *120,000 deaths per year*: Joel Goh, Jeffrey Pfeffer, and Stefanos Zenios, "The Relationship Between Workplace Stressors and Mortality and Health Costs in the United States," *Management Science* 62, no. 2 (March 16, 2016): 608–28, http://dx.doi.org/10.1287/mnsc.2014.2115.

7   *If employers invested in the emotional health of their employees*: Arnold B. Bakker and Juriena D. de Vries, "Job Demands–Resources Theory and Self-Regulation: New Explanations and Remedies for Job Burnout," *Anxiety, Stress, & Coping* 34, no. 1 (2021): 1–21, https://doi.org/10.1080/10615806 .2020.1797695.

7   *in 2017, 19% of employees reported having experienced bullying*: Gary Namie, *2017 Workplace Bullying Institute U.S. Workplace Bullying Survey* (Workplace Bullying Institute, 2017), https://workplacebullying.org/wp-content/uploads /2024/02/2017-WBI-Report.pdf.

7   *By 2024 that number was up to 32%*: Gary Namie, *2024 Workplace Bullying Institute U.S. Workplace Bullying Survey: The National Study* (Workplace Bullying Institute, 2024), www.workplacebullying.org/2024-wbi-us-survey/.

7   *eight times more likely to develop symptoms of burnout*: Lucia Ruhilly, host, *The McKinsey Podcast*, "Beyond Burnout: What Helps—And What Doesn't," interview with Erica Coe, podcast, October 7, 2022, www.mckinsey.com/mhi /our-insights/beyond-burnout-what-helps-and-what-doesnt.

8   *The relationship between stress and performance*: Peter A. Hancock and Joel S. Warm, "A Dynamic Model of Stress and Sustained Attention," *Journal of Human Performance in Extreme Environments* 7, no. 1 (2012): Article 4, www.docs.lib .purdue.edu/jhpee/vol7/iss1/4.

9   *These strategies and approaches our unconscious mind uses*: Estanislao Castellano, Roger Muñoz-Navarro, María S. Toledo, Carlos Spontón, and Leonardo A. Medrano, "Cognitive Processes of Emotional Regulation, Burnout and Work Engagement," *Psicothema* 31, no. 1 (February 2019): 73–80, https://doi.org /10.7334/psicothema2018.228.

11   *almost half of workers are hesitant to speak up*: "News Roundup: 43% of Workers Fear Retaliation If They Speak Up," *Corporate Compliance Insights*, October 17, 2024, www.corporatecomplianceinsights.com/news-roundup -october-17-2024/.

Chapter One: Monday Morning

15   *a notoriously stressful job, especially when markets were volatile*: Wenjuan Ma, Honglei Chen, Lili Jiang, Guixiang Song, and Haidong Kan, "Stock Volatility

NOTES

as a Risk Factor for Coronary Heart Disease Death," *European Heart Journal* 32, no. 8 (April 2011): 1006–11, https://doi.org/10.1093/eurheartj/ehq495.

15 *Mondays are indeed the most stressful day of the week*: Shani Pindek, Zhiqing E. Zhou, Stacey R. Kessler, Alexandra Krajcevska, and Paul E. Spector, "Workdays Are Not Created Equal: Job Satisfaction and Job Stressors Across the Workweek," *Human Relations* 74, no. 9 (2021): 1447–72, https://doi.org/10.1177/00187267209244444.

15 *They are also the day in which incidents of incivility and rudeness in the workplace are highest*: Pindek et al., "Workdays Are Not Created Equal."

15 *More strokes happen on Mondays than on any other workday*: Margaret Kelly-Hayes, P. A. Wolf, C. S. Kase, F. N. Brand, J. M. McGuirk, and R. B. D'Agostino, "Temporal Patterns of Stroke Onset: The Framingham Study," *Stroke* 26, no. 8 (1995): 1343–47, https://doi.org/10.1161/01.str.26.8.1343.

15 *Even deaths by suicide are higher on Mondays*: George Maldonado and Jess F. Kraus, "Variation in Suicide Occurrence by Time of Day, Day of the Week, Month, and Lunar Phase," *Suicide & Life-Threatening Behavior* 21, no. 2 (Summer 1991): 174–87, https://doi.org/10.1111/j.1943-278X.1991.tb00464.x.

16 *Guilt-prone people are often disadvantaged in the workplace*: Scott S. Wiltermuth and Taya R. Cohen, "'I'd Only Let You Down': Guilt Proneness and the Avoidance of Harmful Interdependence," *Journal of Personality and Social Psychology* 107, no. 5 (2014): 925–42, https://doi.org/10.1037/a0037523.

18 *Short bursts of stress can be good for you*: Firdaus S. Dhabhar and Bruce S. McEwen, "Acute Stress Enhances While Chronic Stress Suppresses Cell-Mediated Immunity in Vivo: A Potential Role for Leukocyte Trafficking," *Brain, Behavior, and Immunity* 11, no. 4 (1997): 286–306, https://doi.org/10.1006/brbi.1997.0508.

19 *let's take a slow-motion look at what happened in Tony's body*: Brianna Chu, Komal Marwaha, Terrence Sanvictores, Ayoola O. Awosika, and Derek Ayers, "Physiology, Stress Reaction," StatPearls Publishing for the National Library of Medicine, updated May 7, 2024, www.ncbi.nlm.nih.gov/books/NBK541120/.

19 *if the work stress you experienced went on for months*: "Stress Effects on the Body," *American Psychological Association*, October 21, 2024, www.apa.org/topics/stress/body.

20 *Repeated disruptions to your digestive system could cause heartburn*: Sarah-Jane Leigh, Friederike Uhlig, Lars Wilmes, et al., "The Impact of Acute and Chronic Stress on Gastrointestinal Physiology and Function: A Microbiota–Gut–Brain Axis Perspective," *Journal of Physiology* 601 (2023): 4491–538, https://doi.org/10.1113/JP281951.

21 *our ability to deal with stress is quite elastic*: Danielle Gianferante, Myriam V. Thoma, Luke Hanlin, et al., "Post-Stress Rumination Predicts HPA Axis Responses to Repeated Acute Stress," *Psychoneuroendocrinology* 49 (2014): 244–52, https://doi.org/10.1016/j.psyneuen.2014.07.021.

NOTES

24 *What you (and Tony) are actually doing is task switching*: Danielle Gianferante, Myriam V. Thoma, Luke Hanlin, et al., "Editorial: Multitasking: Executive Functioning in Dual-Task and Task Switching Situations," *Frontiers in Psychology* 9 (2018): 108, https://doi.org/10.3389/fpsyg.2018.00108.

24 Intense stress always taxes your mental operations: Katrin Starcke, Carina Wiesen, Patrick Trotzke, and Matthias Brand, "Effects of Acute Laboratory Stress on Executive Functions," *Frontiers in Psychology* 7 (2016): 461, https://doi.org/10.3389/fpsyg.2016.00461.

27 *Studies found that we tend to think of our future selves as strangers*: Benjamin Ganschow, Sven Zebel, Jean-Louis van Gelder, and Liza J. M. Cornet, "Feeling Connected but Dissimilar to One's Future Self Reduces the Intention-Behavior Gap," *PLoS ONE* 19, no. 7 (2024): e0305815, https://doi.org/10.1371/journal.pone.0305815.

27 *drink a disgusting brew*: Emily Pronin, Christopher Y. Olivola, and Kathleen A. Kennedy, "Doing Unto Future Selves as You Would Do Unto Others: Psychological Distance and Decision Making," *Personality & Social Psychology Bulletin* 34, no. 2 (2008): 224–36, https://doi.org/10.1177/0146167207310023.

Chapter Two: Monday Afternoon

31 *your brain and body respond very differently in each of those mental states*: Sarah E. Williams, Jennifer Cumming, and George M. Balanos, "The Use of Imagery to Manipulate Challenge and Threat Appraisal States in Athletes," *Journal of Sport & Exercise Psychology* 32, no. 3 (2010): 339–58, https://doi.org/10.1123/jsep.32.3.339.

32 *three factors that determine your mindset*: Williams, Cumming, and Balanos, "The Use of Imagery to Manipulate Challenge and Threat Appraisal States in Athletes."

35 *traveling by plane is orders of magnitude safer than traveling by car*: "Is Flying Safer than Driving?" *USA Facts*, December 16, 2024, www.usafacts.org/articles/is-flying-safer-than-driving/.

Chapter Three: Monday Evening

38 *The more distressing or upsetting your workday is*: M. Cropley and L. Millward Purvis, "Job Strain and Rumination About Work Issues During Leisure Time: A Diary Study," *European Journal of Work and Organizational Psychology* 12, no. 3 (2003): 195–207, https://doi.org/10.1080/13594320344000093.

39 *Women make 83 cents on the dollar compared to men*: "Global Gender Pay Gap from 2015 to 2025," *Statistica*, February 2025, www.statista.com/statistics/1212140/global-gender-pay-gap/.

39 *each child under five years old*: Miranda Peterson, "Motherhood Is Hard—Pay Penalties Make It Harder," Institute for Women's Policy Research, August 7, 2024, https://iwpr.org/motherhood-is-hard-pay-penalties-make-it-harder/.

40 *there are several ways to self-reflect*: Susan Nolen-Hoeksema, Blair E. Wisco, and Sonja Lyubomirsky, "Rethinking Rumination," *Perspectives on Psychological Science* 3, no. 5 (2008): 400–24, https://doi.org/10.1111/j.1745-6924.2008.00088.x.

41 *rumination intensifies visceral feelings of stress and angst*: Nolen-Hoeksema et al., "Rethinking Rumination."

42 *Abraham Maslow*: Wikipedia, "Abraham Maslow," last modified May 21, 2025, www.wikipedia.org/wiki/Maslow%27s_hierarchy_of_needs.

43 *It also triggers our stress response*: Nolen-Hoeksema et al., "Rethinking Rumination."

43 *ruminating about work after work hours is associated with significantly higher risks*: Sarah Steiner, "Exploring the Association Between Affective Work-Related Rumination and Cardiovascular Risk Factors," PhD diss., University of Surrey, November 17, 2020, https://doi.org/10.15126/thesis.00853213.

43 *ruminating about work causes sleep disturbances*: Nolen-Hoeksema et al., "Rethinking Rumination."

43 *it even impairs our cognitive and executive functions*: Mark Cropley, Fred R. H. Zijlstra, Dawn Querstret, and Sarah Beck, "Is Work-Related Rumination Associated with Deficits in Executive Functioning?" *Frontiers in Psychology* 7 (2016): 1524, https://doi.org/10.3389/fpsyg.2016.01524.

44 *Tabata training*: Izumi Tabata, "Tabata Training: One of the Most Energetically Effective High-Intensity Intermittent Training Methods," *Journal of Physiological Sciences* 69 (2019): 559–72, https://doi.org/10.1007/s12576-019-00676-7.

46 *Interpersonal conflict has been found to be an especially potent driver of rumination*: Ying Song and Zhenzhi Zhao, "Social Undermining and Interpersonal Rumination Among Employees: The Mediating Role of Being the Subject of Envy and the Moderating Role of Social Support," *International Journal of Environmental Research and Public Health* 19, no. 14 (2022): 8419, https://doi.org/10.3390/ijerph19148419.

47 *unfinished tasks, especially time-sensitive ones, can get ensnared in our brains*: Christine J. Syrek and Conny H. Antoni, "Unfinished Tasks Foster Rumination and Impair Sleeping—Particularly if Leaders Have High Performance Expectations," *Journal of Occupational Health Psychology* 19, no. 4 (2014): 490–9, https://doi.org/10.1037/a0037127.

48 *The more intense those feelings are, the more your thoughts will swirl*: Maxime Résibois, Elise K. Kalokerinos, Gregory Verleysen, et al., "The Rela-

tion Between Rumination and Temporal Features of Emotion Intensity," *Cognition and Emotion* 32, no. 2 (2017): 259–74, https://doi.org/10.1080/02699931.2017.1298993.

49 *Much of the emotional regulation we do occurs automatically and unconsciously*: Jiajin Yuan, Nanxiang Ding, Yingying Liu, and Jiemin Yang, "Unconscious Emotion Regulation: Nonconscious Reappraisal Decreases Emotion-Related Physiological Reactivity During Frustration," *Cognition and Emotion* 29, no. 6 (2014): 1042–53, https://doi.org/10.1080/02699931.2014.965663.

49 *Dysregulation is a temporary loss of the ability to control your emotions*: Claudia Carmassi, Lorenzo Conti, Davide Gravina, Benedetta Nardi, and Liliana Dell'Osso, "Emotional Dysregulation as Trans-Nosographic Psychopathological Dimension in Adulthood: A Systematic Review," *Frontiers in Psychiatry* 13 (2022): 900277, https://doi.org/10.3389/fpsyt.2022.900277.

50 *Suppression is effective but strenuous*: Sally A. Moore, Lori A. Zoellner, Niklas Mollenholt, "Are Expressive Suppression and Cognitive Reappraisal Associated with Stress-Related Symptoms?" *Behavior Research and Therapy* 46, no. 9 (2008): 993–1000, https://doi.org/10.1016/j.brat.2008.05.001.

50 *Over time, using suppression in the workplace*: Moore et al., "Are Expressive Suppression and Cognitive Reappraisal Associated with Stress-Related Symptoms?"

50 *a recent large multinational study*: Maya Tamir, Atsuki Ito, Yuri Miyamoto, et al., "Emotion Regulation Strategies and Psychological Health Across Cultures," *The American Psychologist* 79, no. 5 (2024): 748–64, https://doi.org/10.1037/amp0001237.

50 *The goal of reframing*: Debora Cutuli, "Cognitive Reappraisal and Expressive Suppression Strategies Role in the Emotion Regulation—An Overview on Their Modulatory Effects and Neural Correlates," *Frontiers in Systems Neuroscience* 8 (September 18, 2014): 175, https://doi.org/10.3389/fnsys.2014.00175.

52 *Hardship doesn't automatically boost resilience*: Richard G. Tedeschi and Lawrence G. Calhoun, "Target Article: 'Posttraumatic Growth: Conceptual Foundations and Empirical Evidence,'" *Psychological Inquiry* 15, no. 1 (2004): 1–18, https://doi.org/10.1207/s15327965pli1501_01.

53 *worried participants were instructed to postpone their worrying*: E. J. Masicampo and Roy F. Baumeister, "Consider It Done! Plan Making Can Eliminate the Cognitive Effects of Unfulfilled Goals," *Journal of Personality and Social Psychology* 101, no. 4 (2011): 667–83, https://doi.org/10.1037/a0024192.

54 *a two- or three-minute distraction is enough*: Cheryl L. Rusting and Susan Nolen-Hoeksema, "Regulating Responses to Anger: Effects of Rumination and Distraction on Angry Mood," *Journal of Personality and Social Psychology* 74, no. 3 (1998): 790–803, https://doi.org/10.1037/0022-3514.74.3.790.

NOTES

Chapter Four: Tuesday Morning

57   *Tuesdays were the day positive emotions at work were at their lowest*: Eric Mayor and Lucas M. Bietti, "Twitter, Time and Emotions," *Royal Society Open Science* 8, no. 5 (2021): 201900, https://doi.org/10.1098/rsos.201900.

60   *we favor strategies that are* problem-focused: Shin Hyojung, Yang Min Park, Jin Yuan Ying, Boyoung Kim, Hyunkyung Noh, and Sang Min Lee, "Relationships Between Coping Strategies and Burnout Symptoms: A Meta-Analytic Approach," *Professional Psychology: Research and Practice* 45, no. 1 (2014): 44–56, https://doi.org/10.1037/a0035220.

60   *our automatic coping mechanisms use strategies that are* emotion-focused: Shin et al., "Relationships Between Coping Strategies and Burnout Symptoms."

60   *Our unconscious mind will urge us to act unwisely at times*: Bakker and Wang, "Self-Undermining Behavior at Work."

Chapter Five: Tuesday Afternoon

68   *Using nicknames in the workplace is quite common*: Zhe Zhang and Shuili Du, "Research: The Rules of Using Playful Nicknames at Work," *Harvard Business Review*, October 31, 2024, www.hbr.org/2024/10/research-the-rules-of-using-playful-nicknames-at-work?

69   *Intense job strain sets us up to make more mistakes*: Bakker and de Vries, "Job Demands—Resources Theory and Self-Regulation."

70   *75% of college students struggle with poor time management and procrastination*: "Time Management Statistics for 2025 and What They Teach Us," *Clockify*, www.clockify.me/time-management-statistics.

70   *fondness for procrastination tends to decline with age*: Manfred E. Beutel, Eva M. Klein, Stefan Aufenanger, et al., "Procrastination, Distress and Life Satisfaction Across the Age Range: A German Representative Community Study," *PLoS One* 11, no. 2 (February 12, 2016), https://doi.org/10.1371/journal.pone.0148054.

70   *being even seven minutes late*: "The Average Adult Starts to Feel Stressed if They Are Just Seven Minutes Late for a Social Event or Meeting," *72Point*, October 4, 2021, www.swnsdigital.com/uk/2021/04/the-average-adult-starts-to-feel-stressed-if-they-are-just-seven-minutes-late-for-a-social-event-or-meeting/.

70   *meetings that started late averaged more criticisms*: Joseph A. Allen, Nale Lehmann-Willenbrock, and Steven G. Rogelberg, "Let's Get This Meeting Started: Meeting Lateness and Actual Meeting Outcomes," in University of Nebraska, Omaha, *Psychology Faculty Publications* 199 (2018), www.digitalcommons.unomaha.edu/psychfacpub/199.

71   *Known as* error management: Brandon S. King and Terry A. Beehr, "Working with the Stress of Errors: Error Management Strategies as Coping," *Inter-*

- 222 -

national Journal of Stress Management 24, no. 1 (2017): 18–33, https://doi.org
/10.1037/str0000022.

77   *toiling away for people who seem indifferent to our needs*: Dejun Tony Kong and
Liuba Y. Belkin, "You Don't Care for Me, So What's the Point for Me to Care
for Your Business? Negative Implications of Felt Neglect by the Employer for
Employee Work Meaning and Citizenship Behaviors Amid the COVID-19
Pandemic," *Journal of Business Ethics* 181, no. 3 (2022): 645–60, https://doi
.org/10.1007/s10551-021-04950-w.

77   *workers who feel like they are learning and gaining valuable skills*: Jessica van
Wingerden, Arnold B. Bakker, and Daantje Derks, "The Longitudinal
Impact of a Job Crafting Intervention," *European Journal of Work and Organizational Psychology* 26, no. 1 (2017): 107–19, https://doi.org/10.1080
/1359432X.2016.1224233.

78   *Role curation can also help mitigate the resentment and frustration*: Maria
Tims, Arnold B. Bakker, and Daantje Derks, "The Impact of Job Crafting
on Job Demands, Job Resources, and Well-Being," *Journal of Occupational
Health Psychology* 18, no. 2 (2013): 230–40, https://doi.org/10.1037/a0
032141.

Chapter Six: Tuesday Evening

83   *anxiety makes us overestimate the likelihood of worst-case scenarios*: Jonathan
Abramowitz and Shannon M. Blakey, "Overestimation of Threat," in *Clinical Handbook of Fear and Anxiety: Maintenance Processes and Treatment Mechanisms* (American Psychological Association, 2020): 7–25, https://doi.org
/10.1037/0000150-001.

84   *recovering physically, mentally, and emotionally in the off hours*: Sonnentag, "The
Recovery Paradox."

84   *the more likely we will be to choose* ineffective *recovery strategies*: Sonnentag,
"The Recovery Paradox."

85   *the global average for screen time for television and gaming*: Simon Kemp, "Dig-
ital 2024: Global Overview Report," *DataReportal*, January 31, 2024, www
.datareportal.com/reports/digital-2024-global-overview-report.

86   *Failing to detach from work, whether you are a separator or integrator*: Sonnentag, "The Recovery Paradox."

86   *Recovery efforts aside, failing to mentally detach from work*: Johannes Wendsche
and Andrea Lohmann-Haislah, "A Meta-Analysis on Antecedents and Outcomes of Detachment from Work," *Frontiers in Psychology* 7 (2017): Article
2072, https://doi.org/10.3389/fpsyg.2016.02072.

86   the more stress and pressure you experience during the workday: Sonnentag,
"The Recovery Paradox."

NOTES

87   *conscious experience arises from the dynamic interplay*: Anil Seth, *Being You: A New Science of Consciousness* (New York: Dutton, 2021).

87   *Rituals have also been found to reduce anxiety*: Martin Lang, Jan Krátký, and Dimitris Xygalatas, "Effects of Predictable Behavioral Patterns on Anxiety Dynamics," *Scientific Reports* 12, no. 19240 (2022), https://doi.org/10.1038/s41598-022-23885-4.

87   *and to block out emotional "noise"*: Nicholas M. Hobson, "The Psychology of Ritual: An Empirical Investigation of Ritual's Regulatory Functions and Psychological Processes," PhD diss., University of Toronto (2017), http://hdl.handle.net/1807/89646.

87   *adding a second sense improved pattern recognition by 15%*: Christopher T. Lovelace, Barry E. Stein, and Mark T. Wallace, "An Irrelevant Light Enhances Auditory Detection in Humans: A Psychophysical Analysis of Multisensory Integration in Stimulus Detection," *Cognitive Brain Research* 17, no. 2 (2003): 447–53, https://doi.org/10.1016/s0926-6410(03)00160-5.

87   *the more senses were involved, the quicker pattern recognition occurred*: Adele Diederich and Hans Colonius, "Bimodal and Trimodal Multisensory Enhancement: Effects of Stimulus Onset and Intensity on Reaction Time," *Perception & Psychophysics* 66, no. 8 (2004): 1388–404, https://doi.org/10.3758/bf03195006.

89   *people who wore the white lab coat made a lot fewer mistakes*: Hajo Adam and Adam D. Galinsky, "Enclothed Cognition," *Journal of Experimental Social Psychology* 48, no. 4 (2012): 918–25, https://doi.org/10.1016/j.jesp.2012.02.008.

89   *In a recent study, 74 employees reported*: M. L. M. van Hooff, R. M. Benthem de Grave, and S. A. E. Geurts, "No Pain, No Gain? Recovery and Strenuousness of Physical Activity," *Journal of Occupational Health Psychology* 24, no. 5 (2019): 499–511, https://doi.org/10.1037/ocp0000141.

90   *50% of all workers are expected to respond to emails after hours*: Juliana Menasce Horowitz, and Kim Parker, *How Americans View Their Jobs* (Washington, DC: Pew Research Center, March 30, 2003), www.pewresearch.org/social-trends/2023/03/30/how-americans-view-their-jobs/#how-workers-are-experiencing-the-workplace.

90   *workers spend an average of eight hours a week reading and responding to messages*: Marisa Sanfilippo, "What After-Hours Emails Really Do to Your Employees," *Business News Daily*, updated January 26, 2024, www.businessnewsdaily.com/9241-check-email-after-work.html.

90   *you have to experience a sense of autonomy*: Sonnentag, "The Recovery Paradox."

91   *the mere sight of your phone can trigger associations to work*: Daantje Derks, Lieke L. ten Brummelhuis, Dino Zecic, and Arnold B. Bakker, "Switching On and Off . . . : Does Smartphone Use Obstruct the Possibility to Engage in Recovery Activities?" *European Journal of Work and Organizational Psychology* 23, no. 1 (2014): 80–90, https://doi.org/10.1080/1359432X.2012.711013.

91 *Detaching from work has another benefit*: Johannes Wendsche and Andrea Lohmann-Haislah, "A Meta-Analysis on Antecedents and Outcomes of Detachment from Work," *Frontiers in Psychology* 7 (2017): Article 2072, https://doi.org/10.3389/fpsyg.2016.02072.

92 *Getting good sleep is the foundation*: Faith S. Luyster, Patrick J. Strollo Jr., Phyllis C. Zee, and James K. Walsh, "Sleep: A Health Imperative," *SLEEP* 35, no. 6 (2012): 727–34, https://doi.org/10.5665/sleep.1846.

94 *Accessing important parts of your identity*: Lauren L. Mitchell, Patricia A. Frazier, and Nina A. Sayer, "Identity Disruption and Its Association with Mental Health Among Veterans with Reintegration Difficulty," *Developmental Psychology* 56, no. 11 (2020): 2152–66, https://doi.org/10.1037/dev0001106.

95 *Flow is a psychological state of deep concentration*: Stefan Engeser and Falko Rheinberg, "Flow, Performance and Moderators of Challenge-Skill Balance," *Motivation and Emotion* 32, no. 3 (2008): 158–72, https://doi.org/10.1007/s11031-008-9102-4.

97 *Compartmentalizing is a coping mechanism*: "Compartmentalization," *Psychology Today*, accessed April 10, 2025, www.psychologytoday.com/us/basics/compartmentalization.

Chapter Seven: Wednesday Morning

102 *a term that originated in the 1950s*: "Happy hump day," *Slang Dictionary*, April 5, 2018, www.dictionary.com/e/slang/happy-hump-day/.

102 *68% of people do some work over the weekend*: "Working Weekends a Reality for Nearly 7 in 10 Remote Professionals, Robert Half Research Shows," *Robert Half*, November 23, 2020, www.press.roberthalf.com/2020-11-23-Working-Weekends-a-Reality-for-Nearly-7-in-10-Remote-Professionals-Robert-Half-Research-Shows.

102 *Loneliness was a valid and important concern*: Louise C. Hawkley, "Loneliness and Health," *Nature Reviews Disease Primers* 8, no. 1 (2022): Article 22, https://doi.org/10.1038/s41572-022-00355-9.

103 *the US founder who slept on the floor*: "Narayana Murthy to Elon Musk: Billionaire Insights on Hustle Culture from 70-Hour Weeks to Sleeping in Offices," *MSN*, https://www.msn.com/en-in/news/India/narayana-murthy-to-elon-musk-billionaire-insights-on-hustle-culture-from-70-hour-weeks-to-sleeping-in-offices/ar-AA1qcjUX.

103 *working over 55 hours a week was associated*: Bhairav Prasad and Charu Thakur, "Chronic Overworking: Cause Extremely Negative Impact on Health and Quality of Life," *International Journal of Advanced Microbiology and Health Research* 3, 11–5 (2019).

103   *Karoshi deaths garner much media attention in Japan*: Behrooz Asgari, Peter Peckar, and Victoria Garay, "Karoshi and Karou-Jisatsu in Japan: Causes, Statistics and Prevention Mechanisms," *Asia Pacific Business & Economics Perspectives* 4, no. 2 (Winter 2016): 49–72.

104   *Karoshi is defined as the "sudden death"*: Tori Hiyama, and Masahito Yoshihara, "New Occupational Threats to Japanese Physicians: Karoshi (Death Due to Overwork) and Karojisatsu (Suicide Due to Overwork)," *Occupational and Environmental Medicine* 65, no. 6 (June 2008):428–29, https://doi.org/10.1136/oem.2007.037473.

104   *Most researchers place the cutoff*: Mika Kivimäki, Markus Jokela, Solja T. Nyberg, et al., "Long Working Hours and Risk of Coronary Heart Disease and Stroke: A Systematic Review and Meta-Analysis of Published and Unpublished Data for 603,838 Individuals," *Lancet* 386, no. 10005 (2015): 1739–46, https://doi.org/10.1016/S0140-6736(15)60295-1.

104   *in 2024, Australia passed a* Right to Disconnect *law*: "Right to Disconnect," *Fair Work Ombudsman*, Australian Government, accessed April 10, 2025, www.fairwork.gov.au/employment-conditions/hours-of-work-breaks-and-rosters/right-to-disconnect.

105   *"That's twice the number of hours prisoners in Russian gulags"*: Wikipedia, "Vorkutlag," last modified May 25, 2025, www.wikipedia.org/wiki/Vorkutlag#.

105   *"North Korean labor camps"*: Stephen Evans, "North Korea's Prisons: How Harsh Are Conditions?" *BBC*, June 14, 2017, www.bbc.com/news/world-asia-40269546.

105   *"eighty-five percent less outdoor time than maximum security inmates get"*: Sara Burrows, "We Lock Our Kids Up Longer Than We Do Maximum Security Convicts," *Newsweek*, October 27, 2017, www.newsweek.com/we-lock-our-kids-longer-we-do-maximum-security-convicts-694845.

105   *In a 2024 survey, 44% of respondents said they had to work a second job*: Trendicators, *The 2024 Job Seeker Survey Report* (Engage2Excel, 2024), www.engage2excel.com/resource/1-2024-job-seeker-survey-report/.

106   *12- to 16-hour workdays were the norm*: "Working Conditions in the Industrial Revolution," *History Crunch*, accessed April 10, 2025, www.historycrunch.com/working-conditions-in-the-industrial-revolution.html#/.

106   *laborers rarely lived past the age of 25*: Boundless World History, Child Labor, "Industrial Revolution," in *History of Western Civilization II*, accessed April 10, 2025, https://courses.lumenlearning.com/suny-hccc-worldhistory2/chapter/child-labor/.

106   *In the 1950s, one in three workers was in a union*: Laura Feiveson, "Labor Unions and the US Economy," *US Department of the Treasury*, August 28, 2023, home.treasury.gov/news/featured-stories/labor-unions-and-the-us-economy.

106   *Today, that number is one in ten*: G. E. Miller, "The U.S. is the Most Overworked Developed Nation in the World," 20somethingfinance.com, last updated Jan-

uary 9, 2025, www.20somethingfinance.com/american-hours-worked-product
ivity-vacation/.

107   *managers were tasked with evaluating two groups who had identical perfor-*
mances: Christin L. Munsch, Lindsey T. O'Connor, and Susan R. Fisk, "Gender and the Disparate Payoffs of Overwork," *Social Psychology Quarterly* 87,
no. 1 (2024): 22–43, https://doi.org/10.1177/01902725221141059.

107   *Men who overworked were evaluated as being more committed*: Munsch et al.,
"Gender and the Disparate Payoffs of Overwork."

107   *Here is yet another bias that women face in the workplace*: Madeline E. Heilman,
Suzette Caleo, and Francesca Manzi, "Women at Work: Pathways from Gender Stereotypes to Gender Bias and Discrimination," *Annual Review of Organizational Psychology and Organizational Behavior* 11 (2024): 165–92, https://
doi.org/10.1146/annurev-orgpsych-110721-034105.

107   *and too many others to mention*: Jennifer Y. Kim and Alyson Meister, "Microaggressions, Interrupted: The Experience and Effects of Gender Microaggressions for Women in STEM," *Journal of Business Ethics* 185 (2023): 513–31,
https://doi.org/10.1007/s10551-022-05203-0.

107   *gender parity would only be achieved in 60 years*: William Lutz, "National
Gender Wage Gap Widens Significantly in 2023 for the First Time in 20
Years!" *Institute for Women's Policy Research*, September 12, 2024, www.iwpr
.org/national-gender-wage-gap-widens-significantly-in-2023-for-the-first
-time-in-20-years/.

107   *Black women are exposed to even worse bias*: Alexis Krivkovich, Emily Field,
Lareina Yee, and Megan McConnell, *Women in the Workplace 2024: The
10th-Anniversary Report* (McKinsey & Company, September 17, 2024), www
.mckinsey.com/featured-insights/diversity-and-inclusion/women-in-the
-workplace.

107   *Bias at work causes significant additional stress*: Jian Li, Timothy A. Matthews,
Thomas Clausen, and Reiner Rugulies, "Workplace Discrimination and Risk
of Hypertension: Findings from a Prospective Cohort Study in the United
States," *Journal of the American Heart Association* 12, no. 9 (2023): e027374,
https://doi.org/10.1161/JAHA.122.027374.

110   *A substantial portion of emergency room visits for non-cardiac chest pain*: Guil-
laume Foldes-Busque, Isabelle Denis, Julien Poitras, Richard P. Fleet, Patrick
Archambault, and Clermont E. Dionne, "A Closer Look at the Relationships
Between Panic Attacks, Emergency Department Visits and Non-Cardiac
Chest Pain," *Journal of Health Psychology* 24, no. 6 (2019): 717–25, https://
doi.org/10.1177/1359105316683785.

111   *the more we overwork, the more compromised our functioning will be*: Veruscka
Leso, Luca Fontana, Angela Caturano, Ilaria Vetrani, Mauro Fedele, and Ivo
Iavicoli, "Impact of Shift Work and Long Working Hours on Worker Cogni-

tive Functions: Current Evidence and Future Research Needs," *International Journal of Environmental Research and Public Health* 18, no. 12 (2021): 6540, https://doi.org/10.3390/ijerph18126540.

III   *scientists are making efforts to bring the dodo back from extinction*: Christine Kenneally, "A 'De-extinction' Company Wants to Bring Back the Dodo," *SCIAM*, January 31, 2023, www.scientificamerican.com/article/tech-compa ny-invests-150m-to-bring-back-the-dodo/.

113   *Self-neglect is a concept used primarily by social services*: Wikipedia, "Self-Neglect," last modified March 19, 2025, www.wikipedia.org/wiki/Self-neglect.

113   *Sam Altman, the founder of OpenAI*: Aaron Mok, "OpenAI CEO Sam Altman Says He Worked So Hard Building His First Startup with His Ex-Boyfriend That He Got Scurvy," *Business Insider*, September 25, 2023, https://www.businessin sider.com/openai-ceo-sam-altman-got-scurvy-working-start-up-chatgpt-2023-9.

120   *"harm reduction" approaches are based on the premise*: National Academies of Sciences, Engineering, and Medicine, *Public Health Consequences of e-Cigarettes* (Washington, DC: National Academies Press, 2018), www.ncbi.nlm.nih.gov /books/NBK507185/.

120   *Five years later, when writing my first book*: Guy Winch, *The Squeaky Wheel: Complaining the Right Way to Get Results, Improve Your Relationships and En- hance Self-Esteem* (New York: Walker & Company, 2011).

122   *For decades, canaries were used in coal mines as sentinels*: Kat Eschner, "What Happened to the Canary in the Coal Mine? The Story of How the Real-Life Animal Helper Became Just a Metaphor," *Smithsonian Magazine*, updated by Sonja Anderson on March 7, 2024, accessed April 10, 2025, www.smithso nianmag.com/smart-news/what-happened-canary-coal-mine-story-how-real -life-animal-helper-became-just-metaphor-180961570/.

Chapter Eight: Thursday Morning

125   *the point at which runners often "hit the wall"*: Barry Smyth, "How Recre- ational Marathon Runners Hit the Wall: A Large-Scale Data Analysis of Late- Race Pacing Collapse in the Marathon," *PLoS ONE* 16, no. 5 (2021): e0251513, https://doi.org/10.1371/journal.pone.0251513.

125   *In the workplace, having high EI is associated with*: Bakker and de Vries, "Job Demands—Resources Theory and Self-Regulation."

125   *EI is not just a trait but also a skill*: Pekaar et al., "Managing Own and Others' Emotions."

126   *"Emotionally Savvy Employees Fail to Enact Emotional Intelligence"*: Jie Ma, Zhiliang Zeng, and Ke Fang, "Emotionally Savvy Employees Fail to Enact Emotional Intelligence When Ostracized," *Personality and Individual Differ- ences* 185 (2022): Article 111250, https://doi.org/10.1016/j.paid.2021.111250.

126 *when workers neglected to manage their own emotions*: Bakker and de Vries, "Job Demands—Resources Theory and Self-Regulation."

130 *"Chronic stress and fatigue exhaust our coping mechanisms"*: Iryna S. Palamarchuk and Tracy Vaillancourt, "Mental Resilience and Coping With Stress: A Comprehensive, Multi-Level Model of Cognitive Processing, Decision Making, and Behavior," *Frontiers in Behavioral Neuroscience* 15 (2021): 719674, https://doi.org/10.3389/fnbeh.2021.719674.

130 *A few minutes of slow deep breathing*: Stephen Kaplan and Marc G. Berman, "Directed Attention as a Common Resource for Executive Functioning and Self-Regulation," *Perspectives on Psychological Science* 5, no. 1 (2010): 43–57, https://doi.org/10.1177/1745691609356784.

133 *the more benefit we could derive from short breaks*: Sonnentag, "The Recovery Paradox."

135 *Naps of 10–15 minutes in the early afternoon*: Amber Brooks and Leon Lack, "A Brief Afternoon Nap Following Nocturnal Sleep Restriction: Which Nap Duration Is Most Recuperative?" *SLEEP* 29, no. 6 (2006): 831–40, https://doi.org/10.1093/sleep/29.6.831.

135 *taking breaks is always better for fatigue, attention, and performance*: Albulescu, Patricia, Irina Macsinga, Andrei Rusu, Coralia Sulea, Alexandra Bodnaru, and Bogdan Tudor Tulbure, "'Give Me a Break!' A Systematic Review and Meta-Analysis on the Efficacy of Micro-Breaks for Increasing Well-Being and Performance," *PLoS ONE* 17, no.8 (August 2023), https://doi.org/10.1371/journal.pone.0272460.

135 *Breaks that offer cognitive relaxation and help you detach from work*: Sooyeol Kim, YoungAh Park, and Lucille Headrick, "Daily Micro-Breaks and Job Performance: General Work Engagement as a Cross-Level Moderator," *Journal of Applied Psychology* 103, no. 7 (2018): 772–86, https://doi.org/10.1037/apl0000308.

135 *low-intensity cardiovascular exercise like brisk walking*: Sky Chafin, Nicholas Christenfeld, and William Gerin, "Improving Cardiovascular Recovery from Stress with Brief Post Stress Exercise," *Health Psychology* 27, no. 1S (January 2008): 64–72, https://doi.org/10.1037/0278-6133.27.1.

135 *exercising and stretching for a few minutes*: Zhanna Lyubykh, Duygu Gulseren, Zahra Premji, et al., "Role of Work Breaks in Well-Being and Performance: A Systematic Review and Future Research Agenda," *Journal of Occupational Health Psychology* 27, no. 5 (2022): 470–87, https://doi.org/10.1037/ocp0000337.

135 *taking a stroll in nature, which has been found to lower stress*: Gabriela Gonçalves, Cátia Sousa, Maria Jacinta Fernandes, Nuno Almeida, and António Sousa, "Restorative Effects of Biophilic Workplace and Nature Exposure During Working Time: A Systematic Review," *International Journal of Environmental*

Research and Public Health 20, no. 21 (2023): 6986, https://doi.org/10.3390/ijerph20216986.

135 *and the urge to ruminate*: Gregory N. Bratman, J. Paul Hamilton, Kevin S. Hahn, Gretchen C. Daily, and James J. Gross, "Nature Experience Reduces Rumination and Subgenual Prefrontal Cortex Activation," *Proceedings of the National Academy of Sciences of the United States of America* 112, no. 28 (2015): 8567–72, https://doi.org/10.1073/pnas.1510459112.

135 *Surfing social media was found to be less effective overall*: Lyubykh et al., "Role of Work Breaks in Well-Being and Performance."

136 *Micro-breaks of one to two minutes have been found to reduce fatigue*: Andrew A. Bennett, Allison S. Gabriel, and Charles Calderwood, "Examining the Interplay of Micro-Break Durations and Activities for Employee Recovery: A Mixed-Methods Investigation," *Journal of Occupational Health Psychology* 25, no. 2 (2020): 126–42, https://doi.org/10.1037/ocp0000168.

136 *mindfulness meditation was found to increase executive functioning*: Kaplan and Berman, "Directed Attention as a Common Resource for Executive Functioning and Self-Regulation."

136 *A quick chat with colleagues can boost general well-being*: John P. Trougakos, Ivona Hideg, Bonnie Hayden Cheng, and Daniel J. Beal, "Lunch Breaks Unpacked: The Role of Autonomy as a Moderator of Recovery During Lunch," *Academy of Management Journal* 57, no. 2 (2014): 405–21, https://doi.org/10.5465/amj.2011.1072.

136 *Social support has been shown to lower stress*: Ethan Zell and Christopher A. Stockus, "Social Support and Psychological Adjustment: A Quantitative Synthesis of 60 Meta-Analyses," *American Psychologist* 80, no. 1 (2025): 33–46, https://doi.org/10.1037/amp0001323.

136 *when stress at work compromises our emotional intelligence*: Arnold B. Bakker and Patrícia Costa, "Chronic Job Burnout and Daily Functioning: A Theoretical Analysis," *Burnout Research* 1, no. 3 (2014): 112–19.

140 *getting support in the workplace can fail to provide true emotional recovery*: Lisanne S. Pauw, Disa A. Sauter, Gerben A. van Kleef, and Agneta H. Fischer, "Sense or Sensibility? Social Sharers' Evaluations of Socio-Affective vs. Cognitive Support in Response to Negative Emotions," *Cognition & Emotion* 32, no. 6 (2018): 1247–64, https://doi.org/10.1080/02699931.2017.1400949.

140 *and even to reduce unhealthy snacking and cravings for comfort food*: Mingyue Xiao, Yijun Luo, Weiyu Zeng, and Hong Chen, "Support from a Best Friend Makes People Eat Less Under Stress: Evidence from Two Experiments," *Nutrients* 15, no. 18 (2023): 3898. https://doi.org/10.3390/nu15183898.

141 *one study found that when we're feeling worried or regretful*: Xiao et al., "Support from a Best Friend Makes People Eat Less Under Stress."

141   *Increasing our* emotional granularity: Tse Yen Tan, Louise Wachsmuth, and Michelle M. Tugade, "Emotional Nuance: Examining Positive Emotional Granularity and Well-Being," *Frontiers in Psychology* 13 (2022): 715966, https://doi.org/10.3389/fpsyg.2022.715966.

141   emotional literacy: Melek Alemdarı and Hüseyin Anilan, "The Development and Validation of the Emotional Literacy Skills Scale," *International Journal of Contemporary Educational Research* 7, no. 2 (2020): 258–70, https://doi.org/10.33200/ijcer.757853.

142   *Video calls tend to enable greater feelings of connection*: Lauren E. Sherman, Minas Michikyan, and Patricia M. Greenfield, "The Effects of Text, Audio, Video, and In-Person Communication on Bonding Between Friends," *Cyberpsychology: Journal of Psychosocial Research on Cyberspace* 7, no. 2 (2013): Article 3, https://doi.org/10.5817/CP2013-2-3.

Chapter Nine: Thursday Evening

144   *it's difficult to prevent our tension and bad mood from spilling*: Andrew Li, Russell Cropanzano, Adam Butler, Ping Shao, and Mina Westman, "Work-Family Crossover: A Meta-Analytic Review," *International Journal of Stress Management* 28, no. 2 (2021): 89–104, https://doi.org/10.1037/str0000225.

146   *A 2024 survey found that 55% of employees have job security concerns*: Mark Webster, "Survey Reveals: 55% Of U.S. Workers Have Job Security Concerns," *AuthorityHacker*, October 7, 2024, www.authorityhacker.com/job-security-survey/.

146   *For those in the IT sector*: Webster, "Survey Reveals."

146   *almost 40% of all employees were worried about AI*: American Psychological Association, *2023 Work in America Survey* (October 21, 2024), www.apa.org/pubs/reports/work-in-america/2023-work-america-ai-monitoring.

146   *only 20% to 30% of them will eventually become partners*: "What Percentage of Associates at Big Law Firms Make Partner?" video posted by *BCG Attorney Search*, accessed April 10, 2025, www.bcgsearch.com/videos/11976/What-percentage-of-associates-at-big-law-firms-make-partner-/.

146   *academics face similar years of job insecurity*: Maya Denton, Maura Borrego, and David B. Knight, "U.S. Postdoctoral Careers in Life Sciences, Physical Sciences and Engineering: Government, Industry, and Academia," *PLoS One* 17, no. 2 (February 2022): e0263185, https://doi.org/10.1371/journal.pone.0263185.

146   *Job insecurity is a profound stressor*: Sandra Blomqvist, Marianna Virtanen, Anthony D. LaMontagne, and Linda L. Magnusson Hanson, "Perceived Job Insecurity and Risk of Suicide and Suicide Attempts: A Study of Men and Women in

the Swedish Working Population," *Scandinavian Journal of Work, Environment & Health* 48, no. 4 (2022): 293–301, https://doi.org/10.5271/sjweh.4015.

147   *In one study, the mental health and emotional well-being*: Hans De Witte, Jaco Pienaar, and Nele De Cuyper, "Review of 30 Years of Longitudinal Studies on the Association between Job Insecurity and Health and Well-Being: Is There Causal Evidence?" *Australian Psychologist* 51, no. 1 (2016): 18–31, https://doi.org/10.1111/ap.12176.

147   *subjects had the option to wait to receive a* mild *electric shock*: Gregory S. Berns, Jonathan Chappelow, Milos Cekic, Caroline F. Zink, Giuseppe Pagnoni, and Megan E. Martin-Skurski, "Neurobiological Substrates of Dread," *Science* 312, no. 5774 (2006): 754–58, https://doi.org/10.1126/science.1123721.

147   *70% of employees have trouble accessing the mental health services*: "Addressing Employee Burnout: Are You Solving the Right Problem?" *McKinsey Health Institute*, May 27, 2022, www.mckinsey.com/mhi/our-insights/addressing -employee-burnout-are-you-solving-the-right-problem.

148   *how that news is delivered is too often extremely harsh and humiliating*: Christopher Otts, and Chip Cutter, "When the Pink Slip Comes via Text and Email," *Wall Street Journal*, December 20, 2024, www.wsj.com/business/fired-layoffs -text-email-companies-977f6cf5.

148   *74% of surviving employees experienced drops in productivity* after *layoffs*: "Don't Expect Layoff Survivors To Be Grateful (Survivor's Guilt After a Downsizing)," *Leadership IQ*, accessed April 10, 2025, www.leadershipiq.com/blogs /leadershipiq/29062401-dont-expect-layoff-survivors-to-be-grateful.

149   *we don't adapt to job insecurity*: Ásta Snorradóttir, Kristinn Tómasson, Rúnar Vilhjálmsson, and Guðbjörg Linda Rafnsdóttir, "The Health and Well-Being of Bankers Following Downsizing: A Comparison of Stayers and Leavers," *Work, Employment and Society* 29, no. 5 (2015): 738–56, https://doi.org/10 .1177/0950017014563106.

149   *when managers listened to the concerns and feelings of their subordinates*: Tiffany D. Kriz, Phillip M. Jolly, and Mindy K. Shoss, "Coping with Organizational Layoffs: Managers' Increased Active Listening Reduces Job Insecurity via Perceived Situational Control," *Journal of Occupational Health Psychology* 26, no. 5 (2021): 448–58, https://psycnet.apa.org/doi/10.1037/ocp0000295.

150   *participants were shown pictures of people's bodies and limbs*: Gabriele Buruck, Johannes Wendsche, Marlen Melzer, Alexander Strobel, and Denise Dörfel, "Acute Psychosocial Stress and Emotion Regulation Skills Modulate Empathic Reactions to Pain in Others," *Frontiers in Psychology* 5 (2014), https://doi.org /10.3389/fpsyg.2014.00517.

152   Confirmation bias *refers to our tendency*: Raymond S. Nickerson, "Confirmation Bias: A Ubiquitous Phenomenon in Many Guises," *Review of General Psychology* 2, no. 2 (1998): 175–220, https://doi.org/10.1037/1089-2680.2.2.175.

152 *adults prefer unambiguous characters as well*: Matthew Grizzard, Jialing Huang, Changhyun Ahn, Kaitlin Fitzgerald, C. Joseph Francemone, and Jess Walton, "The Gordian Knot of Disposition Theory: Character Morality and Liking," *Journal of Media Psychology* 32, no. 2 (2019): 100–105, https://doi.org/10.1027/1864-1105/a000257.

153 *Participants who had a greater reaction to stress*: Catherine C. Brown, Candace M. Raio, and Maital Neta, "Cortisol Responses Enhance Negative Valence Perception for Ambiguous Facial Expressions," *Scientific Reports* 7, no. 1 (2017): 15107, https://doi.org/10.1038/s41598-017-14846-3.

153 *our tendency to believe information to which we are exposed repeatedly*: Aumyo Hassan and Sarah J. Barber, "The Effects of Repetition Frequency on the Illusory Truth Effect," *Cognitive Research: Principles and Implications* 6 (2021): Article 38, https://doi.org/10.1186/s41235-021-00301-5.

154 *even if it contradicts our previous knowledge*: Lisa K. Fazio, Nadia M. Brashier, B. Keith Payne, and Elizabeth J. Marsh, "Knowledge Does Not Protect Against Illusory Truth," *Journal of Experimental Psychology: General* 144, no. 5 (2015): 993–1002, https://doi.org/10.1037/xge0000098.

156 *Understanding dissolves anger*: Johanna Wagner, Ulrich Kirchhoff, and Micha Strack, "Apologies: Words of Magic? The Role of Verbal Components, Anger Reduction, and Offence Severity," *Peace and Conflict: Journal of Peace Psychology* 18, no. 2 (2012): 109–30, https://doi.org/10.1037/a0028092.

Chapter Ten: Thursday Night

159 *73% of people said their family took priority over their jobs*: Andy Cerda, "Family Time Is Far More Important Than Other Aspects of Life for Most Americans," *Pew Research Center*, May 26, 2023, www.pewresearch.org/short-reads/2023/05/26/family-time-is-far-more-important-than-other-aspects-of-life-for-most-americans/.

159 *people who prioritized family over work were happier*: Aline D. Masuda and Florencia M. Sortheix, "Work-Family Values, Priority Goals and Life Satisfaction: A Seven Year Follow-up of MBA Students," *Journal of Happiness Studies* 13, no. 6 (2012): 1131–44, https://doi.org/10.1007/s10902-011-9310-6.

160 *they would choose the work dinner*: Julia D. Hur, Alice Lee-Yoon, and Ashley V. Whillans, "Are They Useful? The Effects of Performance Incentives on the Prioritization of Work Versus Personal Ties," *Organizational Behavior and Human Decision Processes* 165 (2021): 103–14. https://doi.org/10.1016/j.obhdp.2021.04.010.

160 *employees spend less than 60 minutes of focused and meaningful time per day*: Hur et al., "Are They Useful?"

160 *including actively undermining them in the home*: Arnold B. Bakker and Evangelia Demerouti, "The Spillover-Crossover Model," in *New Frontiers in Work*

and Family Research, ed. Joseph Grzywacz and Evangelia Demerouti (Psychology Press, 2013): 55–70.

162 *men's work stress impacted their women partners*: Azize Ergeneli, Arzu Ilsev, and Pinar Bayhan Karapinar, "Work-Family Conflict and Job Satisfaction Relationship: The Roles of Gender and Interpretive Habits," *Gender, Work and Organization* 17, no. 6 (2010): 679–95, https://doi.org/10.1111/j.1468-0432.2009.00487.x.

162 *women's work demands can interfere with their duties at home*: Ergeneli et al., "Work-Family Conflict and Job Satisfaction Relationship."

162 *women do far more housework and perform more parenting duties than men*: US Department of Labor, Bureau of Labor Statistics, *American Time Use Survey: 2023 Results* (June 27, 2024), www.bls.gov/news.release/pdf/atus.pdf.

162 *men spend more time on leisure than women do*: US Department of Labor, Bureau of Labor Statistics, *American Time Use Survey: 2023 Results*.

163 *their spouses began developing symptoms of burnout*: Arnold B. Bakker, Evangelia Demerouti, Maureen F. Dollard, "How Job Demands Affect Partners' Experience of Exhaustion: Integrating Work-Family Conflict and Crossover Theory," *Journal of Applied Psychology* 93, no. 4 (2008): 901–11, https://doi.org/10.1037/0021-9010.93.4.901.

166 *intermittent reinforcement has been found to be an extremely potent*: Robin M. Hogarth and Marie Claire Villeval, "Intermittent Reinforcement and the Persistence of Behavior: Experimental Evidence," *IZA Discussion Papers*, No. 5103 (August 10, 2010; last revised May 8, 2025).

168 *One of the boundaries that gets violated most by our employers*: Sanfilippo, "What After-Hours Emails Really Do to Your Employees."

169 *In Japan, for example, workers are more likely to spend their entire careers at a single company*: Yuko Kachi, Akiomi Inoue, Hisashi Eguchi, Norito Kawakami, Akihito Shimazu, and Akizumi Tsutsumi, "Occupational Stress and the Risk of Turnover: A Large Prospective Cohort Study of Employees in Japan," *BMC Public Health* 20, no. 1 (2020): Article 174, https://doi.org/10.1186/s12889-020-8289-5.

170 *Overidentifying with one's employer has all kinds of harmful effects*: Muhammad Irshad and Sajid Bashir, "The Dark Side of Organizational Identification: A Multi-Study Investigation of Negative Outcomes," *Frontiers in Psychology* 11 (2020): 572478, https://doi.org/10.3389/fpsyg.2020.572478.

Chapter Eleven: Friday Morning

171 *Studies show that the number of errors we make at work peaks on Fridays*: Taehyun Roh, Chukwuemeka Esomonu, Joseph Hendricks, Anisha Aggarwal, Nishat Tasnim Hasan, and Mark Benden, "Examining Workweek Variations in Computer Usage Patterns: An Application of Ergonomic Monitoring Soft-

ware," *PLoS ONE* 18, no. 7 (2023): e0287976, https://doi.org/10.1371/jour
nal.pone.0287976.

171 *our productivity reaches its lowest levels of the week on Fridays as well*: Roh et al.,
"Examining Workweek Variations in Computer Usage Patterns."

171 *view behavior we had considered to be objectionable as more reasonable*: Newman
et al., "Moral Disengagement at Work."

174 *Unethical leadership is just one of the factors that corrupt our ethics*: Celia Moore
and Francesca Gino, "Ethically Adrift: How Others Pull Our Moral Compass
from True North, and How We Can Fix It," *Research in Organizational Behavior* 33 (2013): 53–77.

174 *12% of employees admitted to experiencing physical threats or actual violence*:
American Psychological Association, *2023 Work in America Survey*.

174 *96% of employees experience incivility in the workplace*: Christine Porath and Christine Pearson, "The Price of Incivility," *Harvard Business Review* 91 (2013): 114–21.

174 *24% of workers have experienced verbal abuse*: American Psychological Association, *2023 Work in America Survey*.

174 *30% have experienced bullying*: Namie, *2024 Workplace Bullying Institute U.S.
Workplace Bullying Survey*.

174 *22% have experienced sexual harassment, 30% have experienced or witnessed racism*: American Psychological Association, *2023 Work in America Survey*.

174 *women, people of color, and members of the LGBTQ+ communities*: American
Psychological Association, *2023 Work in America Survey*.

174 *19% of employees whose company cultures are toxic*: American Psychological Association, *2023 Work in America Survey*.

176 *Those who are skilled at deceiving others are just as skilled at deceiving themselves*:
Sanket Sunand Dash and Lalatendu Kesari Jena, "Self-Deception, Emotional
Neglect and Workplace Victimization: A Conceptual Analysis and Ideas for
Research," *International Journal of Workplace Health Management* 13, no. 1
(2020): 81–94, https://doi.org/10.1108/IJWHM-03-2019-0036.

177 *38% of workers say they would act unethically*: McCurry, "How Can Trust Survive Without Integrity?"

178 *might act unethically in ways that* solely benefited their manager or company:
Elizabeth E. Umphress and John B. Bingham, "When Employees Do Bad
Things for Good Reasons: Examining Unethical Pro-Organizational Behaviors," *Organization Science* 22, no. 3 (2011): 621–40, https://doi.org/10.1287/
orsc.1100.0559.

178 *several Volkswagen executives were indicted*: Wikipedia, "Volkswagen Emissions
Scandal," last modified June 6, 2025, www.wikipedia.org/wiki/Volkswagen_
emissions_scandal.

178 *One of them even served several years in jail*: Wikipedia, "Volkswagen Emissions
Scandal."

178   *5,000 Wells Fargo employees lost their jobs*: Wikipedia, "Wells Fargo Cross-Selling Scandal," last modified June 5, 2025, www.wikipedia.org/wiki/Wells_Fargo_cross-selling_scandal.

178   *one of the main culprits leading to these kinds of unethical behaviors*: Umphress and Bingham, "When Employees Do Bad Things for Good Reasons."

178   *Identifying with or admiring a charismatic leader who acts unethically*: Saad Basaad, Saleh Bajaba, and A. S. Basahal, "Uncovering the Dark Side of Leadership: How Exploitative Leaders Fuel Unethical Pro-Organizational Behavior Through Moral Disengagement," *Cogent Business & Management* 10, no. 2 (2023): 2233775. https://doi.org/10.1080/23311975.2023.2233775.

178   *cognitive dissonance—an emotionally uncomfortable clash of beliefs and behavior*: Umphress and Bingham, "When Employees Do Bad Things for Good Reasons."

179   *only a third of children are removed from their homes for abuse*: US Department of Health and Human Services Administration for Children and Families, *Administration on Children, Youth and Families, Children's Bureau, Child Maltreatment 2002* (2024): 61, www.acf.gov/sites/default/files/documents/cb/cm2022.pdf#page=61.

179   Emotional neglect *occurs when the emotional needs and experiences*: Kong and Belkin, "You Don't Care for Me, So What's the Point for Me to Care for Your Business?"

179   Professional neglect *occurs when the professional development needs*: Joost Kampen and André Henken, "Emotional Abuse and Neglect in the Workplace: A Method for Arrested OD," *Journal of Organizational Psychology* 49, no. 6 (2019), https://doi.org/10.33423/jop.v19i6.2663.

179   *employees considered ostracism to be more acceptable*: Jane O'Reilly, Sandra L. Robinson, Jennifer L. Berdahl, and Sara Banki, "Is Negative Attention Better Than No Attention? The Comparative Effects of Ostracism and Harassment at Work," *Organization Science* 26, no. 3 (2014): 774–93, https://doi.org/10.1287/orsc.2014.0900.

179   *Shunning is significantly more damaging to employee well-being*: O'Reilly et al., "Is Negative Attention Better Than No Attention?"

181   moral disengagement: Newman et al., "Moral Disengagement at Work."

181   cognitive restructuring: Newman et al., "Moral Disengagement at Work."

182   diffusion of responsibility: Newman et al., "Moral Disengagement at Work."

182   dehumanization: Newman et al., "Moral Disengagement at Work."

182   *Unethical leaders, toxic corporate cultures, and unreasonable performance pressures*: Newman et al., "Moral Disengagement at Work"; Roberta Fida, Marinella Paciello, Carlo Tramontano, Reid Griffith Fontaine, Claudio Barbaranelli, and Maria Luisa Farnese, "An Integrative Approach to Understanding Counterproductive Work Behavior: The Roles of Stressors, Negative Emotions, and Moral Disengagement," *Journal of Business Ethics* 130, no. 1 (2015): 131–44, https://doi.org/10.1007/s10551-014-2209-5.

183 *the stronger our sense of moral identity*: Sam A. Hardy and Gustavo Carlo, "Moral Identity: What Is It, How Does It Develop, and Is It Linked to Moral Action?" *Child Development Perspectives* 5, no. 3 (2011): 212–18, https://doi.org/10.1111/j.1750-8606.2011.00189.x.

183 *primed moral identity by using a rather heavy-handed approach*: Karl Aquino, Dan Freeman, Americus Reed, Will Felps, and Vivien K. G. Lim, "Testing a Social-Cognitive Model of Moral Behavior: The Interactive Influence of Situations and Moral Identity Centrality," *Journal of Personality and Social Psychology* 97, no. 1 (2009): 123–41, https://doi.org/10.1037/a0015406.

183 *identity can be strengthened by going through a process of exploration*: H. A. Bosma and E. S. Kunnen, "Determinants and Mechanisms in Ego Identity Development: A Review and Synthesis," *Developmental Review* 21, no. 1 (2001): 39–66, https://doi.org/10.1006/drev.2000.

185 *counterbalance such losses is a deep sense of self-satisfaction*: Nicholas Stanger, Maria Kavussanu, and Christopher Ring, "Linking Facets of Pride with Moral Behaviour in Sport: The Mediating Role of Moral Disengagement," *International Journal of Sport and Exercise Psychology* 19, no. 6 (2020): 929–42, https://doi.org/10.1080/1612197X.2020.1830825.

Chapter Twelve: Friday Evening

186 *3% of the entire workforce quit their jobs every month*: Maury Gittleman, "The 'Great Resignation' in Perspective," *Monthly Labor Review*, U.S. Bureau of Labor Statistics, July 2022, accessed April 10, 2025, https://www.bls.gov/opub/mlr/2022/article/the-great-resignation-in-perspective.htm.

186 *surge of quitting has since dropped to pre-pandemic rates*: Wikipedia, "Great Resignation," last modified June 7, 2025, https://en.wikipedia.org/wiki/Great_Resignation.

188 *Unemployment and job searches are rough*: Karsten I. Paul and Klaus Moser, "Unemployment Impairs Mental Health: Meta-Analyses," *Journal of Vocational Behavior* 74, no. 3 (2009): 264–82, https://doi.org/10.1016/j.jvb.2009.01.001.

189 *a feeling of belonging in the workplace increases job satisfaction*: Alison M. S. N. Winter-Collins and Anna M. McDaniel, "Sense of Belonging and New Graduate Job Satisfaction," *Journal for Nurses in Staff Development* 16, no. 3 (2000): 103–11.

189 *productivity and that the connection and safety we feel in such situations*: Lee Waller, *A Sense of Belonging at Work: A Guide to Improving Well-Being and Performance* (1st ed., Routledge, 2021), https://doi.org/10.4324/9781003108849.

189 *at CY, a call center with Christian, Jewish, and Moslem employees*: Guy Winch, *Winning with Underdogs: How Hiring the Least Likely Candidates Can Spark*

Creativity, Improve Service, and Boost Profits for Your Business (New York: Mc-Graw Hill, 2022).

189 *feeling shunned or ignored at work creates such significant emotional pain*: John Fiset, Raghid Al Hajj, and John G. Vongas, "Workplace Ostracism Seen Through the Lens of Power," *Frontiers in Psychology* 8 (2017): 1528, https://doi.org/10.3389/fpsyg.2017.01528.

190 *the impairment will be greater if your manager is indifferent to your distress*: Kong and Belkin, "You Don't Care for Me, So What's the Point for Me to Care for Your Business?"

190 *Studies of how rumors and scandals permeate organizations*: Roy Liff and Ewa Wikström, "Rumours and Gossip Demand Continuous Action by Managers in Daily Working Life," *Culture and Organization* 27, no. 6 (2021): 456–75, https://doi.org/10.1080/14759551.2021.1884681.

192 *Researchers call this phenomenon* job embeddedness: Alifah Ratnawati, Ken Sudarti, Mulyana Mulyana, and M. Husni Mubarok, "Job Embeddedness: A Strategy to Reduce Voluntary Turnover Intention," *Jurnal Dinamika Manajemen* 11, no. 2 (2020): 271–82.

192 *Our relationships with colleagues keep us stuck considerably more*: Stefan Korber, Paul Hibbert, Lisa Callagher, Frank Siedlok, and Ziad Elsahn, "We-Experiences and the Maintenance of Workplace Friendships: Being Workplace Friends Together," *Management Learning* 55, no. 3 (2024): 406–31, https://doi.org/10.1177/13505076231181194.

Chapter Thirteen: Saturday

200 *Saturday is the happiest day of the week for most people, peaking at 7:26 PM*: "When do YOU unwind? The happiest time of the week is 7.26pm on a Saturday," *Daily Mail*, February 4, 2011, www.dailymail.co.uk/news/article-1353672/Saturday-evening-7-26pm-happiest-time-week-British-people.html.

200 *the right vacation can boost our general health and well-being*: Jessica de Bloom, Sabine A. E. Geurts, Sabine Sonnentag, Toon Taris, Carolina de Weerth, and Michiel A. J. Kompier, "How Does a Vacation from Work Affect Employee Health and Well-Being?" *Psychology & Health* 26, no. 12 (2011): 1606–22, https://doi.org/10.1080/08870446.2010.546860.

200 *foster creativity upon our return*: Atsushi Kawakubo and Takashi Oguchi, "Recovery Experiences During Vacations Promote Life Satisfaction Through Creative Behavior," *Tourism Management Perspectives* 30 (2019): 240–50, https://doi.org/10.1016/j.tmp.2019.02.017.

200 *reduce the harmful effects of chronic stress, decrease burnout*: Mina Westman and Dalia Etzion, "The Impact of Vacation and Job Stress on Burnout and Absen-

teeism," *Psychology & Health* 16, no. 5 (2001): 595–606, https://doi.org/10.1080/08870440108405529.

200   *increase general life satisfaction*: Chun-Chu Chen, Wei-Jue Huang, and James Petrick, "Holiday Recovery Experiences, Tourism Satisfaction and Life Satisfaction—Is There a Relationship?" *Tourism Management* 53 (2016): 140–47, https://doi.org/10.1016/j.tourman.2015.09.016.

200   *men with cardiovascular disease were followed over nine years*: Brooks B. Gump and Karen A. Matthews, "Are Vacations Good for Your Health? The 9-Year Mortality Experience After the Multiple Risk Factor Intervention Trial," *Psychosomatic Medicine* 62, no. 5 (2000): 608–12, https://doi.org/10.1097/00006842-200009000-00003.

201   *such intrusions almost entirely nullified the vacation's restorative qualities*: Jessica de Bloom, Sabine A. E. Geurts, and Michiel A. J. Kompier, "Effects of Short Vacations, Vacation Activities and Experiences on Employee Health and Well-Being," *Stress and Health: Journal of the International Society for the Investigation of Stress* 28, no. 4 (2012): 305–18, https://doi.org/10.1002/smi.1434.

202   *10 paid vacation days per year*: Eric Czerwonka, "How Many Days of PTO Is Normal?" *Buddy Punch*, March 24, 2025, www.buddypunch.com/blog/how-many-vacation-days-per-year-is-normal/.

202   *almost half of all workers don't use all their vacation days*: Shradha Dinesh and Kim Parker, "More Than 4 in 10 U.S. Workers Don't Take All Their Paid Time Off," *Pew Research Center*, August 10, 2023, www.pewresearch.org/short-reads/2023/08/10/more-than-4-in-10-u-s-workers-dont-take-all-their-paid-time-off/.

203   *make it easier for you to detach from work*: Jan Packer, "Taking a Break: Exploring the Restorative Benefits of Short Breaks and Vacations," *Annals of Tourism Research Empirical Insights* 2, no. 1 (2021): Article 100006, https://doi.org/10.1016/j.annale.2020.100006.

204   *the more exhausted or stressed we are, the longer we'll need*: Jessica Bloom, Sabine Geurts, and Michiel Kompier, "Vacation (After-) Effects on Employee Health and Well-Being, and the Role of Vacation Activities, Experiences and Sleep," *Journal of Happiness Studies* 14, no. 2 (2013): 613–33, https://doi.org/10.1007/s10902-012-9345-3.

204   *the more we spend on a vacation, the more we'll enjoy it*: Atsushi Kawakubo and Takashi Oguchi, "What Promotes the Happiness of Vacationers? A Focus on Vacation Experiences for Japanese People During Winter Vacation," *Frontiers in Sports and Active Living* 4 (2022): Article 872084, https://doi.org/10.3389/fspor.2022.872084.

204   *The benefits of vacations peak after about a week*: de Bloom, Geurts, and Kompier, "Vacation (After-) Effects on Employee Health and Well-Being, and the Role of Vacation Activities, Experiences and Sleep."

204 *taking frequent shorter vacations will be more effective*: de Bloom, Geurts, and Kompier, "Vacation (After-) Effects on Employee Health and Well-Being, and the Role of Vacation Activities, Experiences and Sleep."

204 *experiences promote more happiness than* purchases: A. Kumar et al., "Spending on Doing Promotes More Moment-to-Moment Happiness Than Spending on Having," *Journal of Experimental Social Psychology* 88 (2020): 103971.

207 *Feeling a sense of autonomy and control over how we spend our vacations*: Chen, Huang, and Petrick, "Holiday Recovery Experiences, Tourism Satisfaction and Life Satisfaction—Is There a Relationship?"

209 *the Edinburgh Festival Fringe*: Wikipedia, "Edinburgh Festival Fringe," last modified June 10, 2025, www.wikipedia.org/wiki/Edinburgh_Festival_Fringe.

210 *Those kinds of vacations are especially restorative*: Kawakubo and Oguchi, "What Promotes the Happiness of Vacationers?"

211 *the number of TikTok employees taking mental health leave*: Jason Wingard, "Tik-Tok's Barrage of Mental Health Leaves: Why Is Tech Burning Out?" *Forbes*, March 11, 2025, www.forbes.com/sites/jasonwingard/2025/03/11/tiktoks-bar rage-of-mental-health-leaves-why-is-tech-burning-out/.

211 *mentions of burnout across all industries due to uncaring management had surged*: Daniel Zhao, "Glassdoor Employee Confidence Index: Unsteady Improvements," *Glassdoor*, August 6, 2024, www.glassdoor.com/blog/glassdoor-em ployee-confidence-index-july-2024/.

211 *only 38% of its employees felt comfortable taking breaks during the workday*: Zhao, "Glassdoor Employee Confidence Index."

INDEX

INDEX

ct . INDEX# INDEX

INDEX

detaching from work
after-work rumination, 42, 43 (*see also* rumination)
vacationing for, 207–9 (*see also* vacations)
workday recovery and, 85–86 (*see also* recovery from workday)

diet, unhealthy foods as comfort, 43

diffusion of responsibility, 182

disgust, of ruminative thoughts, 54–56

distraction
as avoidance, 50
from rumination, 53–54

Diversity, Equity, and Inclusion (DEI) initiatives, 107

divorce, 169–70, 201–2

documentation, of vacations, 205–6

dopamine, 166

dysregulation, 49, 130

early warning system, personalizing, 122–24

Edinburgh Festival Fringe (The Fringe), 209–10

elevator example, 1–3

email
overwork and, 104
Red Light, Green Light exercise, 91–93
setting boundaries for, 90–91
See also screen time

emotion
anger, 126–31, 156–58
compartmentalizing, 97–101
defined, 49
emotional confirmation bias, 150, 152–53
emotional drifting, 150
emotional granularity and emotional literacy, 141–42
emotional neglect, 178
emotional recovery gained from social support, 140
emotional regulation, 48–50, 72, 129
emotional wounds, recalling, 41–42 (*see also* rumination)
emotion-focused coping mechanisms, 60
empathy, 51, 156–58
guilt, 15–17, 36–37
intensity of, 48
overwork and effect on, 108–11
See also Emotional Intelligence

Emotional Intelligence (EI, EQ), 125–43
burnout and, 4
defined, 125–26
Emotional Fluency/Work Feelings Chart Exercise, 142–43
naming emotions for, 140–42
reacting vs. emotional checkup, 126–31
recharging opportunities during stressful workdays, 131–36
social support precautions, 136–40
"Emotionally Savvy Employees Fail to Enact Emotional Intelligence" (study), 126

empathy
in personal relationships, 156–58
perspective and, 51

employers
employees' emotional health and benefit to, 7
managerial apathy by, 77

- 244 -

self-care routines, 5–6
self-employment
    burnout in, 6
    case study (*see* Carlos [case study])
    overwork and, 102–3, 105
self-neglect
    Overworking Self-Care Assessment
        Tool, 114–19, 123
    problem of, 112–14, 120
self-reflection, healthy vs. unhealthy,
    40–43
self-sabotage. *See* coping mechanisms
self-talk. *See* mindset
senses
    micro-breaks and, 135
    for work detachment, 87–89, 195
separators, 86
silent weeping, 109–10
silver linings, finding, 50–52
single mother example. *See* Sally (case
    study)
skills, acquiring, 77. *See also* Emotional
    Intelligence
Slack, 211
sleep
    before vacation starts, 203–4
    restorative, 92
social support, precautions about, 136–40
sound
    micro-breaks and, 135
    for work detachment, 87–88
speed bumps, to reduce errors, 73–75
stated priorities, 159–60
stockbroker example. *See* Tony (case
    study)
stress, 15–28
    acute vs. chronic, 18–20
    adaptability for tolerance of, 21–23

bias and, 107
cycle of, 8–11
effect on loved ones, 160–63 (*see also*
    home environment)
fight-or-flight mode, 19, 43, 53,
    144
framing of, 26–28
guilt and, 15–17
mental functioning impaired by,
    23–24
physical sensations of, 42
procrastination as response to,
    24–26
recognizing accumulation of,
    74–75
rumination resulting from (*see*
    rumination)
stress response, efficiency of, 18
See also burnout; coping
    mechanisms; home environment;
    office politics; overwork;
    rumination; unethical behavior;
    individual case studies
stress management
    breathing exercise, blowing bubbles
        for, 92
    counterbalancing stress for,
        76–78
    measuring stress for, 75–76
    mindset and difficulty of,
        29–31
    stress thermometer for,
        75–77
    tools used for, 76
    See also exercises
stroke, risk of, 15
subordinates, setting boundaries with,
    167

INDEX

ABOUT THE AUTHOR

GUY WINCH, PhD, is a psychologist and the author of three books that have been translated into twenty-eight languages, and his three TED Talks have garnered thirty-five million views. He is a gifted storyteller who offers science-based, concrete strategies that empower. His work has been covered in *The New York Times, The Wall Street Journal,* and elsewhere. He lectures widely at corporations, conferences, and government think tanks. His private practice is in New York City.